ARTISTS IN THE AUDIENCE

ARTISTS IN THE AUDIENCE

CULTS, CAMP, AND AMERICAN FILM CRITICISM

GREG TAYLOR

PRINCETON UNIVERSITY PRESS

PRINCETON AND OXFORD

opyright © 1999 by Princeton University Press

ublished by Princeton University Press, 41 William Street,

rinceton, New Jersey 08540

In the United Kingdom: Princeton University Press,

3 Market Place, Woodstock, Oxfordshire OX20 1SY

All Rights Reserved

Second printing, and first paperback printing, 2001

Paperback ISBN 0-691-08955-8

The Library of Congress has cataloged the cloth edition
of this book as follows

Taylor, Greg, 1963–

Artists in the audience : cults, camp, and American film criticism / Greg Taylor.

p. cm.

Includes bibliographical references and index.

ISBN 0-691-00421-8 (cloth : alk. paper)

1. Film criticism—United States—History. 2. Motion pictures—

Aesthetics. I. Title.

PN1995.T339   1999

791.43'01'50973—dc21   98-48593

British Library Cataloging-in-Publication Data is available

This book has been composed in Sabon

Printed on acid-free paper. ∞

www.pup.princeton.edu

Printed in the United States of America

10 9 8 7 6 5 4 3 2

For Klare and Frederick

WHO TAUGHT ME TO HAVE THE COURAGE OF MY CONVICTIONS

CONTENTS

PREFACE

THIS BOOK is not an exhaustive history of American film criticism. Instead, it attempts to explain how and why critics have helped us to see art in movies. The answer, I argue, has less to do with the virtues of movies than with the interests of renegade highbrows, who found in popular cinema raw material for an alternative postwar modernism. In essence, they became artistic, vanguard spectators, remaking the movies in the image of their favored aesthetics. Who needed the leaden pretension of abstract expressionism when America also offered the authentic vigor of shoestring action flicks and the symbolic complexity of Hollywood psycho-mythology? And who needed the authoritative finality of careerist painters when a true avant-garde of cultural critics offered to guide their readers through the untapped riches of pop culture?

The sheer success of this avant-garde has substantially changed the way we regard art, movies, and ourselves, yet its history and motives remain largely unexamined, its formative players largely forgotten. Two of these players form the nucleus of this book. Abstract painter/sculptor Manny Farber and surrealist poet Parker Tyler may not be household names, but this is only because their work has been buried under its own influence. In truth, their key refinements of cultism's radical connoisseurship and camp's creative appreciation substantially enabled art-world discourses to be applied to low-end cultural products such as movies, paving the way for better-known successors—Andrew Sarris, Jonas Mekas, Pauline Kael—to popularize these perspectives during the 1960s and beyond. In tracing the history of vanguard film criticism, we trace the prehistory of our postmodern age; in exploring the neglected contexts of cultism and camp, we see the aesthetic biases fueling contemporary viewing habits. If we now tend to assume pop culture to be innately complex, and empowered/artistic spectatorship to be innately beneficial, we also walk in the footsteps of radical modernists who saw movies as entertaining, malleable junk useful for keeping authentic high culture afloat in middlebrow America.

I have no one but myself to blame for this book, but I do want to thank a number of individuals for their ideas and support along the way.

At the University of Wisconsin–Madison, this project would never have survived its first incarnation without the assistance and inspiration of Tino Balio, Noël Carroll, Donald Crafton, John Fiske, Vance Kepley, Jr., and especially J. J. Murphy (who freed my sensibilities) and David Bordwell (who taught me to be sensible). I also wish to make a special point of thanking David Hayman for guiding me through the complexities of modernist aesthetics.

I have also benefited immeasurably from the scholarship and friendship of Tom Gunning, James Peterson, Klaus Phillips, Murray Smith, and Jeff Smith (whose sound advice, good humor, and tolerance of Marc Bolan deserve special commendation). The staff of Princeton University Press have also been uniformly helpful and understanding: I am most grateful for acquisitions editor Mary Murrell's initial enthusiasm for the manuscript, and for the incisive comments of my readers. In addition, the enormously gifted and dedicated students and faculty of the Purchase College Film Program have provided a constant and much-needed reminder that film art is indeed worth fighting for.

Pavel Tchelitchew's *Hide-and-Seek* is reproduced here courtesy of the Museum of Modern Art. For the reproduction of Kimber Smith's *Sous-Sol*, I owe enormous thanks and appreciation to Gregory Vinitsky of Gregory Gallery. Anthology Film Archives graciously provided the stills from *Meshes of the Afternoon, Pull My Daisy,* and *Wavelength.*

Portions of chapter 7 appeared in a much different form as " 'The Cognitive Instrument in the Service of Revolutionary Change': Sergei Eisenstein, Annette Michelson and the Avant-Garde's Scholarly Aspiration" in *Cinema Journal* 31, no. 4 (Summer 1992): 42–59.

Finally, I must attempt (in words, alas) to thank my wife Renae Edge, whose love of art and film helped to inspire this project, and whose patience, fortitude, and good sense kept it afloat. She can also spot a run-on sentence a mile away. Through fog.

ARTISTS IN THE AUDIENCE

Chapter One

THE SPECTATOR AS CRITIC AS ARTIST

> Surely, criticism is itself an art. . . . The critic occupies the
> same relation to the work of art that he criticizes as the artist
> does to the visible world of form and color, or the unseen
> world of passion and of thought. He does not even
> require for the perfection of his art the finest materials.
> Anything will serve his purpose.
> *(Oscar Wilde)*

CAROL AND MIKE enter the forbidding cave to search for her father. Suddenly Carol sees two human skeletons. *"They're in Michael Jackson's basement!"* exclaims an audience member. Carol and Mike hesitate. Carol steels herself: "I can't go without . . ." *". . . checking to see if there's any meat left on him!"* guffaws another. Another night at the local multiplex? No, merely an episode of cable television's *Mystery Science Theater 3000*. The premise: an unsuspecting clerk has been shot into space by two meddling scientists eager to monitor his mental responses to "cheesy movies," which he watches each week with two lovable robots, Tom Servo and Crow. That these movies are uniformly atrocious enables the show's humor to arise from the characters' comic appreciation of the material screened—in this case, Bert I. Gordon's *Earth vs. the Spider* (1958). In their relentless mockery of the film of the week, Servo, Crow, and the clerk (Joel, later Mike) celebrate their own triumphant power as active, creative spectators. They are not simply making fun of junk; they are making fun *out* of junk.

In fact, they *need* junk for their own vanguard art:[1] the cruder and less involving the movie, the more easily its meanings are resisted, twisted, transformed through an aestheticizing gesture. Already in the 1910s, avant-gardists had begun busily appropriating the detritus of mass culture—newspaper clippings, advertisements, propaganda, pornography—in an effort to display their own rebellious, creative control over the materials of their lives. Such artists (Hannah Höch, Man Ray, Kasimir Malevich, and Kurt Schwitters, to name but a few) remade the mass culture surrounding them, asserting hermeneutic and formal authority over these misshapen, anonymous textual fragments. Most important, they showed that the roles of artist and critic could be collapsed into one, empowering spectators like Tom Servo, Crow, and the rest of us to create a culture better than the one we have been offered.

Hence—apparently—the value of movies. Their existence has enabled vanguard spectatorship of mass culture to ascend from the aesthetic margins to the mainstream. Obscure Hollywood B-films, Bette Davis weepies, and even *The Rocky Horror Picture Show* are no longer discovered primarily through word of mouth. Now cult appreciation and camp response can be gleaned from *Mystery Science Theater*, or from a slew of books, including Edward Margulies and Stephen Rebello's *Bad Movies We Love* ("Big Stars! Big Budgets! Big Hair! Big Mistakes") (1993), Michael Weldon's *The Psychotronic Encyclopedia of Film* (1983), and RE-Search's *Incredibly Strange Films* (1988). The movies, it seems, have enabled us to overturn our culture, to the point where *Earth vs. the Spider* can be aesthetically validated. But what does this say about our regard for cinema? In making art *out* of movies, are we elevating slumming to an art form while implicitly denouncing a medium as aesthetically puerile?

Perhaps we have merely made the best of a bad situation. We know most run-of-the-mill movies are awful, so we try to find a way to love them, *resistantly*. The more we are encouraged to see them, the more expensive and overblown the production design, the more glaringly functional the performances—the more we are tempted to resist the forces of consumerism and seize our spectatorship, either by celebrating more modest, neglected products (which we can at least claim we actively found/chose), or by extravagantly, even aesthetically reveling in the sheer "badness" of the overblown in order to squeeze some personal pleasure, and personal power, out of the cultural experience. Precisely because the films themselves may not be aesthetically sophisticated in their own right, their active use by attuned spectators can assume an aesthetic function. The vanguard consumer calls the shots, asserts oppositional taste as a connoisseurship of trash. In their introduction to *Bad Movies We Love*, Margulies and Rebello carefully set out their field of inquiry, explaining why neither *Plan 9 from Outer Space* nor *Ishtar* will show up in their book:

> Ask anyone who's been to their plex anytime recently and they'll tell you we live in a world polluted by Bad Movies. Occasionally, though, there are Bad Movies that separate themselves from the pack, special Bad Movies: those big-budget, big-star, big-director, aggressively publicized fiascos that have gone wonderfully, irredeemably, lovably haywire. We call them Bad Movies We Love. To rate a special place in our hearts and in this, our tome, not only did the movies have to be jaw-droppingly, astoundingly bad, they had to be fun bad—

the kind of fun that means that, when you're wandering the aisles at the video store looking for a good time, if you're hip to these movies, you can't stop yourself from yanking them off the shelves. (xvii–xviii)

We can almost hear the derisive snickers in the background. These authors have little or no respect for movies that clearly exercise so little aesthetic power *over* them, but at the same time this is what enables them to turn the tables, seizing their own spectatorial power as mass movie consumers. The work is shoddy, it cannot speak to them, it exists only to get them into the theater as paying customers. But at least they have the last laugh.

The movies are a perfect site for this sort of power game, in that they exist on the border between art and consumer culture. Sometimes they cross the boundaries, evincing aesthetic richness while still playing to millions of paying customers. Usually, they do not. We casually categorize cinema as an art form, but the claim often seems a little brazen, and not simply because the medium is not "respected"—as if it automatically deserved respect. The fact is that by aesthetic standards we routinely apply to other arts and artworks, the vast majority of films are woefully inadequate. Most movies are constructed functionally, to be legible and entertaining. They are not built to last but exist very much of their brief, hyped moment in the marketplace. (Hence movies tend to "date" quickly—once it is out of the consumer limelight, a movie's basic aesthetic weaknesses become glaringly obvious. As Margulies and Rebello ask of our old favorites, "Have you seen them anytime lately?" [xviii].) Now, many, many wonderfully rich narrative features have been made, and some have even made money. But separating the wheat from the chaff is difficult, and it leaves us with relatively few works to champion in earnest. Changing the very terms of aesthetic inquiry, from dispassionate judgment of formed works to active, aesthet*icizing* treatment of unformed cultural products, thus has its advantages—in making a virtue of weakness, it actually turns a glut of routine pop artifacts into a vast field for resistant artistry.

Vanguard appreciation of movies has an important history in postwar America, not least because in opening artistic production to all those able to master a liberating aesthetic gesture, it forever changed the face of American art making. We may in fact be so used to making art out of movies that this very gesture now seems like second nature to us, self-evidently appropriate and inherently justified. Yet it certainly did not appear suddenly, fully constituted, at New York's Thalia cinema—nor arrive, in the form of John Waters, on a bus from Baltimore. Hardly as playful and innocent as it seems, it actually arose as a reactionary gesture, a pointed response to consumer-friendly postwar modernism on the part of disaffected highbrow critics eager to assert their relevance to a cultural scene that had seemingly abandoned them. Valid "popular Art" seemed an impossibility to these critics, because high art could not be reduced to a marketable good without a flattening of its innovation or a dilution of its impact. Even creatively refashioned movies were—they could imply—more interesting than a slick abstract expression. A movie was something like a Rorschach blot: you could see in it what you wanted to see, align it with a preferred aesthetic in order to create a cultural product that winked back at you.

In America, this was a bold new way of conceiving of criticism, and even of highbrow influence. It certainly emerged in direct opposition to Matthew Arnold's notion of criticism as "a disinterested endeavor to learn and propagate the best that is known and thought in this world" (1949b, 265). Arnold, after all, had hoped that solemn engagement with the highest culture might act as an effective bulwark against the blind pragmatism of middle-class reformers and the encroachment of a dumbed-down, progress-driven mass culture (Dickstein 1992). Because "the rush and roar of practical life [would] always have a dizzying and attracting effect upon the most collected spectator, and tend to draw him into its vortex," the critic could stay relevant to his age—and to the practical man he served—only by remaining dispassionate and judicious.

> For the practical man is not apt for fine distinctions, and yet in these distinctions truth and the highest culture greatly find their account. . . . The critic must keep out of the region of immediate practice in the political, social, humanitarian sphere if he wants to make a beginning for that more free speculative treatment of things, which may perhaps one day make its benefits felt even in this sphere, but in a natural and thence irresistible manner. (Arnold 1949b, 254–55)

There is indeed a patronizing quality to Arnold's missionary zeal: he saw himself as a kind of prophet of genteel humanism, a leader of like-minded intellectuals in a reformist crusade. Yet while he characteristically framed his cultural crisis through the starkest of oppositions—Culture against Anarchy, "sweetness and light" against mechanistic practicality—at heart he was a liberal too, one who wanted desperately to equip the middle class and masses with a means of enrichment. He insisted that elevated Culture did not seek to "teach down to the level of inferior classes" but instead to "do away with classes, to make the best that has been thought and known in the world current everywhere; to make all men live in an atmosphere of sweetness and light, where they may use ideas, as it uses them itself, freely—nourished and not bound by them" (1949a, 499).

That Arnold's ideals were so profoundly influential on American life—shaping liberal education and spurring the construction of public museums, parks, and libraries (Rubin 1992, 14–20)—only made them the bane of American highbrows fearful or suspicious of broad access to Culture.

It wasn't merely that Arnold was polluting artistic accomplishment by leading the riffraff into museums. More dangerous still was the notion that genuine Taste could be acquired merely with the purchase of a museum ticket, or the Book of the Month. This suggested that art might exist happily within the marketplace, thus rendering the authority of the tastemaking highbrow somewhat redundant.

If we don't take Arnold's ideas too seriously any more, it isn't because highbrows have suddenly abandoned all pretensions to cultural influence, even cultural uplift. They have just changed their tactics, presenting themselves in a more favorable light by offering a sort of uplift different from a simple selection of Great Works.[2] While assailing as elitist the very notion of Cultural elevation (or indeed of Culture as a distinct category of work to be prized and disseminated), many highbrow critics and scholars have instead embraced vanguard ideals, eliminating the troublesome Work and its author entirely while asserting themselves as necessary guides for popular cultural renovation. Here highbrow movie criticism led the way, killing off the traditional author long before Barthes got around to it, while asserting spectatorial liberation as a primary directive. The factory-made movie has proven especially useful to the vanguard highbrow cause; if not artistic in itself, it has provided an anonymous pool of cultural meanings with which the critic/spectator can engage, both resistantly and aesthetically.[3]

The history of movie art in America—at least that made by spectators— thus must begin with a consideration of the aesthetic contexts and vanguard leanings of highbrow film criticism. If, as Andrew Ross (1989) has demonstrated, American intellectuals negotiated their shifting and often precarious status within postwar society through an engagement with popular culture, the movies served as an important nexus of this negotiation.[4] Beginning in the 1940s, key vanguard critics pioneered new models of film appreciation, providing a vision of critic as creative artist, as opposed to distanced judge: now even seemingly *un*exceptional movies could be matched to highbrow aesthetic norms and indeed offered as vehicles for a more active, creative, and implicitly empowering form of spectatorship. The most central of these pioneers are now among the most obscure—so completely were their perspectives absorbed into the vanguard culture that developed in their wake. Yet if Manny Farber and Parker Tyler are all but unknown to today's film scholars, it is hard to imagine film scholarship, or indeed *Mystery Science Theater*, without them. Through their writings we can chart the development of a new outlook on culture, one that would ultimately influence generations of media consumers. While their specific approaches, biases, and indeed critical temperaments differed markedly, they were united by their obvious desire to present their criticism of the movies not merely as a consumer guide but as a vehicle for asserting their own creative, artistic response to the challenge of postwar popular art (i.e., middlebrow culture).

In doing so, they implied that the activist critic could engage in imaginative artistry too, with the materials of mass culture providing raw material for a more authentic and democratic alternative to a growing commercial mainstream of American modernism. Their vanguard critical approaches only grew in popularity and influence with the emergence of the countercultural New York Underground of the 1960s, though now they would be simplified, shaped into more accessible, utilitarian form appealing to antimiddlebrow sentiment within the counterculture. This in turn split the American avant-garde, with a more radical wing successfully retreating into theoretical obscurity, and the pop avant-garde spawned in the Underground gaining still larger audiences on the midnight movie circuit. Together, both halves effectively squeezed out more traditional conceptions of the film artist—*including* that of the autonomous modernist film artist—offering instead a new vision of the artist as creative spectator of movies. Today, the gulfs separating artist, critic, and spectator have narrowed to the point where the special authority of the filmmaker seems an outdated notion: now anyone and everyone, it seems, can make movie art.

THE ASCENT OF THE AVANT-GARDE?

My larger claim is thus not merely that certain American film critics have been "vanguard" in the looser sense of "cutting edge," but that they have actually nuanced and furthered the tactics of the artistic avant-garde. Obviously this suggests that I am defining the avant-garde as much more than simply a style of art, or as a historical movement whose time has long passed. The avant-garde is, more properly, a mode and tradition of art making steeped in modernist precepts yet seeking a more interventionist role for the modern artist as visionary guru who helps others to see the world through a liberating modernist perspective. The avant-garde's goals are self-consciously political to the extent that the democratizing of artistic production is considered a radical act of emancipation from the chains of mass culture, a seizing of everyday spectatorship in the interests of a more aesthetically fulfilling life praxis. This shared philosophy is what unites the various avant-garde movements of the 1920s. In their own ways, dada, surrealism, constructivism, expressionism, and futurism all pursued an oddly elitist antielitism, endeavoring to lead the culturally disenfranchised toward the sweetness and light of aesthetic engagement. The prewar avant-garde's emphasis on populist slogans ("Art into Life!" [Tatlin]; "Literature is a part of life!" [Cendrars]), strident manifestos, and innovative creative procedures reflects a desire to move beyond the perceived dead end of aestheticist autonomy—the bourgeois separation of art and life—by proposing artistic process itself as profoundly relevant *critical* activity. Consider, for instance, this excerpt from Breton's initial surrealist manifesto of 1924:

> Man proposes and disposes. He alone can determine whether he is completely master of himself, that is, whether he maintains the body of his desires, daily more formidable, in a state of anarchy. Poetry teaches him to. It bears within itself the perfect compensation for the miseries we endure. . . . The time is coming when it decrees the end of money and by itself will break the bread of heaven for the earth! There will be gatherings on the public squares, and *movements* you never dared hope participate in. Farewell to absurd choices, the dreams of dark abyss, rivalries, the prolonged patience, the flight of the seasons, the artificial order of ideas, the ramp of danger, time for everything! May you only take the trouble to *practice* poetry. Is it not incumbent upon us, who are already living off it, to try and impose what we hold to be our case for further inquiry? (Breton 1972, 18)

For the avant-gardist, then, it simply wasn't enough for the dada collage or ready-made, surrealist "Exquisite Corpse," futurist poem, or constructivist theatrical production to critique and reconstruct the instrumentalist iconography of modern life—they were also meant to inspire this critical/artistic spectatorship in homes and on the street, where it really mattered. Only when the mass man himself deconstructed advertisements, recognized the artistry of his own mechanized movements, succumbed to the inspiring tumult of his repressed psyche—only then, it was assumed, would the vanguard artist's mission be accomplished.[5]

The avant-garde has staked everything on this claim to radical distinction from their artistic brethren. Yet so long as avant-gardists work in traditional media, they risk having this distinction seem forced and hopelessly utopian. After all, while their own paintings, sculptures, or poems may be formally radical and even reflect a deconstruction of everyday life, they are no more so than those modernist texts which both disrupt and subvert the "prevalent communicative discourse of the sociosymbolic order" (Eysteinsson 1990, 219) and implicitly solicit an appropriately active, critical stance from their audience.[6] Hence vanguard activists have had to assess radicalism not on the basis of form per se, but on the circulation of texts within larger cultural, social, and political spheres. Artworks that allow themselves to be absorbed within—and neutralized by—larger social and cultural forces can be decried as "autonomous," their radicalism viewed as self-contained and onanistic. If this rhetorical stance seems rather shaky (what do we do with the formed works of De Chirico, Ernst, Masson, Brancusi, Picabia, Lipchitz, and Giacometti?), it is also much closer to an accusation of "selling out" than to serious textual criticism. In the end it matters less what a modern artwork looks like, or even what procedures were used to create it, than whether the work has managed to garner acceptance or acclaim from the bourgeois public. Never mind that Jackson Pollock's process and form were radical in themselves—because his paintings became cultural "commodities" in their own right, highly valuable in a nonaesthetic sense, they can be associated with reactionary values, dismissed as culturally and/or ideologically affirmative.

Indeed, the cultural visibility and apparent consumer friendliness of New York School modernism have made it a prime target for vanguard condemnation as the epitome of reactionary autonomy, a corporate style for Eisenhower America. In his influential *Theory of the Avant-Garde* (1984), for instance, Peter Bürger strictly defines the avant-garde as a prewar phenomenon, dismissing American modernism as a false "neo-avant-garde" sparked by bourgeois neutralization of authentic vanguard ideals. Gone are the prewar avant-gardes' replacement of bourgeois art's autonomy and individualism with a "new life praxis" (49) organized from a basis in art. Instead, we merely get affirmative culture in vanguard packaging:

> If an artist today signs a stove pipe and exhibits it, that artist certainly does not denounce the art market but adapts to it. Such adaptation does not eradicate the idea of individual creativity, it affirms it, and the reason is the failure of the avant-gardist attempt to sublate art. Since now the protest of the historical avant-garde against art as institution is accepted as *art*, the gesture of protest of the neo-avant-garde becomes inauthentic. (52–53)

For Bürger, then, American modernism becomes the epitome of *anti*vanguard art, "autonomous art in the full sense of the term, which means that it negates the avant-gardiste intention of returning art to the praxis of life" (58).[7]

Bürger's critique of American art may be justified from the vanguard perspective, but in looking for autonomy in all the obvious places, he fails to notice that postwar America was actually the perfect breeding ground for vanguard revolt against affirmative, consumerist aesthetics. In fact, like-minded attacks on abstract expressionism date from the late 1940s, when they issued from dissatisfied factions of the New York art world itself. Most important, several of these attacks actually voiced a radical, direct, and above all critical response to the apparent fall of American modernism, by reconceiving movie criticism as a vanguard activity. Their success in this endeavor would be enormously influential, altering the course of the avant-garde's development and assuring its place in American cultural life.

For it was in criticism itself that avant-gardists could finally assert artistic, noncommodifiable forms of life praxis liberated from the production of distinct works (and hence from the looming specter of autonomy). Specifically, by reconceiving ways in which Hollywood movies might be viewed, the vanguard critic could promote, through a critical text that was finally *not* an autonomous/consumerist artwork in its own right, a "popular" (democratic) high culture distinct from both mass culture and conventionalized (elitist) high culture. As Bürger notes, prewar avant-gardists such as André Breton and Tristan Tzara had led the way here, moving beyond the relative autonomy of dada poetry and even automatic writing to offer instructions for self-liberation from mass culture through the aesthetic dismantling of the semiotics of everyday life. But in spurring an increasing acceptance of vanguard ideals as a liberating life practice, vanguard movie criticism offered the sort of success Breton could not have dreamt of, and Bürger can never accept.

If claiming the partial success of the vanguard project sounds preposterous, it is only because we have been led by vanguard ideology itself into accepting the ideals of the avant-garde as utopian and unrealizable. Happenings, conceptual art, even earthworks may have taken up the vanguard program too, but we can comfortably accept them as such because they still maintain the authority of the artist while ensuring his minimal sway over the everyday practices of others. Real pedagogical power is harder to embrace. But why? Certainly the avant-garde's messianic populism is severely compromised by its underlying allegiance to the bohemian intelligentsia, and to cultural elitism in general. Certainly its identification with popular culture is hopelessly paternalistic. Yet these facts do not in themselves preclude either the avant-garde's potential influence or indeed the potential success of its agenda.

A quasi-libertarian celebration of the resistant use of shared commercial culture, vanguard culture has actually flourished under American capitalism *because* (not in spite) of its own fiercely individualistic fixation on emancipated, democratic expression. Perhaps its distance from political radicalism didn't hurt, either: by the mid-1940s the consequences of blind devotion to communism and fascism were all too obvious. But the political commitments of prewar avant-gardists had themselves been significantly compromised by their own ambivalence toward constructive political solutions for social change—as witness Breton's decision to flee to America instead of fighting with the French underground.

In its dedication to spectatorial liberation, the postwar American avant-garde was as meaningfully "political" as its prewar ancestors; given its greater influence, perhaps it was ultimately more so. Certainly it had to navigate a sociocultural terrain laced with contradictions. In a society supportive of both democratic freedom and political repression, in a culture that could make modern art a bankable commodity while embracing the mass culture of movies and television, it managed to stake out its own peculiar field of activity by rejecting the acceptable sociocultural alliances of highbrow intellectuals. Instead of siding with democratic freedom and modern art, and against repression and mass culture, vanguard film critics adopted the apparently contradictory stance of siding with *both* democratic freedom and mass culture, and against repression and modernism. In truth, these critics disdained mass culture too—but their willingness to take it seriously, to engage with it intellectually, was still shocking in a culture founded on Arnoldian ideals. In practice, they implicitly sought to supplant Arnold's own prescription for mass culture resistance (instruction in Great Works) with that of an Arnoldian revisionist, Oscar Wilde.

OSCAR WILDE AND THE CRITIC AS ARTIST

Though Wilde is rarely associated with the historical avant-garde at all,[8] his vision of creative, artistic criticism presages the development of vanguard activity into a critical enterprise. Others before him had argued for creative engagement with texts—Thomas De Quincey, for instance, in "On the Knocking at the Gate in *Macbeth*" (1823)—but Wilde, as a disciple of the unapologetic aesthete Walter Pater, insisted in "The Critic as Artist" (1890) that criticism actually be elevated to another form of art, one "creative in the highest sense of the word" (1981, 81). For Wilde, if the artist's material is the world, the critic's material is the artwork—though not necessarily one of inherent value. Indeed, anything will serve his purpose, because he aims not to "see the object as in itself it really is," but rather to "chronicle his own impressions," to produce a "record of [his] own soul" (83).

Wilde contends that the artist's original intention is of little concern to a critic who properly treats the work simply as a "starting-point for a new creation" (85). For the critic's role is not to explicate meanings inscribed in a text by the artist, but to record his own intensely personal impressions of the work:

> The meaning of any beautiful created thing is, at least, as much in the soul of him who looks at it as it was in his soul who wrought it. Nay, it is rather the beholder who lends to the beautiful thing its myriad meanings, and makes it marvelous for us. . . . The beauty of the visible arts is, as the beauty of music, impressive primarily, and . . . it may be marred, and indeed often is so, by any

excess of intellectual intention on the part of the artist. For when the work is finished it has, as it were, an independent life of its own, and may deliver a message far other than that which was put into its lips to say. (86)

Though this comes remarkably close to sounding like later New Critical rhetoric, Wilde's ultimate disregard for the integrity of the original work actually places him at the forefront of the more radical vanguard tradition.

> To the critic the work of art is simply a suggestion for a new work of his own, that need not necessarily bear any obvious resemblance to the thing it criticizes. The one characteristic of a beautiful form is that one can put into it whatever one wishes, and see in it whatever one chooses to see; and the beauty, that gives to creation its universal and aesthetic element, makes the critic a creator in his turn, and whispers of a thousand different things which were not present in the mind of him who carved the statue or painted the panel or graved the gem. (87)

Because relevant meanings are not immanent but *created* out of the work's material by the critic, the text can become a highly fertile site for interpretation. When given the choice, the aesthetic critic rejects "those obvious modes of art that have but one message to deliver" (89) for those which "suggest reverie and mood, and by their imaginative beauty make all interpretations true and no interpretation final" (89–90).

In effect deconstructing the "beautiful form" of the open, liberated text, Wilde's critic makes the work relevant to the age.[9] But this critique also serves as an example of the transcendence of the aesthetic life. If in worshiping beauty he must step outside society's ethical boundaries in order to remain open to "new sensations and fresh points of view" (118), he only wishes to arouse the age "into consciousness, and to make it responsive, creating in it new desires and appetites, and lending it his larger vision and his nobler moods" (126–27). Following Arnold, Wilde directs his ire at the philistinism of the practical life ("we live in the age of the overworked, and the undereducated; the age in which people are so industrious that they become absolutely stupid"[108]); yet here, opposition to this life takes a quite different form, with the critic-artist openly rejecting the vulgar values of middlebrow culture for an impractical, contemplative, even "antinomian" existence. In rejecting "doing" for "becoming" (107), ethics for aesthetics ("even a color sense is more important . . . than a sense of right and wrong" [135]), he brazenly offers himself as a defender of culture and liberty in the crass new world of public opinion.

> I myself am inclined to think that creation is doomed. It springs from too primitive, too natural an impulse. However this may be, it is certain that the subject matter at the disposal of creation is always diminishing, while the subject matter

of criticism increases daily. There are always new attitudes for the mind, and new points of view. The duty of imposing form upon chaos does not grow less as the world advances. There was never a time when criticism was more needed than it is now. It is only by its means that humanity can become conscious of the point at which it has arrived. (130–31)

Ultimately, then, the critic will save culture by promoting the contemplative life, "making special" the world of the everyday, salvaging out of vulgar chaos the transcendent beauty of Art. If conventional creation seems doomed because it remains too close to Life, it is also rendered nearly irrelevant by Wilde's elevation of the critic-as-artist, whose creativity, influence, and ability both to lend Art its meaning and to create a work "flawless in beauty" (82) out of middlebrow material make him the Artist for the modern age. Wilde's critic is, like Arnold's, a cultural activist, seeking to combat the growing dominance of mass values with an aggressive assertion of Taste. Yet in also seeing the critic as a creative artist in his own right, and the public as a field of potential artist-critics, Wilde suggests that Walter Pater's notion of the "art of life" can be extended to large-scale semiotic resistance guided by an elect of aesthetes.

This is essentially the same vision of the critic as superior artist and cultural visionary that would dominate vanguard culture in postwar America. That Wilde happened upon it so early should not surprise us, given his prescient desire to subvert the semiotics of everyday life by advocating an aestheticized lifestyle, manifested in arenas as varied as dress and interior design.[10] Indeed, in audaciously arguing that the critic transforms not just the work but also the world around him, Wilde becomes a model for the vanguard activist whose hope for cultural restoration lies in the artistic critic's freelance aestheticizing of everyday life. For all its apparent naïveté (not to mention its outrageousness in Victorian England), such a hope stemmed from a shrewd observation: that the growth of an industrial mass culture could be opposed, not simply by a counterculture of refined art, but by an aggressive aesthetic reconfiguration of mass culture on the part of its very members, led by a critical elite.

MODES OF CRITICAL ARTISTRY: CULTISM AND CAMP

Wilde's importance for us thus lies less in his influence on specific critics and artists than in his clear, indeed visionary elaboration of the avant-garde's dominant cultural program during the next century. He couldn't have had the movies in mind when he wrote "The Critic as Artist," as they would not make their appearance in England until a few years later (though even given the chance, he is unlikely to have been willing to stoop so low). Nevertheless, his approach was eminently suited to the discussion of cinema as another potentially aesthetic component of everyday life. If aesthetic complexity issues substantially from the soul of the beholder, the movies' apparent lack of sophistication can be rendered moot. But because they are also *authentic* cultural expressions, movies can be pitted against the frieze-dried art of the middle classes: for vanguard film critics of the 1940s, they were as far removed as one could get from the faux sophistication of successful abstract expressionism. The critic could thus become a sort of agent provocateur for a culture of negation, openly refusing any perceived mainstream of taste while providing a model of resistant, artistic spectatorship. The movies could be remade, shaped into resistant vanguard material—and with relative ease, given the appropriate critical approaches.

In practice, two such approaches have dominated: I shall term them *cultism* and *camp*. Though similar in many important respects, these perspectives need to be distinguished clearly. Cult criticism focuses on the identification and isolation of marginal artworks, or aspects and qualities of marginal artworks, that (though sorely neglected by others) meet the critic's privileged aesthetic criteria. Often the marginal cult object is not a traditional artwork at all but a select product of popular culture. Thus the cult critic may generally find Hollywood films of little merit but still find the marginal work of one director, or a particular film, to be of aesthetic interest. At an extreme, cult appreciation can occur at a microlevel: a critic may find a film uninteresting overall yet still fascinating in the details of isolated scenes, shots, or performances.

Cult spectatorship of popular culture is usually thought of as a relatively recent phenomenon, but it has been a fixture of vanguard activity since Picasso and Braque first expressed their selective appreciation of the popular by reproducing fragments of circus and music hall posters in their paintings. Indeed, cult appreciation exploded as a tactical response to the very growth of mass culture: the cultist identifies and refuses "mass" taste by developing a resistant cult taste for more obscure and less clearly commodified cultural objects. The cultist will not be *sold* culture; instead, she displays her power to choose actively among an array of cultural offerings. Yet as cultism is inherently reactionary, cult spectators actively define themselves in relation to the vagaries of the marketplace. They typically respond to commercial co-optation of cult taste by moving *out* or *in*: outward beyond the widened reach of "mass," or inward to the unpillaged nuances of the co-opted taste object.[11]

Cult criticism places a high value on connoisseurship; it glorifies the critic-spectator's heightened ability to select appropriately, and tastefully. Though in the process the cult critic also interprets the mass culture object in order to match it with relevant aesthetic criteria, in effect this facet of cult criticism is usually effaced to the end that the mystique of selection

itself—the connoisseur's talent in finding the prized object or fragment—
is heightened. By contrast, the critical *camp* spectator revels in the inter-
pretation/transformation process while often placing little stake in the
initial selection of mass objects. As with Wilde's artist-critic, often "anything will serve his purpose," because here the pleasure of criticism lies in
forcibly remaking common culture into personal art. Like cultism, camp
asserts dominance over the mass culture field. But camp criticism is more
process-oriented than cultism; instead of celebrating happy exceptions, it
demonstrates that potentially *any* mass culture object can be re-created
aesthetically. Here the process of critical spectatorship comes to the fore,
with metaphoric and especially symbolic complexity accentuated and
even imposed through artistic reception. A movie becomes "activated" as
art by the camp spectator's creative, resistant interpretation.

Because each critical approach favors different skills, the two would
be absorbed into postwar culture differently. Cultism's heavy reliance on
oppositional connoisseurship meant that it could become accessible to a
wider audience only through a clearer focus on hierarchies and canons.
Camp's creative transmutation could become popular only with a reduc-
tion of aesthetic complexity and a heightened emphasis on critical gesture.
In both cases, however, the models provided by pioneering cultist Manny
Farber and camp critic Parker Tyler would be simplified significantly in
order to reach a wider public. Such simplification may be read as corruption, but the *new* cultism and camp epitomized by the approaches of the
1960s Underground's Andrew Sarris and Jonas Mekas actually maintained core vanguard ideals while opening vanguard production to a
broader public now able to seize the movies as aesthetic material.

This very success, however, sparked extreme reactions on two fronts.
To highbrows interested in cinema but unwilling to stoop to middlebrow
discernment of European art films, the popularizing of vanguard strategies sparked a retreat into obscurity, simply by supplementing the old
vanguard approaches with aesthetic positions (minimalism, European
materialism) that were too new, and too difficult, to become highly popular. For those who engaged in Arnoldian discernment of artistic films—
and by the 1950s, this included Tyler himself—the ascent of the new
avant-garde of the 1960s spelled the demise of reliable aesthetic standards
and an irresponsible capitulation of critical responsibility in an age of
important human issues. The movies may have provided highbrow fun in
the 1940s, but vanguard recklessness now seemed far more dangerous,
even ominous. Could America's genuine film art—so bravely pioneered
by promising experimentalists such as Maya Deren, Charles Boultenhouse, and Stan Brakhage,[12] and by select independents like John Cassavetes—survive such a flagrant dismissal of critical values?

That this question still remains highly relevant to today's cultural climate itself suggests that, for better and worse, we now live in an age enormously influenced by the avant-garde's ideals. What is postmodern culture but, broadly speaking, successful vanguard culture? Mass culture's grip on audiences has hardly been eradicated, but the recent slew of feature film versions of TV programs such as *The Brady Bunch*, *The Beverly Hillbillies*, *Sgt. Bilko*, *The Mod Squad*, and *Lost in Space* itself indicates how much cultism and camp now influence mass culture's offerings, as well as spectators' *use* of those offerings. In some respects we may be better off as vanguard critical spectators of our culture, but we cannot assume that the avant-garde's aestheticizing gesture has triumphed without costs, or that its assertion of a particular notion of "artistic" cinema is unallied with specific ideological interests. Like any gesture, it may ultimately prove to be less spontaneous, and more conventional, than it first seems.

The rest of this book is largely an effort to unearth such conventions in order to expose more clearly the contexts, ideologies, and ramifications of the vanguard perspective on movies. My approach is at once narrow and broad. In closely examining the writings and cultural contexts of a few postwar vanguard critics, I offer a specific case study of sorts. But these critics were obviously not chosen at random: they are meant to serve as clear exemplars of vanguard critical traditions of cultism and camp, influential, pioneering highbrows who refined prototypical means of discussing films aesthetically, and oppositionally. Thus, while I will focus most narrowly on specific pieces of criticism, my scope will repeatedly move outward, toward the art and film cultures surrounding them.

Chapter 2 begins by contextualizing the new American avant-garde's emergence within the volatile climate of 1940s American modernism. Artistic film criticism arose from modernist fringes alienated from the palatable, marketable compromise aesthetic of abstract expressionism; by applying the New York School's own dominant interpretive paradigm of freedom and vitality to craft-bound, nonartistic Hollywood films, key members of these fringes could make even mass movies seem as fresh and authentically vibrant as the tired work of New York abstractionists. We turn to film criticism proper in chapters 3 and 4, focusing on the innovative 1940s cultism and camp of Manny Farber and Parker Tyler. In championing the visceral realism lurking in the fringes of Hollywood product, and his own disdain for self-important prestige pictures (i.e., those pictures *marketed* as Art), *New Republic* and *Nation* critic Farber adapted abstractionist norms to a new medium while setting the terms of cultist connoisseurship for a generation of film enthusiasts. By contrast, in developing his own conception of the active, "erotic spectator" who burrowed his way into the symbolic, psychomythic depths of artworks and movies alike, Tyler exposed and shaped the symbolism of everyday life while demonstrating that, like the surrealist artist, the camp critic-spectator might construct something aesthetically rich out of cultural detritus.

By the late 1950s, however, creative, marginal spectatorship was no longer novel in America: film cults and camp appreciation had begun to garner a wider audience of hipsters, some of whom refined the vanguard example for their own purposes. This modification of cultism and camp, and the reaction it provoked, concern us through the rest of the book. Chapter 5 pits Farber's increasingly obscure cultism against the more accessible new model provided by Andrew Sarris, while in chapter 6 a newly Arnoldian Tyler looks on in horror as the French New Wave and Jonas Mekas's Underground alike appear to jettison artistic standards while reveling in an orgy of camp narcissism. The subsequent withdrawal by vanguard critics into academic theory is covered in chapter 7, though I stop short of providing detailed analyses of current academic approaches: my interest is more in situating the avant-garde's move to minimalism and materialism as a culmination of the larger progression examined herein.

Throughout, I assume that highbrow film criticism has been more important, and more aesthetic, than we commonly assume. The movies lie at the nexus of popular, mass, middlebrow, and highbrow; because they can be appropriated by each taste group against the other, they remained for years the prime focus of taste distinctions within our culture. That they could become transformed by a select few into a valid avant-garde, a popular art for a commercial age, has had profound effects on the way we regard art, cinema, and their potential overlap. With this in mind, let us first examine more closely the historical and cultural peculiarities that allowed the movies to be productively aestheticized.

Chapter Two

MOVIES TO THE RESCUE: AMERICAN MODERNISM
AND THE MIDDLEBROW CHALLENGE

The movies—and American movies in particular—stand at
the center of that unresolved problem of "popular culture"
which has come to be a kind of nagging embarrassment to
criticism, intruding itself on all our efforts to understand the
special qualities of our culture and to define our own relation
to it. That this relation should require definition at all is the
heart of the problem. We are all "self-made men" culturally,
establishing ourselves in terms of the particular choices we
make from among the confusing multitude of
stimuli that present themselves to us.
(Robert Warshow)

WHY DO WE take movies seriously? Some may bristle at the question, but the answer is hardly self-evident. Certainly for many academics and laypersons alike, movies still function as casual, superficial diversions from more consequential concerns; indeed, most Hollywood films seem designed accordingly. Regular moviegoers, and the reviewers who serve them, have always recognized the pragmatic craft orientation of film entertainment and have judged accordingly. Was the decor realistic? Were the special effects exciting? Was the script well written, convincingly delivered? But vanguard highbrows, and the vanguard culture they have eventually given rise to, have had a separate agenda. For them, an affection for movies could serve as a radical aesthetic alternative to mainstream, consumer-friendly modernism.

Movies have proven surprisingly useful to different groups seeking to bolster widely disparate social identities; thus highbrow culture critic Robert Warshow could feel justifiably anguished at the problems they posed, and pleasures they offered. At the same time, however, the "particular choices we make from among the confusing multitude of stimuli that present themselves to us" (1970c, 23) are not wholly free, as Warshow implies. They are socially and culturally conditioned choices, highly conventional and historically formed. The decision to embrace the movies as

a serious and implicitly aesthetic culture is one rooted in particular historical and cultural circumstances.

In America, those circumstances involved a reactionary retreat from
the burgeoning success of abstract expressionism on the part of key figures
determined to resist the commodification of modernism and individual
expression. Here the vulgar medium of motion pictures could become a
means to an end, offering the vanguard critic an authentic vibrancy
against which the studied efforts of the fashionable abstractionists seemed
forced and opportunistic. The movies were everything the new modern
art wasn't: craft-oriented, authentically popular, vital, mythically rich.
Were they artworks? No, not in the usual sense—but this was only a plus,
because the commercial, autonomous, supposedly anticraft American artwork was taking modernism down the road to aesthetic ruin. In appropriating popular culture for their own purposes, vanguard critics could actually use the functionalism, accessibility, and sameness of mass-produced
popular culture (Fiske 1991) to their own benefit, hurling aesthetically
rich craft artifacts back in the abstract expressionists' faces.

This disaffection from American modernism stemmed from a deep
sense of betrayal. To its supporters, the New York School may have repre-
sented the ascent of progressive European aesthetics into the "mainstream
tradition" (Rose 1967, 7) of American art and culture—but to its vanguard critics this very desire for mainstream acceptance seemed only to
be producing expensive wallpaper for haut-bourgeois homes. If today's
academics retrospectively see in postwar abstraction apolitical thematics
and conformist expressivism, and not cultural radicalism, in the 1940s it
was not so different.[1] A weak hybrid, the new American art seemed to
have compromised the purity of its constituent influences and aesthetics
in a bid for cultural acceptance and financial success. No wonder it became ripe for ridicule by those who sensed (or hoped) they would be
marginalized in its wake.

ABSTRACTION, SURREALISM, AND THE VITAL MIDDLE

Pitting the movies against Motherwell, craft against liberated expression,
was certainly a loaded gesture.[2] After all, the New York School had itself
rolled in on a wave of anticraft sentiment, defining its progressive aesthetics against the reactionary pull of regional craft traditions and the politicized craft ethos of WPA civic art.[3] The rise of European totalitarianism
had also helped immensely, making Trotskyite modernism seem more renegade than elitist, and—even more important—exiling successful surrealists to New York City. In exchange for temporary asylum, Matta, Mon-
drian, Léger, Breton, Lipchitz, Ernst, and Tanguy lent the New York art
community not simply a European prestige, activist cachet, and ready

supply of works; fundamentally, they offered an example of marketable and potentially popular modern art. This "late" surrealism was on the whole far less openly agitational than its earlier manifestations had been; commercial success and a disillusionment with Stalinism had somewhat moderated this vanguard movement's revolutionary image, allowing the profitable distribution of a slick, high-profile, and relatively apolitical review such as *Minotaure* (1933–39).[4]

Most important, promotional adeptness was also accompanied by a refined rhetoric that could sell seemingly nonfunctional, inaccessible, un*popular* art on the basis of its expression of personal liberty and vitality. In retrospect, the timing was perfect: in a country teetering on the brink of European intervention, liberty and vitality seemed to signify all that distinguished America from the fascist hordes. The new American art that emerged under the promotional tutelage of surrealism could be promoted through open appeal to both qualities. Liberty became expressive freedom, which had been squashed by the Nazis. Peggy Guggenheim highlighted the political implications of her permanent collection by opening her 1942 *Art of this Century* catalog with Hitler's 1937 defense of modernist censorship as "sterilization of the insane" (7). Sheldon Cheney optimistically concludes his *Story of Modern Art* (1941) with "the hope and the belief that in this time of tragedy for Europe, when creation has stopped where once creativeness centered," America's modern artists

> will go on to aesthetic solutions unprecedented, will find ways of carrying on worthily, even magnificently, a tradition made important and splendid more than a half-century ago by Daumier, Whistler, and Cézanne, a tradition enriched by the men of Paris and by the Germans, a tradition accepted and made their own by the Mexicans and the Americans of the United States. (626)

America's natural vitality could be offered as further proof that this was the appropriate country to pick up the modernist torch, rescuing and extending the European aesthetic legacy. Critic and gallery owner Sam Kootz was happily shocked that the newest American art seemed to transcend the "hopeless emasculation" and dearth of "lusty masculine seeing" (1930, 20) of the past, and he couldn't believe that the American public was now hesitating to embrace an aesthetic expressive of both liberal democracy and authentic virility. "We can't understand this apathy and we cry out that the public itself is choking life, refusing to admit the very things that permit life to go on—for without extension, life dies" (1943, 7).

This dual appeal to freedom and vitality was also useful to supporters of American modernism in that it helped to reconcile the hybrid roots of the new American art, uniting surrealism with the abstractionist/cubist tradition that had hugely influenced American modernism. Because these new interpretive norms were so loose and pervasive, and because both had themselves emerged from European modernism, they provided something of a common ground for critics in neighboring camps. The flexibility of this new aesthetic was such that even those critics who still stubbornly refused to come on board as New York School supporters, instead choosing to espouse purer visions of American art, could still inadvertently contribute to a climate of acceptance for America's modernist amalgam.

At one extreme of the New York art world of the 1940s stood loyal abstractionists relieved at the final dissolution of WPA social realism and hopeful for an American modernism that might honor European cubism's example of aesthetic progress. Suspicious of surrealism's faddish popularity, aesthetic simplicity, and obsession with sexual perversion (abstractionist machismo had been inherited from the WPA era), they reserved their praise for the new American art's bold, aggressive, masculine gestures and intelligent resolution of aesthetic problems. Manny Farber would remain loyal to this faction through the 1940s, but for the moment let us briefly consider a far better known (if more temporary) marginal abstractionist, Clement Greenberg.

A loyal Trotskyite, Greenberg consistently favored cubism over surrealism and formal sureness over any exploration of psychomythic depths. Though never wholly apolitical, his criticism for *Partisan Review* and the *Nation* (where he was replaced by Manny Farber in 1949) champions American modernists who share an interest in formal exploration within the cubist tradition. When in 1947 he declares Pollock to be "the most important so far of the younger generation of American painters," it is not the painter's exploration of mythic concerns that impresses him. Rather, "as is the case with almost all post-cubist painting of any real originality, it is the tension inherent in the constructed, recreated flatness of the surface that produces the strength of his art" (1986, 125). Skeptical of much American modernism through the 1940s, Greenberg reserved his praise for particular artists who managed to build on the European example while exuding freedom and vitality within a controlled, reductivist aesthetic framework. The baroque excesses of David Smith's mid-1940s work had not pleased the critic, but by 1947 the sculptor had managed to express "spareness and speed" within a newly unified style, and without "emasculating his invention."

> His sculpture for all its energy presents an elegance like that of Picasso's and Braque's high cubism: there is a similar clarity and a similar plenitude, both of which come from the artist's certainty of having a style that is able to say everything he has to say with the maximum of economy. (141)

In measured tone and careful attention to Smith's cubist elegance and economy, Greenberg certainly reveals his formal, abstractionist leanings, while in his concern for the speed, power, and (explicitly masculine) invention of the work, he is clearly also appealing to the liberty/vitality paradigm. Important too, these qualities lie very much near the surface of the artwork; indeed, for the abstractionist connoisseur they are palpable, an expression of the work's skillful kinetics. By contrast, the mainstream surrealists seemed to eschew true vitality for spurious hidden significance cloaked in crude symbolism. For Greenberg, such reliance on illustrated anecdote was retrograde in the extreme, branding these poseurs as "revivers of the literal past and advance agents of a new conformist, and best-selling art" (1986, 230). To committed cubist abstractionists, the surrealist alternative could be as stultifying as those provincial traditions that had gripped American art for most of its history.

To the surrealists, however, Greenberg's complaints must have seemed terribly old-fashioned, steeped in a formalism that their own exploration of textual substrata had attempted to transcend. They too saw liberated, vital expression at the root of vanguard art making, but for them aesthetic vigor and freedom lay not in the warp and woof of a work's surface form, but in the work's revelation of that psychomythic content usually held in check by a mind's, or culture's, repressive forces. Surrealism sharply redirected attention away from the *product* of skilled art making (à la Greenberg), to the liberating *process* of artistic creation. As a result, the artist himself became a sort of critic, freeing and analyzing the interior life of himself or his culture via an artwork that itself functioned as a living, active participant in this ongoing discovery.[5]

To a core group of artists and critics in the 1940s New York art scene, surrealism, and not cubism—and *certainly* not abstract expressionism—stood as the victorious center of the new American art. Again, this was not the "classic" surrealism of the 1920s but an updated, marketable, less radically political and more truly "artistic" model. Indeed, Breton himself (who seemed to many in New York cowardly, arrogant, and altogether unpleasant) had ultimately proven less influential on the American version than an earlier surrealist revisionist, Eugene Jolas. An American expatriate and editor of the Parisian journal *transition*, Jolas had certainly shared orthodox surrealism's interest in the dream state and the unconscious as a creative realm, but he had become wary of what he perceived to be its downplaying of deliberate, skilled artistic guidance in favor of automatic expression.[6]

Because it preserved a central role for artistic training and talent, and played off an existing bias for Jung over Freud, Jolas's more traditional aesthetic would actually prove quite influential in the burgeoning New York art scene.[7] But it was more pointedly honed elsewhere, by poet Charles Henri Ford and his surrealist journal *View*. Officially a venue for surrealist-flavored art, poetry, and criticism, *View* published Matta,

Breton, Ernst, Tanguy, Nicolas Calas, and Kurt Seligmann. More broadly, however, it actually positioned itself against Greenberg's (and *Partisan Review*'s) abstractionist traditionalism by presenting its surrealism as loose and thoroughly modern, encompassing the efforts of a wide range of European nonabstractionists.[8] Parker Tyler, a close friend of Ford's and a *View* writer and coeditor, would later recall that

> anything stylish is *View* style except Abstract Expressionism. . . . We print Chirico's autobiographical prose and Mario Praz's criticism. We have a Belgian Surrealist issue, a Latin American issue, a Paris issue, a British issue, a post-war Italian issue. Our covers (in color except for a Man Ray photograph) are by leading exiled and American modernists: Brancusi, Calder, O'Keeffe, Léger, Duchamp (to whom an elaborate issue is devoted), Tchelitchew, Seligmann, Noguchi, Jean Hélion, Léonor Fini, Esteban Francés. (1967a, 423–24)

The *View* agenda was to promote not a narrow visual style but new ways of thinking about art and, ultimately, the world. If Jolasian aesthetics encouraged some of its critics to engage in formal analysis, it allowed others to delve brazenly into the complex symbolic matrix of a work, revealing through a kind of participatory reverie the layered hidden meanings of the text, while also in a sense re-creating the text for the reader. Surrealism had permitted the artist to become a critic of psyche and society, but conversely it had also entreated the critic to display his artistry, producing an interpreted, "liberated" version of the work that highlighted and *extended* the original artist's vital subterranean invention.

Surrealist criticism could thus provide heightened challenges for the writer: if for Greenberg (and some *View* critics) elements of the freedom/vitality paradigm could be discerned on the surface of a work, for the radical surrealist critic they must first be unearthed, then incorporated into the surface of his *own* work. Consider this excerpt from Breton's own lengthy analysis of Duchamp's *Mariée mise à nue* (*The Bride Stripped Bare*), which *View* reprinted from a 1935 issue of *Minotaure*:

> The bride, by means of the three nets above her (the draft pistons) exchanges *orders* with the bachelor machine, orders that are transmitted along the milky way. For this, the nine mâlic moulds, in the appearance of waiting, in red lead, have by definition "received" the *lighting gas* and have taken *moulds* of it; and when they hear the *litanies of the chariot recited* (the refrain of the bachelor machine), let this lighting gas escape through a given number of *capillary tubes* placed toward their top. . . . The gas, being thus brought to the first sieve, continues to undergo various modifications in this state until in the end, after passing through a kind of *toboggan* or *corkscrew*, it becomes, as it comes out of the last sieve, *explosive* fluid. . . . During the whole of the operation just

described, the chariot (formed of rods of *emancipated metal*) recites, as we have seen, its litanies . . . while at the same time performing a to-and-fro motion along its gutter. (1991, 128)

Such a clearly creative, poetic critical approach to surrealist art could be readily accepted because such works seemed to openly invite participatory input, even interpretive reverie; as James John Sweeney remarked about Tanguy, "he sets the stage and we dream onto it" (1991, 48).

If such a radical vision of criticism was not adopted by the hybrid mainstream of abstract expressionism, it may have been because modern artists themselves had not yet become established as a viable force in American culture; it was radical enough that they were daring to assert their own expressive liberty and involvement in the vibrant psychomythic depths of the collective unconscious. Pollock's psychologically expressive, vibrant drip method is an obvious example here, but these notions pervade the movement. William Baziotes claimed that his canvases, lined up against his studio wall, told him "what [he was] like at the moment" (1990, 241); Herbert Ferber insisted that the "surrational space" of the creative imagination was "charged with form, sprung, tense as a steel coil, from those layers of being not subject to the censorship of verisimilitude" (Margo 1990, 136).[9]

Because a loosened appeal to liberty and vitality could be so instrumental in promoting the possibilities of a nonfunctional, less accessible artistic future for America, the aesthetic discourse of the New York School would finally be much broader and more encompassing than those of *View*'s surrealism or Greenberg's 1940s cubist abstractionism. If anything, the influence of Jung's "visionary mode" of artistic creation so widened the scope of aesthetic freedom and vitality as to push art making toward a kind of transcendentalist celebration of the life force itself.[10] For Barnett Newman, the artist's problem was now "not the pure line, straight and narrow," but "the idea-complex that makes contact with mystery—of life, of men, of nature, of the hard, black chaos that is death, of the grayer, softer chaos that is tragedy" (1990, 108). Peter Grippe claimed to "seek to express the life rhythm which is ever-changing, ever-growing" ("The Idea of Art" 1990, 151); for Hans Hofmann, the magic of painting could never be "fully, rationally explained," because it is "a process of metabolism, whereby color transubstantiates into vital forces that become the real sources of painterly life" ("Catalogue" 1975, 148).

To the loyal surrealist and abstractionist alike this may have seemed a grotesque, simplistic distortion of the European legacy, but the increasing exposure of this discourse in the late 1940s both reflected and heightened the new movement's rapidly accumulating cultural capital.[11] The rising prices of work by key artists and the success of the 1948 and 1950 Venice Biennales correspond to a steady increase in coverage of abstract expressionism in both popular media and specialized journals.[12] Within the New York art community itself, the growth, consolidation, and success of the school were marked by the introduction of artist-run periodicals modeled on the little magazines of the New York literary world. Journals such as the *Tiger's Eye*, *Possibilities*, and *Instead* served as influential forums for critical and theoretical discussions of the emerging expressivist aesthetic, and for the reproduction of paintings, photographs, poetry, and drama, the printing of artists' descriptions of their own working methods, and occasionally the transcription of group discussions such as 1950's "Artists' Sessions at Studio 35."[13] By the early 1950s, the New York School had acquired not simply a promotional rhetoric defensible on ideological grounds but also access to publishing venues necessary for the dissemination of this rhetoric. Now able to sell themselves effectively, the abstract expressionists garnered national, then international fame and prestige, and created a huge American constituency for expressive painting, sculpture, dance, theater, and music. Once the province of a marginal avant-garde, aesthetic liberty and vitality would soon be distributed to an unprecedented audience, and on an unprecedented scale.

RECLAIMING THE FRINGE

This was obviously not the bright future that the surrealist and abstractionist loyalists had predicted for American art. From authentic avant-gardism had emerged something altogether monstrous—a genuine American sellout, a weak mishmash of European ideas thrown together with some heroic bluster and marketing panache.

In response, key members of the marginalized wings elaborated their own alternative, spectator-centered vision of vanguard American art. Though couched in aesthetics, their objections to mainstreamed abstraction were implicitly ideological, rooted in a genuine fear that mass culture was working its way up the ladder of taste and would soon claim the rarefied space of serious art. This avant-garde, like those of prewar Europe, saw as its enemy the very notion of popular, commodified art. But kitsch had never seemed quite so close to home: the rapid postwar growth of a middle-class, consumerist audience for once-restricted forms of culture (abstract art, modern dance, "serious" plays and novels, modern jazz) suggested that aesthetics might actually find a home within commodified culture. This was a problem insofar as it threatened highbrow tastemaking privileges and suggested that commerce and cultural authenticity might actually be compatible. In response, highbrows could only hope to hold their ground by stressing commodified art's necessary inauthenticity. It could not be considered genuine high culture, because it had been co-opted and therefore defused by the forces of capitalism; yet neither could it be rescued as authentic popular culture, because it reeked of an intellectual self-importance that rendered it antipopular (if not necessarily *un*popular). Commodified art was, in essence, frozen out, stranded between tweezed and burly brows.

In a sense, *middlebrow* owed much to the Arnoldian genteel tradition, which had insisted that Culture could be acquired by all who were willing both to invest the necessary time and to accept the paternal guidance of the old-guard intellectual elite. Yet consumerism had itself fatally tainted the ideals of gentility, replacing traditional ideals of discipline and self-restraint with an emphasis on spontaneity and personal gratification, and ultimately rendering intellectual guidance somewhat superfluous. The new cultural gatekeepers were of a different order, employees of the Book of the Month Club (Radway 1988, Rubin 1992), members of the Academy of Motion Picture Arts—or perhaps judges for Pulitzer, whose prizes inevitably went to pretentious efforts like *Our Town* and *The Old Man and the Sea*. For Dwight Macdonald (1960), these books typified midcult's "tepid ooze" (609): here was formula-bound mass culture gussied up in an all-out effort to pass as highbrow, tackling Serious, Universal Themes and indulging in Sophisticated Stylistic Effects. This ignorant attention to the superficial reflected the tastes of rising classes who "imitate the forms of culture without understanding its essence" (610). While midcult may have pretended to "respect the standards of High Culture," it only diluted and vulgarized them into Bauhaus cafeterias, beatnik poetry, and the obscenely successful *Horizon: A Magazine of the Arts*. Authentic mass culture was at least tolerable because it expressed a quaint vitality, and because it never pretended to be more than it was—but midcult actually threatened to "fuzz up the distinction" (628) between High and Low, and thus had to be isolated and delegitimized.

Middlebrow, then, is not a fixed category of taste but a loose, oppositional epithet that continues to be wielded by all manner of highbrow intellectuals.[14] As Ross (1989) suggests, its expression of highbrow derision functioned during the postwar period as a "containing structure" (61) protecting cultural and intellectual authority, even as such authority was itself contained within the Cold War ideology of liberal pluralism. Nevertheless, gaining authority over what "popular art" might mean in America was no minor feat, as it allowed for a larger reconception of highbrow culture along vanguard lines. Indeed, the effort to reclaim Art from the creeping middle has fundamentally defined our culture of today, by offering in place of consumer-friendly modernism (and classicism) a notion of the cultural spectator as aesthetically empowered consumer of nonaesthetic material. "Popular art" could thus become not the art made by sellouts and sold to the would-bes, but the art that *we* make out of the stuff we see and buy.

For certain disgruntled highbrows of the 1940s, this "stuff" included movies. Here was an unsullied, authentic pop form that seemed positively refreshing next to the dull mannerism of mainstream abstract expressionism. In refining their own alternative modernism, an effective vanguard stance for postwar America, the two critics we will now examine opposed American art's middlebrow encroachment by gesturing back to the people, and to the legitimate vitality of popular craft culture. This was still manufactured mass culture, but because most movies lacked even the minimal aesthetic integrity of middlebrow art, they were available to be revisioned, transformed by discerning eyes into an alternative, vanguard vision of popular art. The movies, in short, could assume the position of the new avant-garde, though only on paper—or in the eyes of these enlightened, indeed "producerly" spectators. Manny Farber and Parker Tyler were not organized into an identifiable movement comparable to the prewar avant-gardes; during the 1940s, they remained isolated individuals working from the fringes of postwar modernism. Nor was their vanguard critique explicitly political, because the distasteful memories of 1930s radicalism, and the aesthetic biases associated with it, were still too fresh. But their stance was still *im*plicitly political, to be sure; it engaged the vanguard tradition's aesthetic activism (its forcible reengagement of art with the praxis of life) as convincingly as the prewar factions ever had.

There were, after all, other options for critics interested in the movies. One could simply assess Hollywood films for entertainment value. Alternatively, one might aim to apply more traditional (even traditionally modernist) standards of discernment to the broader field of contemporary releases, with a view toward more distanced aesthetic judgment. In rejecting both options, these two vanguard critics were not happening upon the "right" approach (even if it seems so from today's perspective); they were participating in a historically and culturally determined response to a specific set of circumstances. In flaunting their cultist and camp perspectives, Manny Farber and Parker Tyler hitched their own spirited bid for vanguard cultural authority to the wagon of mass culture. Each tried to imply that the vitality and freedom associated with the dominant abstract expressionist aesthetic could be found—by them at least—within popular cinema. For Farber, the cheapie action flick might serve as a superior alternative to much of what passed for action painting, expressing all the palpable, kinetic virility but none of the pretentiousness of the work of Pollock and Kline. For Tyler, the most banal Hollywood melodrama—unlike most New York School art—could be seen to harbor the subterranean vigor, symbolic complexity, and mythic import of authentic surrealism.

In their tastes, personas, and allegiances, they were miles apart—Farber a hard-boiled abstractionist painter/sculptor, Tyler a symbolist poet and self-styled aesthete. But together they pioneered sophisticated vanguard film criticism in America, incorporating the movies into modernist discourse in the absence (initially) of a cohesive New York modernist film scene.[15] In effect, they rescued the movies for criticism, albeit for reasons that had as much (or more) to do with American modernism as with movies themselves. They were looking for an alternative high culture outside the bounds of mainstreamed high culture, and they found it in films that few had theretofore taken seriously. Tyler could revel in the surreal currents flowing beneath an ordinary Hollywood product; Farber could pursue a connoisseurship of hidden vitality lurking on the fringes of scenes, films, or genres. Yet both spoke from the margins, defining their tastes against a new nemesis, commercial art.

In the process, both critics revived meaningful vanguard activity outside Europe and suggested a bold new direction for American modernism—beyond abstract expressionism, but also beyond abstractionism and surrealism as well. When in 1939 Clement Greenberg had pitted the avant-garde against the forces of kitsch, he was opposing modernist painting to all mass culture, from movies (lumped with magazine covers and tap dancing) up to the "high class *kitsch*" (1990, 343) of middlebrow *New Yorker* pieces. By considering mainstream modernism itself a form of kitsch, the new vanguard critics validated a resistant perspective for those who similarly cringed at the New York School's increasing cultural centrality and embarrassing assumption of the "avant-garde" mantle.

Indeed, the new critical art would irrevocably alter the very dynamics of high culture in America. Our influential pioneers were not actually aiming quite so high: in refining models of aesthetic refashioning, they were merely illustrating that *another* liberating, vital, and authentically American art was available to the tasteful, cultured highbrow, provided one had the skills needed to retrieve it. Nevertheless, their models of democratic insurgence would soon be successfully appropriated by others who felt a similar need to resist (or explode) Establishment aesthetics. What this later success ultimately tells us about the value and nature of the avant-garde—not to mention the movies—is something we will need to reconsider later. First, let us examine these trailblazing critical approaches more closely, beginning with Farber's rough-hewn cultism of the 1940s.

Chapter Three

LIFE ON THE EDGE: MANNY FARBER AND
CULT CRITICISM

> *Dear Sirs:* Your Manny Farber is, in my opinion, one of the most
> thoroughly annoying critics I have ever read. The term critic
> hardly does him justice: he is more of a professional
> pessimist and finger-pointer. . . .
> I have looked long and earnestly through dozens of *Nations*, hoping to
> be able to find one favorable criticism, one ordinary comment like
> "this picture is pretty good," or "the acting left something to be de-
> sired but the point went over," or even "you might possibly enjoy this
> one." But no. He obviously long ago reached the conclusion that no
> picture ever produced or likely to be produced in Hollywood has any
> merit whatsoever, all directors are sneaky and inept mechanics, all per-
> formers puppets or automatons, and all dialogue drizzly, dreary, man-
> gled, or downright idiotic. And he couches all his remarks in such re-
> condite language that he comes out sounding pretty profound.
> I could forgive him his dissection of *Riding High*, or even his snap-
> pings at the motives and techniques of Capra, Huston, Reed *et al.* But
> when he laces into *The Men*, *Home of the Brave*, *No Way Out*, and
> some of the others, the man is just raving. I daresay there is some good
> (perhaps not *art*) even in the run-of-the-mill Hollywood output; how
> much more so in these authentically produced, deftly
> acted, and altogether competent films?
> *(Max Bart)*[1]

MANNY FARBER may have read Mr. Bart's letter to the editor of the *Nation* with some confusion. Was he being accused of having too much taste, or not enough? It was not the first time Farber had been assailed in print. One disgruntled *New Republic* reader had charged him with harboring the absolute standards of a ranting "old Granny" (Kelly 1943, 121). Even Hollywood screenwriter Dudley Nichols had penned a mocking, drawling thank-you on behalf of all back-woods film factory workers: "Main thing is we hain't got [Farber's] vision and his private telephone connection with the Creator, so we cain't talk with his kind of finality and absolute authority" (1943, 640). But Bart's

missive is particularly pointed in its expression of a frustration many readers must have shared. (Who did this Farber think he was, anyhow?) It
also raises some interesting questions pertinent to film criticism.

First, does the film critic *evaluate* or *analyze*? Today, we associate the
former with journalism, the latter with highbrow or academic writing.
Yet if academics must start with at least an implicit value judgment (the
film is worth examining more closely), so journalistic reviewers must also
analyze. Still, for the journalist, analysis remains a means to an end. Like
most movies, movie reviewing highlights function and craft, analyzing
only to evaluate those craft elements most directly relevant to the consumer (usually acting and scriptwriting, but often editing, special effects,
and set design as well) in relation to desired effects, such as realism, sus-
pense, even eroticism. And while the reviewer will openly share her enthusiasm or distaste for the material, these judgments tend not to be
grounded in an explicit aesthetic bias; rather, they are carefully framed by
rhetorical strategies designed to establish the reviewer's credibility, arouse
reader interest, and justify through inductive or deductive proof (Bordwell 1989). Even the temper of the reviewer's own style and persona—
however flamboyant—will usually not be so extreme as to compromise
the spirit of generosity and objectivity that anchors his appeal and (in
many cases) keeps him employed. Because each movie is evaluated on the
basis of a mélange of craft elements, each is regarded afresh, with final
judgment less a sweeping claim than a carefully weighed, pragmatic assessment ("the acting left something to be desired but the point went
over"; "you might possibly enjoy this one").

This emphasis on pragmatism, however, presents something of a problem for the aesthetically biased reviewer, because if movies are indeed
evaluated according to broad aesthetic criteria, the resulting criticism may
seem too judgmental to be useful to the average reader. To Bart, indeed,
Manny Farber seems less a critic (as he understands the term) than a
"professional pessimist and finger-pointer" whose blanket assessment of
Hollywood product blinds him to the good stuff not simply in run-of-the-
mill movies but even in "altogether competent"—i.e., well crafted—films.
Like fellow reader Paul Gardner, who attacked Farber's "compulsion to
be devastatingly iconoclastic at all costs" (1949, 97), Bart sees a critic
sacrificing valuative cogency for polemical fury. To put it bluntly, Farber
seemed to hate the movies.

Farber, of course, would have vehemently disagreed. He didn't hate the
movies; he respected them enough to subject them to serious discussion
and judgment. But this still doesn't give Max Bart what he wants, which
is practical, useful criticism, using criteria generous enough to offer adequate consumer choice, and to validate existing standards of elevated
taste for the popular. Farber crosses the line when he "laces into" superior

Hollywood films *The Men, Home of the Brave,* and *No Way Out*: now he is "raving," wildly contemptuous of those reasonable standards of discernment indicative of civility and gentility. Here discriminating taste has been taken too far, into willful eclecticism. To Bart, Farber stubbornly insists on grading Hollywood films with a scale on which far too few will register. But for Farber, those special few are all that matter.

We should not really be surprised that this apparent refusal of accepted standards could raise such ire. After all, it was meant to. Farber's was an openly, tauntingly oppositional stance that pioneered new standards of connoisseurship in order to carve out a marginal niche. His vanguard cultism wore its disdain for the hopelessly middlebrow tastes of America's Max Barts as a badge of honor. Aggressiveness lies at the heart of cultism—for the cult gesture is nothing if not an assault on the conventions and order of taste.

Taste itself is a curious and complex notion. For many, it remains a natural quality: you either have it or you don't. But this is already to imply certain ideal objects of taste, as well as intermediary arbiters needed to determine and reinforce the elevated status of these objects. Taste judgments may be spontaneous, they may be informed, they may be particular, they may even be aesthetically, ethically, spiritually *justifiable*—but they are certainly not wholly natural. Taste distinctions are made for a variety of reasons, because they are influenced by culture and class as much as by personality.

Still, such distinctions are not so narrowly restricted by culture and class as to prevent individuals from making unorthodox, "inappropriate," even resistant assertions of taste. Lynes ([1949] 1980) and Gans (1974) both found that American culture's class mobility also opened it to a marked fluidity in taste cultures—though as liberals they both hoped that most "cultural straddling" (Gans, 109) would be upward, with the socially disadvantaged gaining access to a rich high culture of which they had been deprived. In retrospect, however, the last fifty years have been marked with as much *downward* as upward straddling, with the former emerging as something of a marginal highbrow response to the latter (then spreading beyond the highbrow arena altogether). As a key instance of downward straddling, cultism assails normative taste distinctions by refusing suitable taste objects, instead seeking out inappropriate objects from a lower taste culture, or from the lower recesses of one's own taste culture.

Among other things, cultism offers a naked assertion of high cultural capital when economic capital is scarce. Thus it attracts those enticed by high culture's aesthetics yet disaffected from its ideological values, providing these individuals an effective, aggressive means of cultural distinction. It makes sense, then, that cultism's roots would lie in bohemia and the avant-garde. If, as Bourdieu (1984) has noted, the avant-garde takes the negative refusal at the heart of all taste distinctions to a logical extreme, offering "the sum of the refusals of all socially recognized tastes" (294), cultism turns that refusal into a bold affirmation of resistance. For Telotte (1991), the cult film "is a way we have of crossing boundaries, even if we let others share in that brief, satisfying transgression. Such sharing still expresses our yearning for distinction; we at least want to *feel* different from the norm and from the conventional self we are supposed to become" (12).

In this light, it is not surprising that film cultism emerged in the postwar climate as a means of valiantly expressing difference within an expanding culture of sameness. The prewar avant-gardes had certainly embraced a popular cultism of their own: futurism, constructivism, dada, expressionism, and surrealism all variously celebrated the vitality of popular life, as embodied in amusements such as the circus and cabaret, and in the explosive energy of industrial technology. The vanguard drive to emancipate the common man from the forces of "mass" provoked a refinement of taste for authentically popular culture that might be remade into the vanguard work's manifestation of an ideal, liberated populism.

As connoisseurs of marginal art, including the aesthetically malleable fringes of nonart, vanguard cultists celebrate the power of spectators to define their own culture in opposition to prevailing standards. Yet whereas the prewar avant-garde could also celebrate a truly marginal art of their own, postwar avant-gardists have defined themselves *against* the modern art in their midst. Even as the growth of America's "lonely crowd" made the need for popular resistance to cultural hegemony especially urgent, fashionably alienated abstractionists' apparently eager capitulation to middlebrow commercial values made cultism an appealing choice for a new intellectual and cultural avant-garde.

Certainly for Manny Farber, criticism and creation were on more equal footing, implicitly complementing each other. A cultist's cultist known for his remarkable influence on the tastes of filmmakers, buffs, and other critics (Jonathan Rosenbaum simply calls him "the most important American film critic" [1995, 62]), Farber initially took up art and film criticism at the *New Republic* and the *Nation* largely as a means of supporting his own painting and sculpture. But his movie reviewing, in particular, ultimately proved a far more powerful means of expressing his own vanguard stance vis-à-vis an emerging mainstream of watered-down, consumerist high culture.

Farber's cultism certainly reflects a mixture of allegiances common to members of the American middle classes, especially during the socially conscious 1930s. The son of Arizona shopkeepers, he pursued sportswriting and football (at UC Berkeley), art (at Stanford, the California School of Fine Arts, and the Rudolf Schaefer School of Design), and carpentry (apprenticing in the Brotherhood of Carpenters and Joiners). Relocating to Greenwich Village in 1942 with Janet Terrace,[2] he befriended the likes of Saul Bellow, Alfred Kazin, Edmund Wilson, Alexander Calder, Harold Rosenberg, Robert Motherwell, Hans Hofmann, Clement Greenberg, and William Baziotes. Though he would never be properly recognized as an important artist in his own right, he participated closely in the development of the New York School and was included in several of its early group shows. More important for us, because he was immersed in its evolving promotional discourse, he would be able to use the aesthetic ideals championed within that discourse as a standard against which to highlight the new work's increasing affectation and fatigue.

ART OR WALLPAPER?

From the start, Farber was a cultist of art as well as cinema, favoring the margins over any perceived cultural mainstream while still strongly supporting the freedom/vitality paradigm dominant in American modernist aesthetics. Typically, his favored artist refused to stoop to convention by eschewing style-heavy mannerism in favor of the unpretentious, vigorous expression of a work's inner content through appropriate form. In the early 1940s, before abstract expressionism had emerged as a school in its own right, Farber could still associate mannerist lethargy with the passé provincialism of Eakins, Homer, or Benton (a "bush league painter" with a "flair for publicity" [1942c, 542]), or with the "mundane, stodgy, hopelessly unimaginative" (1943c, 916) romanticism of Bingham, Kent, and Cowles. Bogged down by pretentious literariness and heavy-handed symbolism, classic American painting was as "dead-serious as a Dreiser novel, as undecorative as a wash basin and as afraid of free-running instinct as Dorothy Dix's lovelorn advice. . . . Somewhere, and for puritanical reasons, our painting got tied up with preconceived ideas—moral, literary, and economic" (1942e, 610).

By contrast, modernism could offer freshness and vitality: Léger and Chagall, for instance, produced work that expressed "freedom, bounce and their own personality," with the former manipulating form to suggest a feeling of "sophisticated virility" (1942e, 610). Was there hope yet for American art? Perhaps so—Motherwell's early work displayed uninhibited good cheer and "valuable recklessness" (1944a, 626), while Pollock's pre-drip paintings suggested an "effect of virile, hectic action" (1945, 871). But Farber was not one to ride bandwagons, and by 1946 he was already charting American modernism's decline. The conventionalism that had always doomed American art was pulling the young proto–abstract expressionists out of the avant-garde, into the commercial mainstream. Perhaps Motherwell still painted with "vitality and enjoyment," but the surface of his work had become vacant. Most of the American art featured in MOMA's 1946 retrospective exhibited

> characteristics that usually appear in American art—repression, lack of arro-
> gance, limited display of emotion, picayunishness, sternness and sobriety. Most
> of the pieces carefully avoid crude, spontaneous or troubling notes. There is so
> much restraint of feeling, so much impersonality, so much coldness and empha-
> sis on technique that you are made very uneasy and nervous by all the quiet,
> regulated creativity. (1946a, 485)

The huge, sleepy canvases of Jackson Pollock, Robert Motherwell, Mark Rothko, and Hans Hofmann indicated that these New York paint-ers were already falling victim to the very sluggishness and stylistic rigidity they had purportedly sought to escape. In turning the freedom/vitality paradigm back on them, Farber found only a tired past aesthetic repack-aged for a new age and audience. By the mid-'40s, he later recalled, these intrasubjectivists had "perfected their slap-happy, wall-paper technique to an elegant point, dangerously close to the empty stylishness of aca-demic art." The work seemed "cold and persistent," generated on an as-sembly line by "young Americans out to 'succeed' " (1951b, 162). George Constant's paintings so resembled one other, they seemed "unpieced sec-tions of a gigantic jigsaw puzzle"; Rothko's had become vacant, "noise-less decorations" (1951c, 384).

Farber's cult sensibilities simply prevented him from supporting artists who seemed to be proudly courting fame and acceptance at the expense of artistic integrity. By 1949, we should note, Pollock had appeared in *Life*, Rothko was selling paintings for a thousand dollars, and periodicals such as the *Tiger's Eye* and *Instead* were actively promoting New York School art. Was this really an overthrowing of past traditions, or merely the rise of a new Establishment? In reality, it was an *amalgamation* of past and borrowed traditions, but for Farber even this was intolerable. With the purity and unrestrained Kootzian vigor of masculine abstrac-tionism increasingly diluted into navel-gazing intrasubjectivity, the few remaining stalwarts (and here Farber could include himself)[3] were being pushed back into the cultist margins. By 1951 Farber could provide a list of recommended exhibitions that featured Gorky and Dubuffet, but no established Americans. Instead he offers overlooked underdogs: Kimber Smith's "cold density of color" can be "heard six blocks block away," Robert DeNiro's abstractions "obliterat[e] form with small bent strokes," Weldon Kees's "shrill rubbed-color foregrounds" seem to "boomerang into solid gloomy backgrounds" in a manner reminiscent of "Fatha" Hines playing "Cement Mixer" (1951a, 92).

In praising a white abstract painter by associating him with the authen-tic vitality of black jazz, Farber is also showing us that he needs to be hip to low as well as high if he is ever to gauge aesthetic vigor in serious art. His downward straddling kept him attuned to the popular energy of

1. "Cold density" from an underdog abstractionist. Kimber Smith, *Sous-Sol.* 1955. Oil on canvas, 79' × 58'. Photograph © 1996 Gregory Gallery, New York.

music, comic strips, and movies, expressive forms built on movement and powered by the "free-wheeling American inventive genius which is cramped by most of the traditional and established arts" (1951d, 477). Comics had been a popular favorite of select American highbrows since Gilbert Seldes threw down the gauntlet in 1924, declaring George Herriman's *Krazy Kat* to be the "most amusing and fantastic and satisfactory work of art produced in America to-day" (Seldes [1924] 1957, 207).[4] For Farber, they now provided ample evidence of the comparative provincial stolidity of native art.

> Top comic-strip artists like Al Capp, Chet Gould, and Milt Caniff are the last
> in the great tradition of linear composers that started with Giotto and continued
> unbroken through Ingres. . . . Today the only linear surgeons carrying on the
> practice . . . are the pow-bam-sock cartoonists, whose masterful use of a dash-

ing pen line goes virtually unnoticed in the art world. . . . The rococo, squiggling composition of the average comic strip is too intricate, difficult, and unorthodox for cultured eyes grown lazy on the flaccid drawing-with-color technique and the pillow-like form of modern painting. (1951e, 572)

Farber's terms of comparison here were typically loaded: Ingres had been a strong influence on Gorky, Graham, and De Kooning (Polcari 1991, 270–72), and thus to imply that it was actually Al Capp and Chet Gould who were the rightful heirs to the Giotto/Ingres tradition was to lampoon the abstract expressionists' Europhilic pretensions, especially as promoted by fellow critic and retrograde cubist Clement Greenberg.[5]

It was the movies, though, that provided the ammunition Farber would need if he were to have any hope of derailing the modernist gravy train. Certainly the film industry was an unabashedly commercial enterprise, but it also offered products that successfully appealed to authentically robust popular tastes. That Hollywood ignorantly lumped its most virile, exciting work in with its most overblown failures—or, worse, openly consigned such work to the cultural margins—only made Farber's own cultist discernment all the more necessary. For Farber, Hollywood (like American art) succeeded only despite itself, when it dropped its embarrassing penchant for mannered "art" making and allowed its unsung technicians to pursue their craft unmolested. That filmmaking *was* still a craft made it particularly attractive, enabling the oppositional critic to support authentic, vigorous cultural expression without having to rehabilitate premodern provincialism. Yet this also meant that Farber would need to position (and reposition) his critical stance against Hollywood's own attempts to transcend craft for the rarefied air of Art. His favored films may have exhibited aesthetic qualities that implicitly aligned them with the neglected true vanguard of American modernism, but he didn't consider them artworks in themselves, simply because the Hollywood machine remained incapable of true aesthetic shaping. Those favorable qualities he found in movies characteristically lurked on the unflattened fringes; these were wild, untamed elements that had escaped the slick packagers of studio merchandise. It was precisely because they hadn't been commodified into "art" that they made movies worth watching in the first place.

MOVIES ON THE MARGINS

Farber's stance was thus doubly oppositional. In displaying his affection for popular movies, he openly defied conventional highbrow taste. But in attacking those films which Hollywood marketed as art, he was equally resisting middlebrow taste and asserting his own privileged authority over Hollywood's popular aesthetics. Here he was working in a long line of oppositional film critics who had similarly sought cultist alternatives to gloss and spectacle (understood as the hallmarks of Hollywood Art), both in neglected films and in unheralded "minor" elements of otherwise problematic films. In 1921, Robert E. Sherwood celebrated the "vigorous appeal" of Rex Ingram's *Four Horsemen of the Apocalypse* by pitting it against the "grandiose posturings" (114) of Griffith and DeMille. For many 1930s leftist humanists, vitally depicted social realism could be found lurking in the most unexpected places—in the likes of Capra's *It Happened One Night* (1934), for instance, or in cultist obscurities like *Riff-Raff* (1935), *The Devil Is a Sissy* (1936), *Mary Burns, Fugitive* (1935), and even *Tuesday Brown* (1940), an independent that for Meyer Levin in 1940 seemed "muscular" and "direct" (239), and in its sheer freshness and originality comparable to Joyce's *Ulysses*. Next to the overstuffed costume dramas and leaden literary epics ladled on unsuspecting middlebrows, such unpretentious, marginal movies—gangster films, gritty urban dramas, cheap fast comedies—seemed a breath of fresh air.

Film cultism might also become a means of defining a marginal self-image. With Otis Ferguson, a distaste for pretension and a gruff, iconoclastic personality went hand in hand. The *New Republic* film critic from 1934 to 1942 (he died at sea soon after) and a major influence on both Farber and Andrew Sarris, Ferguson was an anti-intellectual intellectual who cultivated a popular, even vulgar taste in opposition to the highbrow, politically fashionable, stifling New York intellectual milieu that surrounded him on all sides.[6] Alfred Kazin recalls Ferguson as

> one of the real roughs of the Thirties—not because he had been a sailor, but because he feared or despised high culture. His jazz, radio and movie pieces, wild monodies called *Nertz to Hertz*, crammed with weird and orgiastic puns, the general razzle-dazzle of his style—all this, wonderful as it was as force, as farce, as musical sound, was his way of saying *nuts to you, everybody*. (1965, 30–31)

Ferguson's movie reviews manifested his struggle to celebrate lowbrow culture in the face of highbrow snobbery (not least among *New Republic* staffers) by promoting low-budget or independent efforts as simply more exciting and realistic than A-line spectacles, at the very least depicting the "solid human truth" lurking beneath costumes and stage-craft (Ferguson 1971, 188). He wore his eclecticism as a badge of honor: he could praise Joris Ivens's "unquenchable feeling for the life of people, at war or at work" (191) in *The Spanish Earth* (1937), and in the next breath welcome "the sidelights on life in the city" (192) in Wyler's *Dead End* (1937). Sometimes he seemed downright eccentric, denigrating *The Wizard of Oz* (1939) as "painfully literal" (270) while lauding *Snow White and the Seven Dwarfs*'s "realism of the everyday" (210). Yet his judgments consistently stemmed from a conviction that the best film dramas manage to eschew overblown theatricality, instead capturing and expressing the reality of human life.

Ferguson even turned authenticity into a property of the film medium, rendering hokum not just dull but actually uncinematic. The camera eye couldn't be fooled—it relentlessly revealed any falsity in content or style, "literally throw[ing] it at your head, back row or front" (408). This meant that the camera itself could level the playing field, freeing the critic to spot bloated spectacle in unlikely places. We might expect Ferguson to have disliked Alexander Korda's *The Thief of Bagdad* (1940) ("a picture for children of all ages up to six" [325]), but he was equally contemptuous of *Citizen Kane*'s regressive, theatrical flash, noting that "the picture somehow leaves you cold even while your mouth is still open at its excitements." Instead he recommends Hawks/Wyler's *Come and Get It* (1936) and Kanin's similarly flashback-laden *A Man to Remember* (1938)—which, though made in a couple of weeks and for $100,000, managed to keep "the real life in it, the skill and the heart too" (370).

In his passion for upsetting canons of "quality" filmmaking, Ferguson often singled out low-budget B-movies, whose economy of means allowed smaller players to enter the movie game and forced larger players to forgo the usual gloss coat. The low budget inevitably proved a boon, evaporating middlebrow pretensions and freeing up vital cinematic elements in neglected treasures such as George Nicholls Jr.'s shoestring epic *Man of Conquest* (1939), and the RKO quickie *Boy Slaves* (1939), whose harrowingly authentic depiction of life in a turpentine camp suggested the "illusion of participating in something with real and troubled people" (249). "When you can make a feature film and get out for little more than what it cost to feed the elephants in *Gunga Din*," Ferguson mused, "nobody is going to worry so much if you happen to get a good idea of your own" (248).

Farber idolized Ferguson and would later credit him as the "expert voice" of a 1930s "underground" audience able to distinguish between "perceptive trash and the Thalberg pepsin-flavored sloshing with Tracy and Gable" (1971i, 24). For the younger critic, Ferguson's fierce, even macho resistance to dominant standards of cinematic sophistication provided a model of oppositional tastemaking in a medium blessed by its affinity for gritty reality, but cursed by a submission to middlebrow mores and Hollywood sheen.[7] Like Ferguson—and like his French contemporary André Bazin—Farber would also seek to root his oppositional tastes in the inherent realism of the film medium.[8] But while Farber certainly shared Ferguson and Bazin's distaste for middlebrow aesthetics and affection for popular amusements, his own forays into realist film theory would also be substantially shaped by his own parallel interest in American art—specifically, his desire to preserve and promote the artist's unfettered, vigorous self-expression within a climate of compromise.

Middlebrow compromise was bad enough in the high-art world; in the authentically vital popular art of cinema it was unforgivable. For Farber, those form-heavy extravaganzas obsessed with conveying their contrived artiness simply did not allow style to express content but imposed the same superficial pattern on all works, squashing the vigorous expression of studio personnel and offering the spectator only the impression of aesthetic significance. The "flamboyantly artistic setting" (1943e, 255) of *The Constant Nymph* only belied its hollow core; Carol Reed's *Young Mr. Pitt* was even worse, an "impotent" amalgam of "hundreds of good-looking, accurate stills" (1943g, 382), arranged with bloodless precision.

The problem lay in studio precensorship, which in turn stemmed from an enslavement to "middlebrow attitudes about what makes a good movie" (1953a, 57). What a shame, when the medium itself offered so much more, presenting naturally the very dynamic visual expression and vigorous human realism that the best modern artists (Kimber Smith, Weldon Kees) were striving to inject into their work. In a lengthy 1942 defense of the medium (and a sharp retort to fellow critic Elmer Rice), Farber carefully grounds his antiestablishment populism in an expressive vitality endemic to the movies.

> Every art is defined by the nature of its mechanics: painting has to do without time and sound, writing without color and line. But . . . the very boundaries of an art produce its most basic advantages. In the movies the basic advantage is the movement of visual images, which the cameras, players and technicians make possible. . . . In the peculiar quality of each image, and the movement created by their succession, exists the particular expression of each artist, the human breath and thumbprint Mr. Rice says isn't there. . . . Mr. Rice is looking at one art through the eyes of another, or he would not be blind to a real spontaneity peculiar to movies, the lack of which he insists on. (1942b, 546–47)

To the casual reader this may have seemed pretentious grandstanding. But for Farber (as indeed for Bazin), this sort of theorizing about cinema was a helpful accompaniment to reviewing, allowing him to work through and justify the broad aesthetic positions that fueled and distinguished his criticism. Certainly on paper, cinema could be shown to exhibit the same formal dynamism and authentic expression of human behavior characteristic of cutting-edge modernism. Of course, the proof was in the movies themselves—those movies, or parts of movies, left after the critic had sifted through the dross of industry product.

Again, thorough sifting was necessary because the industry itself inevitably got it wrong, misfiring on all cylinders. War dramas, for instance, had presented Hollywood a perfect opportunity to combine dynamic action with the realistic depiction of individuals struggling to defeat fascism. Yet most were predictably mired in restrictive conventionalism: during a war fought in the name of freedom, it seemed painfully ironic that "the most popular medium of expression [was] nowhere free" (1944b, 20). The "melodramatic attitude, patriotic narrowness and glibness" (16) of American war films only highlighted Hollywood's fear of truth and penchant for lush fantasy. As for the documentary/newsreel (a significant influence on Bazin as well),[9] the photographs in MOMA's June 1942 *Road to Victory* exhibit doubtless suggested that the movies might similarly take advantage of the "basic camera function for reproducing and analyzing" in order to "shoot a scene for what it is fundamentally" (1942a, 798). But where were the American answers to Britain's *I Was a Fireman*, which conveyed an "exact respect for the instinctive behavior and responses of men working" (1943f, 687), and *Desert Victory*, whose "photography sees the outside world of texture and light values in the same way as the human eye, leaving the business of drama and working up of emotions to the context of the event itself" (1943d, 476)? War's virile violence and brutal human realities made it a natural for cinema; yet with the exception of *Prelude to War* (1942), American depictions of wartime life were smothered by an industry enamored with overstuffed middle-brow spectacle and blind to the movies' real potential.

> While Hollywood in its story films depended entirely on cast-iron plots of flashy incident to get their pseudo-life and pseudo-movement, no one, not even the newsreel companies, examined human actions and behavior in detail with the motion picture camera. Whereas Eisenstein in Russia, Ivens in Holland and Grierson and Legg in England were watching the daily life in fields, factories and coal mines with their cameras, not only in documentaries but in story films as well. So that American directors generally, without their preconceived plot to use, are unable to film actuality and get from it its meaning and emotion, a technique which can't be acquired in a day. (1943h, 447)

This was an extreme position, to be sure. But foreign documentaries had at least spurred Farber's continued reflection on the nature of cinema, and on Hollywood's failings. Echoing Ferguson, he could now claim that because the camera is "a machine for recording the visual diary of an event" (1944c, 212), any decent documentary or film drama "will express the essential nature of the subject, which is human life in one form or another" (1943a, 48). He was transposing his art-world liberty/vitality sympathies to a new medium, though with one crucial change: because cinema was at heart a passive medium, the expression of a movie's inner content could occur only if the camera were treated not as intrusive dynamo (the action painter's brush) but as impersonal witness to "spontaneous, unalterable happenings," so that the event captured might seem "propelled solely by factors within the event itself" (1944c, 211). Whereas the visual artist openly, honestly expressed, the film artist tried not to get in the way. He only *facilitated* expression, created a climate in which expressive materials might be captured by the camera.

Most movies failed, Farber insisted, not because they were movies, but because they had been ill-conceived. The passive spectatorship encouraged by Hollywood's "cleaned and plucked movie art" stemmed from the studios' inability or unwillingness to recognize the cinematic value of the unhindered, vital expression of the filmed world.

> This turning of the spectator into a receiver rather than a co-worker occurs in the conception itself of the subject matter: the too-fortunate and conscious view that the camera takes of events, so that you feel the artist is merely copying an action he thinks of as already accomplished; the manipulation of characters into patterns of action, so that you feel the ostentation; and the lack of individuality in the texture of the photography, so that you feel it is not expressing the spirit of the idea but merely making a clear reproduction of a reenactment of the idea. The result is that no matter what you are shown . . . your feeling is that you are seeing a posed, not a spontaneous, action. (1943b, 653)

Farber recognizes that the camera must inevitably manipulate, and he clearly advocates deft cinematographic artistry. (He wants us to feel individuality in the "texture of the photography.") Still, the hand of the film artist must be subtle and skillful—not intrusive—in order to facilitate expression of the "spirit of the idea."

Farber may not have been a film theorist per se, but nonetheless this is film theory—here employed to support the cultist's bold assertion of superior yet oppositional discernment. The cultist hardly wants to seem to be skimming the margins for the sake of it, or just in order to seem different: the cult object must be seen to be important in itself, authentic, aesthetically interesting, though inexplicably neglected by others. It is not simply a question of the cultist's superior access to the obscured recesses of culture, but his superior taste, required to rescue from obscurity an inherently valuable artwork. Determining that work to be closer to the nature of the medium (more cinematic) than those heralded by others can be highly useful to this process. On a microlevel, the cult critic can use theoretical insights to bolster an appreciation of aspects of a work, even fleeting moments that suggest aesthetic interest still distinguishable *despite* the collective efforts of its creators. Thus Farber can deem *Casablanca* (1942) and *Lifeboat* (1944) to be hopelessly overburdened by theatricality, while still finding cultist interest in their presentation of a "visual fact, that of watching vital, invigorating-looking people" (1944c, 212).

Similarly, while active spectatorship is a mainstay of vanguard rhetoric and film theory alike, for the postwar cultist it could be put to practical use, activated within a connoisseurship of all superior entertainments. When Farber assails Lewis Milestone's unbearably sensitive war drama *The North Star* as a film in which "the food has not only been cooked for you but eaten and digested" (1943b, 653), he is echoing Clement Greenberg's earlier excoriation of kitsch in *Partisan Review*, while addressing a cultural product Greenberg would never have deigned to analyze in such detail.[10] Farber was willingly engaging the movies because his primary goal was not to rescue high culture wholesale (à la Greenberg) but to delineate the oppositional margins of popular culture by approaching the movies critically and aesthetically. In this light, his criticism was perhaps more practical than it had appeared to poor Max Bart: though it failed to offer the generosity of conventional movie reviewing, it did provide like-minded readers a means of negotiating the treacherous seas of postwar culture by empowering themselves as active members— and indeed creators—of that culture.

Thus, as a cult critic, Farber could rely on theoretical notions without becoming much of a theorist in his own right. This is why his realist discernment was far less constrained and somewhat more eclectic than Bazin's (refined at roughly the same time). Bazin was also interested in promoting viable cultural alternatives to middlebrow extravagance, but he was ultimately more theorist than cultist—particular directors, films, and movements were often subject to his overriding aesthetic and spiritual program. Farber preferred to shoot from the hip, lauding *Open City*'s newsreel realism and "oil-dump fire" intensity (1946f, 46) and *The Miracle*'s "hail storm" vitality (1951f, 45), yet openly deriding the cloying sentimentality of *The Bicycle Thief* (1948). And because he saw cinematic realism in terms of conception and working of material, and not deployment of specific devices such as deep focus and the long take, he could justifiably dislike *Citizen Kane* and *The Magnificent Ambersons* (both Bazin favorites); as Ferguson had noted, Welles's approach courted style-heavy pretension, not vital realism. *Ambersons*'s characters may have been three-dimensional, but the film as a whole was theatrical and lethargic in the extreme, running

> from burdensome through heavy and dull to bad. It stutters and stumbles as Welles submerges Tarkington's story in a mess of radio and stage technique. The radio comes in those stretches of blank screen when the only thing present is Welles's off-screen voice mellifluously setting the period and coyly reminiscing, talking and drooling, while you sit there muttering let's get on. . . . Meanwhile, for something to do, you count the shadows. (1942d, 173)

Farber's attitude toward widescreen was also freer and more nuanced than Bazin's. The new format did seem truer to cinema's antitheatrical, documentary nature (1952, 337), but its value could ultimately be determined only from its use in individual films. Cinemascope certainly did not help *The Robe*: elephantine, humorless, and composed of "spectacular, mural-type photographs" (1953b, 318), it was just philistine calendar art. In practice, widescreen might hinder more than help, smothering internal life with decorative lethargy as effectively as the pillow art of contemporary abstract expressionists. Such was the fate of *How to Marry a Millionaire*, whose few bright lines were enveloped by "dead landscapes and uninteresting masses of interior decoration" (1953c, 574).

In the end, Farber's realist theory and antimiddlebrow bias are difficult to separate, as each supported the other. Yet he refused to be unduly constrained by either. Because the cultist's superior discernment—even more than the casual reviewer's—must seem creative and individual, never guided by formula, Farber's opinions are rarely easy to predict, and his reviews are peppered with surprising recommendations of films he should have hated. His cultism boldly placed the future of American culture in the hands of the critic—and, by implication, the critically attuned spectator. He certainly assumed that no cultural product of any significant aesthetic value would be knowingly produced by the mainstream of the American culture industry. The value of connoisseurship lay in rescuing from obscurity those aesthetic elements which had happened to worm their way into theaters thanks to the dogged efforts of unpretentious technicians. This also meant, however, that Farber would accept no rival assertions of fringe activity, even from a practicing independent filmmaker such as Maya Deren.[11] Film artists actually pose a potent threat to cultist privilege—because cultist "film art" can exist only as claimed, defined, indeed *shaped* by the critic, filmmakers can be championed so long as they remain blind to the aesthetic nature of their activity.

The inherent instability of cult material actually makes the vanguard cultist's job rather difficult. She must always be on her toes, continually reassessing the margins and adjusting her taste objects, or aesthetic, accordingly. It is easier to adjust one's taste objects, but this is possible only when one's aesthetic remains marginal: Farber could support Kimber Smith and Robert DeNiro as vital fringe alternatives to the lethargic abstract expressionists because the latter had abandoned the authentic margins for the creature comforts of middle-class life. The acceptance of one's *aesthetic* by others, however, proves much trickier to handle. The cultist should be pleased that his authentic alternative has been embraced within the larger culture; but as this threatens the cultist's raison d'être, it must be rejected. Luckily, he can claim that in its diffusion into the mainstream, the aesthetic has been diluted, corrupted, rendered affirmative instead of oppositional. Yet there is still a problem. Sticking with the aesthetic, even in its slightly purer form, is now of dubious value, because the cultist's distinction from mainstream culture has been fatally compromised. But dropping this aesthetic for a new one is itself not a simple matter, especially if the old one has been carefully grounded in the very nature of the medium.

FROM MARGINS TO MAINSTREAM

Such was the dilemma facing Farber in the late 1940s, when the major studios finally played off the currency of wartime documentaries by releasing feature narratives that flirted with the harsh human realism the critic had clamored for. Only a few years earlier, gritty masculine dramas had still been marginal enough to warrant cultist support. *The Blue Dahlia* had done a fine job conveying the behavior of people "going through the motions of every-day living" (1946c, 806), while *The Killers* had refused to whitewash social reality, hurling its raw truths at the spectator:

> Besides its brutality, it has the noise, the jagged, tormenting movement of keyed-up, tough, flashy humanity that you get from a walk through Times Square. . . . Though there is a cheapness about *The Killers* that reminds you of five-and-ten jewelry, its scenes of sadism and menacing action have been formed and filled with a vitality all too rare in current movies. It is a production that is suspense-ridden and exciting down to tiny details in the background. (1946b, 415–16)

Yet as the decade wore on, the studios had begun mainstreaming hard-edged realism, flaunting stylized cinematography and lighting in pop-Freudian thrillers such as *The Locket* and *Follow Me Quietly* (1949). They had even taken to the streets, injecting artificial documentary flavor into thrillers like *The Naked City* (1948), *Between Midnight and Dawn* (1950), and *Detective Story* (1951), and into self-important dramas such as *Champion* (1949) and *The Next Voice You Hear* (1950). Farber's response was predictable, but again his critical hands were tied. Hollywood had pushed him into a corner: so long as he stuck by his aesthetic convictions, there was little to do but to assail the fashionable faux realism as preachy, listless, and hopelessly theatrical. *Champion* and *The Set-Up* may have seemed gritty, but they were ultimately "dehumanized by an effort at newsreel realism and a compulsion to grind away at a message. Attempting to describe the sadism of the ring, the directors exaggerate the savagery inherent in prize fighting, dragging in enough peripheral mayhem to scare the officers of Buchenwald" (1949, 538). Even worse was the hapless suicide drama *Fourteen Hours*. In its desperation to seem realistic and relevant, the film had placed its self-destructive protagonist

2. "Keyed-up, tough, flashy humanity." *The Killers* (1946).

high on a ledge, then overwhelmed his solemn predicament with an assault of "contrived wit, mush, camera gymnastics, and self-conscious 'natural' acting" (1951h, 306).

These were classic attacks on middlebrow. What Farber objected to most strenuously was that these films were just too forced—they strained to make their points and to display their effects. Yet to be fair, they were also presenting aesthetic material on their own terms, in a manner accessible to wider audiences. They simply refused to be the kind of movies Farber was most comfortable with; if he had to denigrate them as unauthentic, it was because he found it exceedingly difficult to claim aesthetic authority over them. The middlebrow scourge had thoroughly infected cinema, with the new middle-class art audience actively redefining movie art, and weak-kneed apologists like James Agee biting the bait.[12] In response, the irascible Farber only deepened his trench in the sand. To hell with Max Bart and his ilk! These spectators didn't want to mine crevasses in popular junk; they wanted their art up-front and comprehensible, overdone like a tough steak.

Now sensing real competition in cinematic tastemaking, Farber sharpened his ire, declaring war on the new wave of bombastic pseudorealists most favored by the dreary middle. Obsessed with the Big Statement, Joseph L. Mankiewicz burdened *All about Eve*'s actors with "impossible dialogue abounding in clichés" and "forced cleverness that turn[ed] each stock character into the echo of an eclectic writer" (1950, 397). Fred Zinnemann squandered *Teresa*'s nonactors on a script written by someone who seemed to "know about every uncomfortable thing that is bothering mankind, and spell[ed] it out in neon lights" (1951g, 237). No one seemed to care about making rough'n'tumble two-fisted cheapies anymore. Filmmakers now felt compelled to offer their sensitive take on the human condition; in doing so, they overstepped the bounds of the medium, pushed Hollywood movies further than they were meant to venture. What had happened to the subversive fun of moviegoing?

> For me 1953 was the year in which Hollywood almost lost me as an irritable non-paying customer. The simple reason for my disaffection with H-movies— I ceased to be a foreign-movie fan when foreign films became so pretentiously unpretentious—is that there were few pictures last year in which the "human element" wasn't swallowed up by production values. In this era of hard, tight semi-documentaries embroidered with fancying-up touches that seem controlled almost to rigidity, only an occasional *Roman Holiday* turns up with enough individual flourish to make one interested in any craftsmen but the lead actors. (1954, 37)

Hollywood did indeed lose Farber as an irritable, nonpaying customer shortly thereafter, when he left weekly reviewing to return to painting and carpentry. Though he would not stop writing about films, he would now concentrate his criticism in longer, sporadic position papers written for publications such as *Commonweal*, *Commentary*, and *Film Culture*. Until he retooled his aesthetic to reclaim a vanguard cult fringe, he could do little more than attempt to hold his ground against a growing legion of film aficionados easily impressed by the posturings of the Antonionis and Kazans, but also increasingly savvy to the authentic vitality of Hawks and Fuller. In many ways these later critical provocations (to be discussed in chapter 5) were sharper, bolder, altogether tougher. They had to be, if Farber were to maintain his credibility as spokesman for the vanguard "underground audience" of the past.

Farber was obviously not an old-time avant-gardist; his activism was solitary, and largely contained within his own critical work. Yet as a reviewer he had still positioned himself on the cutting edge of an antiestablishment tradition, playing on the sympathies of his readers while relentlessly assaulting their middlebrow tastes. The fear of middlebrow, of a "mass culture of the educated classes," as Robert Warshow (1970b, 34) put it, was only the earlier avant-gardists' fear of a culture of commodified zombies, brought closer to home; in pushing his readers to look deeper into movies, or past mainstream releases for fringe product, Farber furthered the vanguard agenda without the need for leaflets or soirées.[13] And while his aims may have been considerably less audacious than those of prewar avant-gardist Dziga Vertov, who had hoped to use cinema to foster the "perfect electric man" (Vertov 1984, 8), Farber and Vertov both drew on the same vanguard impulse to liberate the spectator from the "sweet fog" (48) of mainstream culture and return him to an idealized, revitalized version of his own folk traditions.

Farber's cultism offered itself as a countergesture for savvy hipsters, and he kept it marginal enough to make sure the nonhip remained rigorously excluded. Yet this certainly didn't prevent his stance from influencing a wide range of critical spectators, some of whom would modify and soften movie cultism in the coming decades, enabling it to become an altogether accessible means of asserting one's power to choose within the marketplace of culture. This new cultism would be different from Farber's, to the extent that it openly reified hierarchies, pantheons, and auteurs of mass movies. Its widespread influence, however, would be undeniable.

We will look more closely at the dissemination of vanguard techniques in later chapters. Now let us leave Farber and cultism temporarily to examine a parallel and equally influential vanguard perspective on pop culture—namely, camp. It too was refined by an American critic writing from the margins of 1940s modernism, popularized in a modified, user-friendly form in the 1960s, then purified by film academics seeking to reclaim the avant-garde for themselves. But by then poetic spectatorship, like cultism, had already become broadly available as a means of asserting personal dominance over the movies, creativity within the constricting bounds of consumerism.

Chapter Four

HALLUCINATING HOLLYWOOD: PARKER TYLER

AND CAMP SPECTATORSHIP

> The eyes of the masses are always perfect, though they never
> know just what it is they see.
> *(Parker Tyler)*

I N SEIZING cinema for his own use, the vanguard critic was assuming that he alone could make popular movies artistic. Because middlebrow threatened this assumption by suggesting an alternative conception of popular art, it had to be assailed as inauthentic, fatally corrupted by market forces. For film art to belong to the critic—and to those spectators willing to listen to and learn from him—the judgments of middlebrow's rival tastemaking institutions would have to be considered, at best, irrelevant. So what if the Academy of Motion Picture Arts and Sciences knew that Art sometimes made good business?

Actually reclaiming film art from the academy wasn't easy, but it could be done. Consider *The Best Years of Our Lives*, produced by Samuel Goldwyn and released by RKO in late 1946 amid a flurry of publicity. Here was an eminently respectable film: directed by prestige specialist William Wyler and almost three hours long, *Years* attempted a serious, realistic examination of America's homecoming experience. And of course it swept the subsequent Academy Awards, winning Best Picture, Direction, Actor, Supporting Actor, Editing, and Score. Nonactor Harold Russell, an amputee himself, was even presented a special award for his inspiration to other veterans.

Manny Farber could have rejected the film outright: sappy and overblown, it shouldn't have been his cup of java. Yet instead he chose a riskier tactic, bringing *Years* back down to size by audaciously recasting it as just another fierce little movie.[1] Its expression of vital, realistic behavior made it seem not at all a "Hollywood job"; the actions of lovers Dana Andrews and Teresa Wright seemed to "arise out of natural, human, instinctual responses" that defied convention. Even minute tics of performance could be singled out for praise. Fredric March's "knifelike movements" nicely accented his portrayal of a self-loathing alcoholic; Wright played "so completely from the inside" and had "so labile a face" that her scenes rocked with emotion (1946e, 723). In offering such an unusually sympathetic take on a socially conscious prestige picture, Farber was keeping his readers guessing, emphasizing his own Fergusonian iconoclasm but also his ability to spot aesthetic interest in the most unexpected of places.[2] He was still implicitly asserting that *his* criteria, and his own critical discernment, were what mattered most. He just happened to like this movie—so what of it?

Farber had reined the film in, containing it within his own aesthetic purview. Yet one could also reclaim it by digging it up. Sure, the film was an official, sanctioned success, but *real* aesthetic interest still lurked beneath the surface, in material audience members saw but didn't notice. In his own openly creative analysis of *Years* for the *Kenyon Review*, Parker Tyler resituated the film within the "inexhaustibly protean" (1947c, 317) psychomythic matrix of Hollywood cinema. The very touches Farber had praised as realistic, when processed through a film factory fueled by stereotype and cliché, might produce a kind of "naive symbolism" (320) fascinating for its mythic depth and dreamlike energy. To the academy, Harold Russell's handless veteran may have signaled authenticity, but to Tyler he evoked the subhuman qualities of Frankenstein's monster. Because the cinema was rooted in the far deeper reality of collective myth and unconscious psychic processes, *Years*'s attempt at realistically depicting social issues was misguided and fruitless: in the end, it reveled in Hollywood myth patterns as much as any other movie.

> It has the bad dream ("war"), the trance, the sex triangle, the bedroom scene (thrice in crescendo), the crucial sex innuendo (also thrice in crescendo), and the sex "ethics" leading to stalemate . . . the last is the breakdown in the film's realistic pattern into sheer tarnished nonsense, not at all lifelike. . . . The fact is that all these flat human mores, lacking the true dimension of experience, are of unusual interest and win a certain verisimilitude of treatment simply because they have been put in question by forced physical abdication from them. (322–23)

The film wasn't really any good, but it was still pretty interesting. Its crudeness, its tarnished nonsense suggested intriguing complexities and depths of which its makers were surely ignorant.[3] Through his criticism, Tyler had helped release—or perhaps helped produce—a much more interesting and daring movie than the one Wyler himself had managed to come up with.

Should we be surprised? Like Manny Farber, Parker Tyler was an artist both within and beyond his criticism, and like Farber, he too was intensely committed to promoting an authentic highbrow modernism. Both critics adhered to aesthetic agendas abandoned (in their eyes) for the compromise of mainstreamed abstract expressionism: if Farber saw himself as an uncorrupted abstractionist, Tyler's allegiance was to European surrealism. Most important, however, both were able to sustain these traditions, at least on paper, by refining vanguard approaches to the movies. Farber's cultism had allowed him to discover expressive vitality not simply in the work of lesser-known New York artists but in neglected nooks and crannies of Hollywood product. For Tyler, a poet, playwright, and novelist, art and film criticism served more openly as creative ends in themselves; his *camp* approach encouraged the critic to "complete" the work creatively, actively reworking and augmenting its material into a new aesthetic form. The transformed movie was hardly dull and prosaic—it suggested the freedom, vitality, depth, resonance, rhythm, and even metaphorical/symbolic complexity common to surrealist art and sophisticated poetry.

Tyler's camp, like Farber's cultism, thus facilitated creative, aesthetic discussion of popular cinema. Yet Tyler took movies themselves even less seriously than Farber did—he openly regarded them as material for his own creative, psychological-mythic reverie. He was seeking only to add method to the movies' madness. The movies themselves were aesthetically *out* of control, an entertaining maelstrom of meanings and sensations that could be shaped only from without and after the fact, by the properly attuned critical spectator. Tyler's art was thus not one of cultist discrimination (locating aesthetic bits in the margins of films or genres) but rather of visionary, poetic revelation of a Hollywood cinema marked not by visceral expression but by the symbolic richness characteristic of the best surrealist work. As a result, his approach accepted a much wider body of films, but it was also more complex in that it necessitated a much trickier alternation between open disdain for movies' nonaesthetic surfaces and a camp fascination with their psychological and mythic depths.

(More) Notes on Camp

This camp fascination was thus also fundamentally aesthetic in nature, as camp is fundamentally an aesthetic declaration of the spectator's ability to choose and manipulate the cultural meanings surrounding her. Camp has been so appealing to dominated subcultures, notably that of gay males, precisely because it powerfully asserts control over one's own symbolic identity. But it is this symbolic appropriation, and not any particular use or instance of it, that defines camp activity and situates it at the heart of vanguard traditions.[4] As an active refashioning of mass culture into something personal and aesthetic, camp offers a homemade challenge to the art foisted on the public by the culture industry. Unlike cultism, which emphasizes the oppositional connoisseur's ability to discern (and define) authentic aesthetic material lurking in low culture products, camp revels in the critic's skill in reclaiming the entire mass cultural field as one's own—as when the drag queen aggressively reclaims his "feminine" gay identity from dominant culture by donning women's apparel (and the meanings circulating around it) strictly on his own terms.[5]

Unlike cultism, camp does not need to be choosy; it loves/hates all junk equally. Yet the more banal, impersonal, and naively "obvious" the mass cultural artifact, the more clearly it will emphasize the camp spectator's playful revelation of this artifact as ill-formed, uncontrolled, barely managing its own meanings. It is, indeed, so hopelessly *non*aesthetic as to warrant the spectator's charity, which she provides in the form of a half-affectionate, half-mocking personal aesthetic makeover. All she asks in return is the opportunity to claim the text as her own, reshuffling its meanings until they reflect her own radical, marginalized voice. Camp's affection for aesthetic crudeness is thus self-serving: because radical meanings must underlie obvious ones, the poorly controlled text will usually prove more rewarding than the tightly managed artwork.[6]

This is what Sontag (1966a) is getting at when she locates in the camp sensibility a tender (but also detached) appreciation of "success in certain passionate failures" (293). The extravagance, wild ambition, "virtually uncontrolled sensibility" (285) of a work can attract the camp spectator even as they derail the work itself, because they provide the raw, unfettered vitality that fuels the "coarsest, commonest pleasures" (290) of mass culture. By contrast, even minimal aesthetic *success* (fulfillment of sophisticated intentions) can disqualify a work from true camp appreciation, insofar as the spectator willingly submits to the work's own devices and thus relinquishes the distance and disdain central to camp pleasure.[7] Correspondingly, the aging of popular texts also frees them up for camp appropriation because it loosens the control culture (in particular, advertising) exerts over their meanings, allowing them—in Andrew Ross's words—to "become available, in the present, for redefinition according to contemporary codes of taste" (1989, 139).

Hence camp's "attitude toward kitsch" (Long 1993, 86) was also, in the postwar period, a vanguard attitude toward middlebrow culture, whose pathetic pretensions to offer aesthetic fulfillment could be answered with highbrow "Art Pop"—pop culture made available for active hermeneutic play.[8] If cultism sought to rebuild a legitimate American high culture out of a connoisseurship of detritus, camp could in effect treat the field of low culture as if it were high culture, worthier of attention than the dry, lethargic labors of the *purportedly* passionate, extravagant, wildly ambitious abstract expressionists. Though, as Ross suggests, the postwar camp intellectual may have been asserting his own aristocratic image in defiance of his declining influence within the "ruling bloc," and upon the "conventional morality and taste of the ascendant middle class" (1989, 146–47), Tyler's case demonstrates that highbrow aesthetic activism could still prove remarkably successful and influential, nuancing prewar vanguard strategies in order to reinvent modernist culture—here, as psychomythological movies.

THE ARTWORK THROUGH THE EYES OF A POET

Indeed, Tyler's camp criticism of the 1940s is particularly useful in highlighting the crucial links between camp and vanguard modernism, even though he was hardly the first avant-gardist to explore camp's possibilities. In offering up mass culture as raw material for aesthetic creation, camp had already heavily informed the tactics of the European avant-gardes—especially surrealism, which emphasized liberated critical spectatorship (of the self, the work, and culture) as a fundamental aid to aesthetic production. Surrealism had assumed that the artist was a critical observer of the psychomythic universe (Dali had even called himself a "critical paranoiac"),[9] but also that the surrealist critic was himself an artist, actively reengaging in the process of creation. (Recall the excerpt from Breton's 1935 analysis of Duchamp's *Mariée mise à nue* in chapter 2.) Yet if indeed the critic created too, and in the same way—scrambling psyche, myth, and the symbolism of everyday life into a rich, expressive stew—the original artist wasn't really necessary any more. As the surrealist artist already knew, raw material appeared in many forms.

Here pop culture, and especially movies, came in quite handy, allowing the surrealist critic to explore camp in earnest. Movies weren't complete, rounded works; they were grab bags of images, sounds, and emotions. That the trashiest films were unable to master their meanings only helped matters, heightening the suggestive power, wonder, monstrousness of their images, even allowing Breton and his friends to become fugitive spectators of film spectacle who entered and left theaters between plot points. In ignoring storytelling (the central craft focus of classical filmmaking), surrealist spectators were characteristically asserting their own disdain for the material, refusing to respond to it on its own terms. Storytelling got in the way of reverie—dragging down, literalizing, stifling the images (which themselves were uncrafted magical apparitions). It was up to the surrealist camp critic to purify the medium, play up its mysterious dreamlike nature, emphasize the uncanny ability of the cinematic apparatus to transform the ordinary into the *marvelous*. The critic thus liberated the movie behind the movie; it was not the movie everyone else saw, the one Hollywood technicians thought they had made. *That* film was terrible; it was worth watching only because it might be remade into something much more interesting, aesthetic even.[10]

Parker Tyler was a surrealist, too. Yet his particular brand of camp criticism, as well as his considerable success in refining the camp approach, owe much to his own personal take on surrealist aesthetics, one fundamentally guided by his core commitment to the importance of poetic form. Tyler had been involved in American poetry and art since the 1920s: born in New Orleans in 1904, he moved to New York while still in his youth and was soon publishing poems and essays in the *Bookman*, *Voices*, the *Saturday Review of Literature*, *Japm*, and *Contemporary Verse*.[11] As an assistant to Charles Henri Ford at the aggressive young journal *Blues*, he became influenced by the revisionist, Jungian surrealism promoted by *transition*'s Eugene Jolas, whose writings *Blues* reproduced amid poetry, artwork, and wild attacks on rival publications (*New Masses*, *Poetry*) and revered figures alike.[12] Jolas's own rebelliousness would have appealed to a young poet whose sensibilities embraced symbolism as much as surrealism: seeking to push surrealism beyond the tradition of spontaneous, accidental art making epitomized by automatic writing, Jolas insisted that subconscious material be not merely unearthed in all its chaotic splendor but consciously shaped into aesthetic form.[13]

This insistence on controlled aesthetic shaping became a cornerstone of Tyler's notion of surrealism, as fundamentally important as psyche and myth. In "Beyond Surrealism," Tyler insists that the "functional inadequacy of the Surrealistic esthetic philosophy" (1935, 2) had been that its anarchic social creed had shortchanged artistic skill, omitting "from art its craftsmanship" and "from the emotion of the artist his pride of craftsmanship." The amateur, backslapping, "interior impressionistic criticism" (4) of the European surrealist circles had served only to retard artistic development. In the end, the surrealists hadn't taken themselves seriously enough, at least as artists—for only superior aesthetic arrangement of psychomythic and formal materials (a *reasoned* derangement of the senses, à la Rimbaud) could produce valid art. Or valid criticism, for that matter.

Indeed, Tyler's adamant revisionism suited his subsequent stint as art/movie critic at Ford's surrealist journal *View* (1940–47), whose motto proudly announced aesthetic vision "Through the Eyes of Poets." *View* provocatively positioned itself on the cutting edge of a truly alternative and aesthetically legitimate notion of American modernism; this was by no means old-style surrealism but a revamped and much broader model through which Ford and New York might revive and extend the European legacy. Hence most of the American artists promoted in *View*'s pages were not really orthodox surrealists at all but iconoclasts such as Edward Hopper, Alexander Calder, Georgia O'Keeffe, Florine Stettheimer, and Philip Lamantia, who now found themselves published alongside the better-known European émigrés.[14]

Correspondingly, the better-known local modernists could be roundly derided as inferior artists offering only superficial, lifeless reproductions of European styles. To Tyler, Saul Steinberg specialized in "blushless parodies" of Picasso and Klee (1946, 37), while Charles Sheeler could manage only a "slanderous impressionism" of authentic cubism. Stuart Davis's way of improving landscape was only "a notch or two above the Commissioner's way of improving parks" (1945b, 41). Those who embarrassingly trod in the surrealists' much larger footsteps—let alone followed the Jolasian line—obviously fared even worse. Gorky had simply been derivative; now Jackson Pollock was producing abstract work the way lunch kitchens produce daily specials. Was it any wonder his paintings suggested not inspired psychic release but "an air of baked-macaroni" (1945c, 30)?

For Tyler, however, *View* provided a venue not simply for the valuation of individual artists but for an enhanced vision of the productive, artistic critic. This was something new for America: though some of Tyler's mythological precepts would have been long familiar to many contemporary literary critics,[15] the notion of a critic productively engaged with the aesthetic liberty and vitality of his surroundings enjoyed little currency, even within the art world. In "A Gift from Max Ernst" (1942), for instance, Tyler uses his poetic skills to depict the European artist's inner self as unstable, dynamic, even explosive. "Nowhere at rest is the violent home of Max Ernst," he notes. "He creates only the malcontented image developing, in its hated home, the first limb of rebellion." Tyler then proceeds to interpret the figures in *The Robing of the Bride* (and probably also *Napoleon in the Wilderness*), revealing their symbolic value within a dynamic, mythic narrative expressive of Ernst's creative, psychobiological self.

> And one morning the bride, whom we all know by her hair and her flesh, has a train of feathers whose gentle aspiration has utterly usurped her face and added insolence to majesty. The wish always attendant at her elbow is the bird she is about to recognize with her owl's eye, holding an historic weapon: sabotage ... Ah, what an adorable discontent: pliant statues purporting to be women; feathers sprouting in the utopia of paint; paint spreading propaganda of stone, leaf, Max Ernst; paint haunting the frame like a detective; and somewhere a child carried off. Somewhere the bare face of the ballet of change, simple as a lock of white hair. (1942b, 16).

Now, in deciphering the hidden allegorical content of the painting, Tyler is certainly aided by Ernst's allegorical, figurative style, penchant for symbolism, and romantic image as an artist expressing inner truths. Because the work itself is assumed to be a controlled expression of the artist's subconscious, the critic feels justified in producing a work of criticism that is itself a controlled expression of the artist's, work's, *and* critic's subconsciouses. Through the use of poetic devices such as metaphor and rhythm, the critic can hope to *extend* the work by reexploring and reexpressing—as an attuned and creative spectator—the dynamic, psychomythic landscape of the artist's/work's interior. For Jung archetypal patterns exist across the length of the poetic communication chain, "as configurations in the poet's unconscious, as recurring themes or image sequences in poetry, and as configurations in the reader's or audience's unconscious" (Hyman 1948, 143); thus the Jungian critic, in liberating and expanding the work's inner self, can assert her own place in this chain while conveying its associative chaos and organic vitality. The disjunctive rhythm of Tyler's critical prose, and his use of simile and metaphor in phrases such as "paint haunting the frame like a detective," help to reexpress, aesthetically, the work's, artist's, and critic's inner tensions.

Tyler's approach here is inspired by the work's form—it seeks to help us understand it by plunging us into the psychomythic maelstrom guiding its production. Nevertheless, because the critical text, like the work itself, is a conscious and careful (re)shaping of unconscious forces, the critic does not simply engage in poetic free association but meticulously structures his interpretations, assuming formal/thematic unity as the fundamental aesthetic criterion for both artwork and critical analysis. In approaching Pavel Tchelitchew's *Hide-and-Seek* (1940–42), for example, Tyler first establishes that the painting is governed by a formal law ("hide emotions and seek forms") and a thematic principle (*"la condition humaine . . .* To Be"). These unifying guidelines then allow him to move on to symbolic-mythic interpretation of specific motifs, while again drawing on his own poetic skills to reveal and enhance the work's inner spirit.

> Between the fingers of the branching hand, as rootlike as it is mature, emerge the children of the womb of space, insouciant accidents, hazards of air more daring than those that mother and father the airman, including one whose flying flames, between the third and fourth fingers, are like the catastrophes of matches one lit in secret when a child, hoping to be transmuted in the flames of the magic box from inferior childhood into overwhelming grownness. In all the elements provided for them in *Hide and Seek*, the child plays hide and seek with the adult as the adult plays hide and seek with the child. (1942a, 10)

Tyler the critic is an attuned spectator with tremendous poetic flair. Yet here again we should note that he is employing an interpretive method well suited to the text at hand. All spectators of *Hide-and-Seek* will find themselves confronted with an openly symbolic canvas whose relentlessly intertwined symbolic motifs (hands, feet, veins, children's heads, tree limbs and trunks, leaves, flowers, even an apple and fetus) invite identification and interrelation. In offering a personal guide to the work's implicit meanings, Tyler applies an approach designed to decode while preserving and extending the work's own complexity, vitality, emotional resonance, and associative, subconscious roots through the essay's aesthetic (poetic) style.[16]

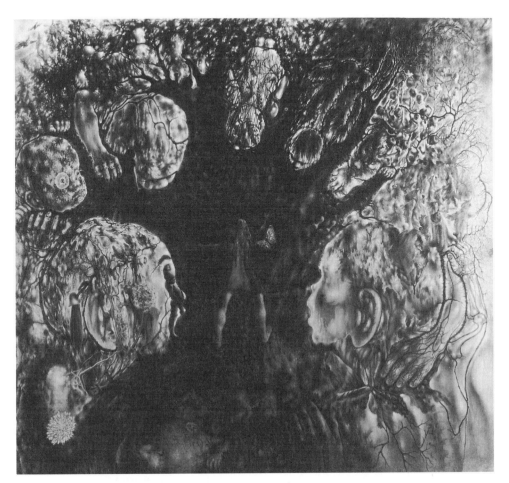

3. Pavel Tchelitchew. *Hide-and-Seek* {Cache-cache}. 1940–42. Oil on canvas, 6' 6½" × 7' ¾" (199.3 × 215.3 cm). The Museum of Modern Art, New York. Mrs. Solomon Guggenheim Fund. Photograph © 1999 The Museum of Modern Art, New York.

The implicit conception here of critic as intermediary between artist and spectator certainly suits Tyler's own desire to support, and explore, interesting work; as we have already noted, because the critic is also a productive, creative intermediary sharing creative responsibility, criticism can still prove fruitful in the absence of an original artist or formed work. Indeed, citing Proust's implication of the role of the active, "hallucinative" imagination in the transformation of reality into art, Tyler had already argued for such a radical extension of the critic's creative and aesthetic license by aligning critic and artist as creative, "erotic" spectators. If the artist is an erotic spectator whose desire collaborates with nature to transform the world into metaphor, Tyler suggested, the critical viewer of the work is also a "connoisseur of sight" able to "carry his perceptive faculty to the independent interpretation of images fugitively perceived in painting itself." In the end, "what is true of the artist, the erotic creator, is thus also true of the spectator, the erotic critic; a situation of collaborative vision exists" (1944a, 76).

As a partner in this "collaborative vision," the critic becomes an artist who assumes a sizable share of creative responsibility—and, potentially, *full* aesthetic responsibility. So long as he is placed on a par with the artist as an agent of hallucinative, aesthetic transformation, the artistic critic no longer requires the finest materials; as Wilde had suggested, "anything will serve his purpose." The erotic spectator is clearly a surrealist, but his vision is also thoroughly camp, downplaying aesthetic judgment while highlighting creative apprehension. Because the critic now interweaves unconscious and conscious thought in his collaborative creation of the work, he can reveal and sculpt hidden mythic/symbolic content that had never been formally placed in the work in the first place. This might mean that even an apparently nonsymbolic, nonauthored text, or even a cultural icon such as a movie star, could warrant careful decoding. The banality of popular culture could thus be reshaped and personalized by the dissident highbrow modernist.

SYMBOLS FROM THE CENTRIFUGE

> What material is not good enough for creative transmutation?
> *(Parker Tyler)*

In placing such faith in the creative perception of the erotic spectator, Tyler might be seen to be suggesting a radical democracy of artistic production, an opening of art making to nonartists, and potentially to anyone. Yet nothing could have been further from his mind. The *movies* may have been made by nonartists, but the erotic spectator was still a special individual, a new version of the gifted artist who now used culture as raw material. As with Farber, Tyler's approach was fueled by the vanguard desire to lead but not be followed: this may have been an example of creative, resistant spectatorship, but ultimately it was one whose purity, in practice, could be maintained only by an elite.

In building on the European example, Tyler refined surrealist vanguard spectatorship into a camp method sophisticated enough to serve as his chief means of aesthetic expression during the 1940s. While he didn't share Farber's predisposition toward popular entertainment, his writing clearly displays a certain measured fondness for cinema, coupled with the same condescension implicit in Farber's stance. His tone is very much tongue-in-cheek—he wants us to know that he is having creative fun with movies, not providing a method for judging "high or low esthetic content" (1947b, xix) in what are finally pop entertainments. Indeed, the movies could safely serve as material for critical transmutation largely because their inherent artistic worthlessness was never in doubt: these were not *poor* American artworks but *non*works that failed to display the "deliberate and controlled imprint of a single intelligence" (1944b, 12) and sacrificed individual vision to the law of the "centrifugal collective" (7). They provided psychomythic content without aesthetic shaping, allowing the critic to liberate the hidden symbolic complexity that factory filmmaking shared with high culture, while again contributing his own enriching, poetic form to the shapeless text.[17]

Reconstructed through criticism, the film might now seem closer to legitimate art than cultural trash, but it had been so reborn through creative, critical revelation. In themselves, movies were merely undeniably entertaining though largely formless amalgams of mythic, psychic, and physical energy. Echoing European predecessors such as Artaud and Goudal, who had noted the ability of devices such as editing and close-ups to liberate the marvelous in commonplace objects, Tyler saw a popular cinema "intoxicat[ed] with its technical powers," drawn toward a spectacular extreme of "form regardless of content" and "expression regardless of skill" (1944b, 11). This wild, "super artistic" vigor, coupled with the medium's overwhelming powers of illusion, engulfed the viewer in a "maze of symbolic emotions" issuing from the screen "in free forms that seduce and entangle by their universal repercussiveness" (20–21). But the protean energy had also splintered the text into a cyclone of symbolic fragments, which the erotic spectator might organize and combine with her own "dreams, half-remembered associations of our past, or subconscious or conscious literary memories" (35).

This was Tyler's *Hollywood Hallucination.* His first complete book of film criticism, published in 1944 while he was still at *View,* announced the camp critic as America's new vanguard artist, and the movies as a field ripe for aesthetic reclamation and transformation. In highlighting the "uncoördinated and inadvertent elements of grandeur" (220) in the charged subsurface of Hollywood movies, he isolates material for a new work powered by primitive dynamism and organized through the poetic arrangement of symbol and myth. On a broad scale, such arrangement will order textual components such as voice, music, clothing, and facial expression into an oppositional series[18] of affinities and disparities, interrelated through associated texts, myths, and metaphors. Wrenched from their functional, hopelessly prosaic placement in the movie, these components are revealed to have a symbolic and semantic depth of their own. In their newly organized extracinematic form, they also express the aesthetic resonance that a centrifugal collective, wastefully spinning energies outward into the surrounding culture, is both unwilling to acknowledge and unable to control.

A particularly clear example of Tyler's camp reclamation can be found in the *Hollywood Hallucination* chapter "Of Mickey and Monsters," which pits the Frankenstein myth (a particular favorite of Tyler's) against its modern antithesis, that of Mickey Mouse. The critic begins by suggesting a simple physical opposition—Mickey is "tiny and agile," whereas Frankenstein's monster is "huge and unwieldy"—but he quickly moves on, interpreting similarities and differences that relate the figures to art, myth, and society. Though both are members of the "same allegorical class by token of their marginal relation to the animal kingdom," Mickey represents the Aesopian tradition's "aggrandizement of a beast," whereas the monster suggests the "debasement of a man" (137). While Mickey, like the monster, is also a machine—the product of a creator—*The Brave Little Tailor* (1938) prefers to play out a parodic *inversion* of the Frankenstein myth:

> Whereas Mickey illustrates the comedy of the mechanical resources of the underdog, Frankenstein is the late nineteenth-century myth of reaction against mechanization—mechanization, that is to say, as an enemy of the human spirit rather than its ally. Today, in the world drama of war, we see exactly this latter situation: mechanization as an agent of destruction, and the German and Japanese armies in the esthetic guise of so many million "Frankensteins" while our own boys are "Davids." (141)

The Brave Little Tailor's mythical relevance has thus been revealed. Here was something quite different from Hollywood's old take on Frankenstein as a simple folk symbol of the subhuman rapist: Mickey suggested an interesting inversion of the mechanical principle, even a kind of fantasy of "musical reciprocity" between man/mouse and nature, each manipulating, and manipulated by, the other. But wasn't it odd that such a fantasy should prevail at a time of war, in an era seemingly dominated by the mechanical principle at its most stultifying?

> Alas, then! Mickey is a *peace-time* morality. . . . But in the more pertinent sense of his myth, Mickey is the peace-time individual, indulging in a dream of pure escapes from material dangers in which at the same time he has the most strenuous fun. Consequently he represents sport as a morality, no less than morality

4. Peacetime morality and protean joy. *The Brave Little Tailor* (1938).

as a sport. . . . When the mechanical principle is symbolically dedicated to the consummation of peaceful happiness and delight in leisure, its protean joy becomes wonderfully manifest. Then its coördination of deliberate skill with spontaneous reaction is on an esthetic-moral level; it is musical and profound. (143–44)

Note how Tyler is careful to root this protean joy, aesthetic-moral dimension, and even profundity in the manifestation of the mechanical principle in the Mickey Mouse myth—not in any deliberate artistry on the part of individuals at the Disney studio. His associational method, justified by an assumed interrelation among psyche, culture, and myth, allows him to discuss a film against a series of backgrounds (sociological, historical, mythic, cultural, psychological) limited only by the constraints of a larger organic structure without requiring specific attributions of agency. Here the organic structure is formed by the governing "Mickey Mouse / Frankenstein's monster" opposition, from which follow a host of suboppositions ("agile/unwieldy," "aggrandizement of beast / debasement of man," "David/Goliath," "Allies/Enemies," "Peace-time fantasy / war-time morality") and related associations (animation as mechanization—*Brave Little Tailor*—David—Allies). Obviously, this method allows the critic to introduce an enormous range of topics, and to move freely between textual and transtextual levels of myth, story, and even production context.

Though the resulting critical text can become a little daunting, at times even baffling in its seemingly casual meandering through the psychosymbolic matrix, its reverie is justified as a means of unearthing the mythic depth lying beneath the fragile surface of the mass text. (In the lengthy analysis of *Of Mice and Men* [1939] that follows, Tyler narrows his central opposition to "Dr. Frankenstein / the Monster," which allows him to critique heterosexual myth by allying George/Lennie with "American male / docile wife," and "Adam/Eve.") The critical text's own opacity is itself evidence of the artist-critic's active contribution to the material. The meandering oppositional/associational structure is also fundamentally an *aesthetic* structure, and "Of Mickey and Monsters" is, in its own way, a work of art.

By the mid-1940s, Tyler had developed erotic/camp spectatorship to the point where the critic might adopt the stance of a freelance intellectual capable of integrating insights from a number of fields into a single critical essay centered on the symbolic structure of a particular film. A film's symbolic content might, however, rest not simply in character but in narrative structure, sound, or mise-en-scène. The romantic social myth of the Single Instance (marriage as a "monolithic act of nature" [46]) may be embodied in the central Scarlett/Ashley opposition of *Gone with the Wind* (1939), but it is further elaborated through costume, voice, and physique: she becomes an acquiescent somnambule whose silent, submissive body contrasts with his repressive masculinity, expressed through his dominant and outwardly reassuring body, eyes, and voice. Even Leslie Howard's wardrobe plays a role here, suggesting "a true symbol of that sexual tact which Ashley (being married to Melanie) was supposed to be applying to Scarlett, for whom he felt a sharp animal desire" (70). In a critical approach that thrived on metaphor, costume offered a particular appeal, flimsily wrapping the psychic realities of screen characters in false, overlaid meanings that cried out for symbolic interpretation.

The actor's face presented similar possibilities, which Tyler explored more fully in his second book of film criticism, *Magic and Myth of the Movies* (1947). Because Hollywood's use of the human mask was so inept as to "disguise" character, it could inadvertently reveal some hidden psychological and/or mythic truth, for which the often placid performer acted as naive conduit. Indeed, the sheer power of an imaginary situation might induce seemingly instinctual reactions among performers, as in the case of the young men aboard the stifling, claustrophobic submarine in *Gung Ho!* (1943):

> The sign of reaction on their faces was one of passive appeal with a profound worry just below the surface. The sublevel of their aquatic vehicle brought to their own surfaces a sublevel of themselves, there being no mask of war to hide it. They were returned to a state of childhood, and for these boys it was naturally to that state when, depending on their mother's benevolence, they were accustomed to ask bounty and loving protection from her. So their faces assumed that mask of innocent and pure appeal that little boys wear specifically to attract and compel the good will of their mothers. (1947b, 155)

Tyler's assumption of the interpenetration of individual and collective unconscious allows him to slide subtly between conceptions of the young men as actors and characters within a movie myth. The implication is that like spectators, the performers in the film have been so mesmerized by the mythic/cinematic situation that they too have regressed to an anterior state of consciousness. (The "method" indeed!) Yet Tyler does not have to contact the actors to confirm his suspicions; it is enough merely to reveal the facial expressions that reside on the visible, symbolic surface of Hollywood's inadvertent "charade." Further, because he is *reforming* this symbolic content aesthetically, even poetic or pun-based symbolic relationships ("the sublevel of their aquatic vehicle brought to their own surfaces a sublevel of themselves") can enhance not simply the symbolic richness of the movie text but the aesthetic richness of the critical text.

A New Challenge

By the time *Magic and Myth* was published in 1947, however, Tyler was finding himself increasingly isolated as a vanguard critic. New York surrealism was dissolving around him. Enormous debt forced *View* to fold that spring. Many of the key European surrealists, including Breton, had already returned overseas. The New York School, itself steeped in the looser psychomythological surrealism promoted in *View*, would soon find its own voice in the *Tiger's Eye*, *Possibilities*, and *Instead*. Perhaps most ominous, a newfound popular interest in human psychology and psychoanalysis had spawned a growing number of movies with related themes, including *Now, Voyager* (1942), *Lady in the Dark* (1944), *The Seventh Veil* (1945), *Spellbound* (1945), *The Dark Mirror* (1946), and *Possessed* (1947). As with Farber's own affection for realistic action, Tyler's vanguard, oppositional tastes were seemingly being overtaken by the mainstream. What had once been championed by the discerning connoisseur—

in this case, psychological depth—was quickly becoming an acceptable norm of art and moviemaking.

Tyler could not accept this, because he had always assumed that Hollywood's charade was naive; without the mediation of the vanguard critic, the chaotic psychomythology of the movies remained puerile, even dangerous. A few years earlier, he had ended *The Hollywood Hallucination* with a biting critique of the movies' "daylight dream" as a second-rate psychic experience, another mechanism by which modern industrial society stifles the burgeoning inner world of the average worker.[19] Hollywood was the mass unconscious, but "scooped up as crudely as a steam shovel scoops up the depths of a hill, and served on a helplessly empty screen" (1944b, 238). The ritualized daydream was a barren experience that could not compare with the "luminous and authentic monstrosity of a little child's drawings or the paintings of the insane" (245).

Nor could daydream ritual compare with the authentic artistry of the vanguard critic. "I affirm that only reasons for being too good for the movie theater and for its vibrating messages about the modern psyche are the best in the world," he announces in *Magic and Myth*—"and the best in the world is the exclusive property, at this juncture of planetary time elapse, of the exceptional and validly accredited individual" (1947b, 120–21). How could one trust Hollywood to provide its own psychic, mythic, or symbolic richness? One couldn't, of course—the studios couldn't even manage mystery and horror, treating them as naively rational and readily revealed (as in the sled at the end of *Citizen Kane*), rather than subconscious, metaphysical, beyond the purview of the camera. New cinematic excursions into psychoanalysis were, naturally, even worse; here a hollow exoticism reigned, as in the clichéd dream sequences from *Lady in the Dark*, *Spellbound*, and *Yolanda and the Thief* (1945). Next to these scenes, Tyler's own superior insight into a text's psychic depths seemed self-evident—at least to himself.

> One of my present purposes is to reveal a weightier entertainment value in films than Hollywood itself is aware of. And in this respect [these] analyses . . . are in competition with the *Spellbounds* that have been and the *Spellbounds* to come. If I aim, however, at orientating my analysis of movies to a deeper psychological truth than routine dream interpretation, it is because Hollywood's dream products (or films) are much more complex than its script-writers lead, and are led, to suppose. (114–15)

As we saw in the case of Farber, mainstream/middlebrow encroachment on the critic's vanguard territory can force the critic to up the ante, emphasizing his superior powers of discernment and connoisseurship. Here, a "deeper psychological truth" than that recognized by the film is available to the critic via those patterns and symbols which do *not* serve as vehicles for the text's own superficial psychoanalysis. Hollywood's increasing willingness to use its own crude symbolism as clues to psychological trauma forced the critic to work even harder to find alternative, obscured symbolic matrices within mainstream cinema. Consequently, it also allowed him to refine an alternative to the oppositional series of symbols as an organizing tool for criticism.

COMPLEX STORIES AND HOLLYWOOD DREAMS

The new organizing form was allegory. Here, a film's "surface" narrative is seen as an (again unintended) allegory for the underlying psychomythic narrative pieced together by the critic. As with the oppositional series, the appeal to allegory accommodates a substantial amount of textual material, while the sheer stability of the interpretation's overall structure lends credibility to individual components. It also allows the critic to avoid engaging with a movie's middlebrow symbolism on its own terms, offering a side route into the subsurface of the text via the gaps or inconsistencies (usually from insufficient character motivation) in its bumbling narrative. Tyler had already tentatively explored this possibility in *The Hollywood Hallucination*, claiming that the "pseudo-divine" happy ending of *Meet John Doe* (1941) glazed over the film's underlying psychological complexities (1944b, 186). But the movies' newfound psychological pretension induced him to tackle their narrative ineptitude in earnest, revealing his own symbolic subnarrative as the text's authentic core. Mildred's "rather excessive passion" for her daughter Veda in *Mildred Pierce* (1945) is powerful enough to lead to her degradation and ruin but is insufficiently explained by the film. Tyler can do better, by offering a Freudian narrative, the Electra complex, and a key Freudian concept, displacement:

> Mildred imagines herself as Veda, in love with her own father, Mildred's husband, as *Mildred* was in love with *her* father. The passionate desire to give Veda everything, to see her grow up happy and successful in every way, is an ordinary case of displacement; paradoxically Mildred wants to give her every charm and chance to accomplish that which *she* was prevented from accomplishing, union with her father. But the desertion of Mildred by Pierce, Veda's father, lends extra neurotic energy to Mildred's aim, and it is not till late that she realizes she must supply Veda with another "father" to complete her own (Mildred's) incest pattern. This she does by marrying Beragon; sure enough, this brings Veda and Beragon together, and Mildred duly surprises them in an incestuous embrace. But in the shock of the moment Mildred wakes up, so to speak, from her complex and objectifies her own guilt as a daughter, identifies Veda as her own past,

5. A "rather excessive passion." *Mildred Pierce* (1945).

and changes at this moment into the outraged mother that her own mother would have been had she caught her (Mildred) in the arms of her own father. (1947b, 226–27)

Tyler's underlying narrative thus reveals a psychological richness, a depth of character invisible to the casual spectator. It was also clearly invisible to the film's screenwriters, who had concluded *Mildred Pierce*'s surface story not with Mildred's murdering Beragon or even Veda—both credible outcomes of the hidden psychodrama—but with Veda's murdering Beragon instead.

Logically it is Mildred . . . as a betrayed mother and wife who would have killed her husband, Beragon, and not Veda, who actually commits the murder according to the movie. If Mildred seeks to protect Veda, it is because Veda is a form of herself and for some reason has taken on her incest crime. Since it is implausible to believe that Veda would really have had the nerve to commit such a crime, the whole movie may be accepted as Mildred's dream of guilt, from which she exonerates herself, in conspiracy with Hollywood, by walking out of the hall of justice a free woman; that is . . . *by waking up into an optimistic, daylight reality.* In this way every dreamer exonerates himself of dream guilt. A Hollywood guilt dream, of course, is paradoxically done à la Ziegfeld. (227)

Remarkably, Tyler turns the apparent failure of his Electra narrative to explain the murderer's identity into an unlikely victory. Again, Hollywood incompetence ultimately becomes a boon to the critic: the implausibility of Veda's guilt pushes Tyler to accept the film in a new way, as Mildred's projected guilt dream.

Yet there is also the suggestion here that Hollywood may *not* be so innocent, that in some way it has conspired with Mildred to avoid the ugly implications of the movie's psychology. Are the movie industry, and the movie itself, simply ignorant of the reality of *Mildred Pierce*'s characters and their true motivations? Or are they at some level aware of these deeper truths but finally unwilling to face them head-on? Tyler wants to have it both ways. In order to show that he understands the text far better than it understands itself, the camp critic engages in a struggle with the text for ownership of its meanings. If the text does not seem *completely* passive but at least attempts to keep its filthy underside unexposed, the critic's efforts will seem all the more valiant, his struggle hard-won.

Unfortunately, however, keeping the text "active" in this sense will also raise the troubling specter of agency. It is one thing to assume that cultural meanings, shared in a collective psychomythic unconscious, can rise into movies *despite* the misguided actions of naive craftsmen. It is another to suggest that the industry, the film, perhaps even the craftsmen themselves, have shared the same dream fantasy and covered up the evidence ("secondary revision" at work), waking Mildred, the spectator, and themselves into an "optimistic daylight reality." The dream analogy is tempting for the camp film critic, because in putting a movie on the couch, it places appropriate emphasis on the critic's ability to organize the symbolic chaos manifested on its surface.[20] But as soon as we remember that dreaming is an activity which only animals—as opposed to inanimate objects and institutions—engage in, we run into difficult questions. If the film is a dream, who is dreaming? If the *filmmakers* are dreaming, have they gone to the trouble of arranging and editing their own dream material? If so, how are they different from surrealist artists?

I admit this line of questioning is a trifle unfair to the spirit of Tyler's approach, which was always meant, first and foremost, as a fun, creative way to look at artifacts that otherwise fail to "dominate or satisfy our esthetic instincts" (1944b, 67). This was spectatorship as poetic inspiration: the work that ultimately results from Tyler's analysis of *Mildred Pierce* is, I would venture to say, not *Mildred Pierce* itself but a psychologically enriched, ambiguous, poetic, and racy *version* of the film. (*Pierce* remade as a proto–"art film," even.) As a poet, Tyler believed strongly in such a fluidity and interpenetration of forms. His nine-canto *The Granite Butterfly*, published one year after *The Hollywood Hallucination*, mixes a variety of verse styles with prose and drama, even including staging instructions and filming notations ("Cut!"; "Iris in") while intermingling references to classic myths (Oedipus, Medusa, Narcissus) and Hollywood movies. The poet who walks onstage after the second act of "Boredom" (the play that constitutes the third canto) notes in the middle of his monologue that "to me . . . speech is a wound."

> Contrary to a certain popular notion that I personally am inclined to be verbose, I say only what is absolutely necessary, for it pains me a great deal to say anything. You see, I may not say it properly. I may not say exactly what is in my head. . . . But the main thing with artists is that something be in the head, something tremendously difficult to exhume, like a mummy in the heart of a pyramid. At first, I did not mean to say anything figurative in this prose speech, but you see, I have. And it has a great deal to do with the scheme of the poem. . . . One of my traits, I say without shame (and without shame simply because it must be said), is that I am perverse. I am perverse enough to believe in the twentieth-century revelation (or did it happen before?) that whatever a person thinks should be expressed in a convenient and communicable form. This form is the form that he chooses from moment to moment. (1945a, 19)

For Tyler, movie criticism could itself become another convenient form of personal expression for the modern poet, one that mixed poetry with prose in its exhuming of personal and cultural psychological-mythic interiors. As in *The Granite Butterfly*, it drew on the poet's knowledge of his own ties to the mythical roots of culture in order to facilitate self-expression. Yet the criticism of *The Hollywood Hallucination* and *Magic and Myth of the Movies* also went further, developing self-expression as resistance to a form of culture for which the critic had only limited respect. This is what marked it as camp, a gesture just as aggressive as the cultism we examined in the previous chapter. Tyler wants us to believe that he has liberated the complex, poetic underside of *Mildred Pierce*, but in fact he has thrown out much of the film on the screen, replacing it with one he finds aesthetically pleasing, and challenging. Though not a filmmaker, he has ably constructed his own cultured cinema out of the materials available.

Camp fundamentally requires such a feeling of cultural and intellectual superiority over the mass culture text and its meanings. This is also an *aesthetic* superiority, as the camp critic-spectator plays with the hierarchies and emphases of textual meanings in order to remake the text as a product of his own personal expression. The specific nature of textual refashioning will differ with the various personalities and aesthetic biases of camp spectators; not all, certainly, will favor psychomythic subtexts as much as did the surrealist-influenced Tyler. Nevertheless, many will focus on semantic iconography as shared and readily identifiable surface meanings that can be identified as symbols to be decoded, or simply as conventions to be mocked and overturned. This form of spectatorship can be quite fun, as most readers will already know. It is also empowering, to an extent. But for Tyler, it served first and foremost as a means of sustaining vanguard aesthetics within an increasingly narrow and oppressive culture. His own Hollywood "remakes" were as openly mythic, psychological, (homo)erotic, and artistically complex as *The Granite Butterfly*; in the face of an art scene that was, by 1950, already swapping its integrity for middle-class patronage, they expressed the unyielding stand of the authentic artist determined to wield pop mythos as an assault weapon.

THE MOVIE ARTIST AS TRAMP

If Tyler's camp criticism depended on his assumed superiority over the movies, what would happen if he were confronted with a filmmaker who seemed more authentic artist than anonymous cog in the Hollywood dream machine? As a self-styled aesthete, he was certainly not too proud to herald artistic filmmaking when he saw it; however, he would have to be prepared to alter his critical assumptions and procedures accordingly. Camp was simply not designed to deal with real art. Indeed, because it aimed to provide a means of highlighting the critic's own artistry, *non*art—myth-laden, mass-psychotic cultural clay—was much easier to work with.

The emergence of European and American modernist cinemas in the 1950s would eventually force Tyler's hand, encouraging him to leave movie camp to the vulgar and fashion-conscious in order to pursue a far more serious, even Arnoldian discernment of Great Works. Yet we see him preparing for this move already in the late 1940s, adjusting his methods in order to embrace an existing film artist, Charlie Chaplin. Tyler's discussions of Chaplin thus represent something of a transition between the two halves (and personas) of his career as a film critic: as much as they echo the Hollywood hallucinations (most obviously in their emphasis on psychology and personal mythology), they simply lack the disdain and condescension of the camp perspective. Chaplin made popular movies, but it was still safe for American highbrows to respect him as a legitimate artist (especially after *Monsieur Verdoux* [1947], which could be fiercely defended as an incisive, mature work [Maland 1989]). It obviously didn't hurt that the comic had also been a favorite of the European surrealists.

Tyler submitted Chaplin to the one psychoanalytic critical approach acceptably applied to great artists: psychobiography. This granted the gifted performer/director/producer the autonomy he had earned, and the credit he deserved (as active agent determining the content and aesthetic shape of his films), while still leaving the critic ample material for study. Psychobiography had been a mainstay of American literary criticism for decades, enjoying an initial heyday in the 1920s with the publication of Katherine Anthony's *Margaret Fuller: A Psychological Biography* (1920), Van Wyck Brooks's *The Ordeal of Mark Twain* (1920), Raymond Weaver's *Herman Melville, Mariner and Mystic* (1921), and Joseph Wood Crutch's *Edgar Allan Poe: A Study in Genius* (1926). With its psychoanalytically informed reevaluations of the work of Dickens and Kipling, Edmund Wilson's *The Wound and the Bow* (1941) demonstrated that this approach could still be considered current twenty years later, among a new generation of literary intellectuals.

In recasting Chaplin as the tortured artist, Tyler may have had in mind Brooks's study of Twain, an early classic of the critical genre and a key influence on many of Tyler's contemporaries. For Brooks, Twain's "unconscious desire to be an artist" (2) had from the start resisted the business career planned for him by society and his mother, and acceded to by his conscious self. The resulting heroic struggle between creative unconscious and stifling superego is played out in the plots of Twain's stories, and in fictional surrogates such as Pudd'nhead Wilson and Huckleberry Finn.

Tyler revived this struggle quite productively in his own *Chaplin: Last of the Clowns* (1948). As with Twain, the screen clown's expressive abilities must compete with his business acumen; the Public Artist must struggle with the Private Poet. Like Brooks, who had relied extensively on Albert Bigelow Paine's 1912 Twain biography, Tyler eschewed original research for his study, relying instead on established biographical narratives as a base from which to launch his own psychoanalytic interpretations. Anecdotes related by others—notably Gerith von Ulm's account, in *Charlie Chaplin: King of Comedy* (1940), of Chaplin's 1904 encounter with Sir Arthur Conan Doyle—become central to his interpretation of the comic's life, regardless of their basis in historical fact. Tyler merely relates the Doyle story, then remarks:

> I hardly pause here—as hardly elsewhere—to consider if this incident be a "true" one. It is enough that it is consistent both with a *profound* and *my* conception of Chaplin. This conception has for one of its premises the hypothesis of the unconscious as it exists in all of us; therefore, it is possible to detect in the above-mentioned incident a shadow of the impulse to bargain with the fa-

ther for an equal share of the mother. . . . Like many an occurrence one might invent for a man's life, if it did not happen it should have—and, indeed, it might as well have. (1948a, 58–59)

Clearly the critic's critical assumptions have not changed all that drastically—the myths of Chaplin's biography and fictional personae can themselves become valid objects of interpretation. The artist-critic still wishes to exercise creative control over the reality he is analyzing; as with the poststructuralists whose ideas Tyler anticipates, the historical "reality" of Chaplin's life (as we commonly understand it) can finally be accessed only through the discursive, " 'biographical truth' of Chaplin's career" (61).

This "biographical truth" is now subject to creative interpretation along archetypal lines. The pampered infant's "aristocratic" nature is initially squashed by the death of his comedian father and his subsequent forced entry into the world of "child serfdom" (32), but it bravely fights for survival, reemerging in the form of Chaplin's poetic/romantic ideal, the Tramp. But the aristocrat can never return completely, and the tragedy of Chaplin's career will be his own necessary alienation from the Tramp's idealized vision. Chaplin-the-artist-worker's own relationships with women fall far short of the Tramp's vision of idealized romance, and the Tramp's global success can be experienced by his creator only "*by proxy*" (125). By *Modern Times* (1936) the artist-worker's insane jealousy has driven him to tyrannize the Tramp, forcing him to submit to the "crucible of the work-world" (131). This tyranny reaches even greater heights in *The Great Dictator* (1940), before Chaplin eradicates the Tramp completely in *Monsieur Verdoux*.

If this struggle between poet and artist-worker mirrors Tyler's own struggle to maintain his integrity as an intellectual poet-critic within a postwar climate tyrannized by crass artist-professionals, it also more generally suggests the artist under siege, fighting to define and maintain an identity within a climate of middlebrow conformity. For Tyler, Chaplin can become the culture industry's alienated virtuoso, a figure who, like the camp critic himself, struggles to escape the pressures of pulverizing consumerist mediocrity. In *A Little Boy Lost: Marcel Proust and Charlie Chaplin* (an essay published in 1947 as a low-circulation Prospero Pamphlet), Tyler makes the implicit connection even clearer, reading Chaplin's Tramp outfit as the artist's own form of camp resistance. Here Tyler reconceives personal identity in almost Wildean terms, as an "attempt to master the problem of costume," with the true "secret of clothes-wearing" as the naturalizing of artifice. Self-expression becomes a matter of personalizing the meanings of mass-produced material. Chaplin, like Proust, is Blake's "Little Boy Lost" from the Songs of Experience; each possesses the Muse of the Child but the outer shell of the wizened man.

Seen side by side in a photograph, the young Proust appropriates the costume of the backward-gazing dandy, while Charlie seems the "daddy-envious presumptuous child who steals his father's pants," the "adult-disguised boy at large, bent on reconquest of the symbolic mother" (1947a, unpaginated). If in the end neither has "mastered" his apparel, this very disunity of self has allowed for enormous artistic success by enabling aesthetic expression, metaphorically expressed as radical personal chic.

Now elevated to camp cultural critic in his own right, Chaplin can be rescued as a film artist of real depth and importance, a genuine erotic spectator of his world comparable with Proust and even Kafka.[21] This enabled Tyler to shift his own perspective even further, if he so desired: because filmmakers might be worth respecting on their own terms, for their own creative work, the critic might retreat to the more traditional role of intermediary, assessing and interpreting a work in elevated terms for the receptive spectator. Unlike most Hollywood movies, sophisticated art did not require the camp perspective to make it interesting or aesthetic. When in the 1950s and 1960s an increasing number of richly artistic films appeared from both Europe (in the form of refined, often provocative features) and America (from solitary independents), Tyler would move from cultural (re)producer to connoisseurist consumer, becoming an "elder statesman" of aesthetic culture capable of taking films seriously, on their own terms, and committed to passing his recommendations on to others. Like Chaplin, the best of these new film artists assumed the primary role of erotic spectator and psychomythological critic themselves, making Tyler's own transmutative work unnecessary. Now the critic could step back and engage in the deferential discernment inappropriate for pop movies but crucial to any serious art criticism. That many others who purported to take films seriously would apparently not share this changed attitude would now seem to Tyler not just frivolous but flatly irresponsible. With the trendy middle lapping up polluted versions of camp and cult attitudes like cheap champagne, the bold reassertion of good taste, and of the enlightened critic's heightened access to it, would be needed more than ever. If film could be taken seriously as art, the time for critical fun was over.

Chapter Five

FROM TERMITES TO AUTEURS:
CULTISM GOES MAINSTREAM

> Any day now, Americans may realize that scrambling after
> the obvious in art is a losing game.
> *(Manny Farber)*

A S WE HAVE SEEN, the camp and cult wings of American film criticism arose as vanguard gestures at a specific time, and within a
specific cultural climate. Manny Farber and Parker Tyler may
have enjoyed movies, but they most certainly did not consider them distinct artworks in their own right. This is precisely why they proved so
eminently useful in the struggle over authentic highbrow art in America.
The movies could be appealed to as a standing repository of authentic
surface vitality, masculine strength, psychomythological depth—all the
characteristics highbrow American modernism *should* have contained in
America, and might have contained, had the temptation of money, com-
fort, and success not erased the European legacy and driven American
painters toward a dead end of middlebrow conformity.

The rhetorical gesture inherent in this stance is quite daring. The critic,
as vanguard intellectual, offers himself as spearhead of a richer culture, a
critical culture, one in which detritus can be appreciated (albeit with effort) from an aesthetic perspective. He must, however, be prepared to
sift and/or dig—sift through cultural product to find an aesthetic match
(cultism), dig beneath a text's deceptively bland, functional surface in
search of underlying aesthetic complexity (camp). As developed by Farber
and Tyler, cultism and camp provided, in effect, a homegrown American
art cinema contemporaneous with the early modernist films of Maya
Deren and Kenneth Anger, and decades before the likes of *Shadows*
(1960), *Mickey One* (1965), and *Easy Rider* (1969). However—and this
is the crucial point—Farber and Tyler's art cinemas required no gifted
film artist aesthetically expressing herself either within or beyond the Hollywood system; only the movies, critical skill, and an artistic imagination
were needed.

The critic was freed to become a re-creator of culture in the vanguard
tradition, an artist whose "work" was not the original movie, prior to

critical selection and transformation (just as the urinal Duchamp selected was not a work before it became his *Fountain*), but rather the transformation process itself, offered as an example to others. The avant-garde elevates the romantic/modern ethos of renewed vision (through the eyes of the artist) to a pedagogical extreme: the vanguard work actually seeks to *teach* us how to regard our world differently. We have learned the lesson when we accept the work, grasp its gestured message, and apply it to our own life experience, thus creating our own culture along the vanguard model.

The main difficulty facing both the European avant-gardes and Farber and Tyler's wartime insurgence was that few students seemed willing to sit through the lectures. Vanguard art requires, ironically, an educated audience resistant to dominant aesthetic trends; the sheer novelty (even outrageousness) of modernist styles through the 1940s had ensured that this audience would remain quite small. The rise of an extensive, educated middle-class art market in postwar America, by contrast, provided a significant oppositional constituency for the avant-garde among those increasingly disaffected from a homogenous glut of officially acceptable, financially successful, even popular art.

By 1960, such art (and, by extension, aesthetic discernment) had become available to anyone with a television, a J. D. Salinger novel, or even a ticket to an Elia Kazan or Fred Zinnemann film. Again, here was a rival notion of "popular art" to that suggested by the avant-garde: if this rival notion seemed poised to emerge victorious during the postwar decades, it was (highbrows could surmise) because middlebrow art exhibited the sameness and seductive shallowness of mass art. Middlebrows were really lowbrows burdened with rather embarrassing aspirations to cultural authority. The crude earnestness of New Deal aesthetic populism had seemingly been resurrected wholesale. Popular film art, for example, was typically tarted up with enough obvious symbolism, flashy style, and social "relevance" to impress the undiscerning. Leslie Fiedler captured the prevailing sentiment: middlebrow was a faux art born of a sniveling fear of traditional distinctions and a disturbing "drive for conformity on the level of the timid, sentimental, mindless-bodiless genteel" (1957, 547). If the authentic masses were too ignorant to know their plight, the upwardly mobile masses now seemed to crave homogeneity.

Mass culture wasn't just junk anymore, which to vanguard highbrows signaled that "their" culture was being stolen from them. But these highbrows were also feeling threatened on another front as well: their vanguard ranks were filling with hordes of middlebrows alienated from the mainstream of their own aesthetic culture. On the sizable fringes of popular art was arising a *popular avant-garde* teeming with individuals hungry for strategies of self-empowerment and eager to reclaim as their own the trash culture their middle-class brethren had so eagerly rejected. To the vanguard purist this more popular, accessible form of resistance naturally spelled a corruption or at least compromise of dearly held principles, but it also directly threatened the subcultural authority of the avant-garde's older practitioners and practices. Seized consumerism would not only shape the youth styles of the "white negro" hipster and flower child; it would help popularize vanguard film spectatorship in ways Farber and Tyler could not have envisioned in the 1940s.

In the rapidly expanding American film culture of the postwar decades, taking films seriously was no longer in itself outrageous or even novel, even when it came to routine products of the Hollywood system. In 1940, there had been 27 film societies in America; by 1948, there were 84, by 1955, 300, and by the 1960s, over 4,000.[1] In the 1930s, MOMA's Circulating Film Library had begun distributing 16mm prints of more "artistic" Hollywood fare in almost total isolation, but after the war interest in film art was sufficient to support a number of rival operations. One of the most significant of these, Amos Vogel's Cinema 16, specialized in experimental shorts but pursued an extreme cultism in its own crowded New York screenings, often mixing experimental work with science films, political documentaries, obscure features, and more mainstream classics that had fallen out of circulation (MacDonald 1987). For those who preferred to stay home, even television could be reappropriated as a source of vanguard fun, turning living rooms into private revival houses for a gamut of old Hollywood features.

The rise of an oppositional vanguard market could make the vanguard film critic a key cultural player, but only if he agreed to live up to his pedagogical obligations, modifying his strategies of provocation for the wider audience. The rewards—including real cultural influence—might be significant, but more widespread acceptance would prove difficult for the diehard avant-gardist to swallow, even suggesting the avant-garde's own absorption into the middlebrow sphere. As we shall see over these next two chapters, vanguard veterans such as Farber and Tyler would have to work hard to renegotiate their positions within this new climate. Tyler would take the stronger stand, dumping camp criticism for more refined discernment when he realized there were artistic films worth critiquing as such; from the murky margins between the avant-garde and middlebrow, he could then comfortably assail the newly fashionable camp posturing of Jonas Mekas's New York Underground. Farber instead dug in his heels, choosing hermeticist avoidance over direct confrontation, ignoring the fashionable cultist auteurism of Andrew Sarris while pursuing ever more esoteric strains of vanguard activity. Yet at least he was still stubbornly sticking to his vanguard ideals: Farber's longer position papers of the 1950s and 1960s would reveal a critic determined to hone cultism into a form obscure enough to keep pseudosophisticates at bay. Even if they too rejected the pretentious, symbol-heavy European art cinema, could they ever see movies as termite mounds?

BUGS ON THE LOOSE

For Manny Farber, the ascent of middlebrow within Hollywood made authentically expressive movies even harder to spot, and cultist integrity and leadership more necessary than ever. He had already sensed the middlebrow danger in the early 1950s, when faux realism began peppering arty Hollywood releases such as *Fourteen Hours* and *Detective Story*. Indeed, he left regular reviewing shortly thereafter, concentrating instead on his own painting and sculpture. His film criticism now became more sporadic, appearing in a variety of publications (*Commonweal*, *Commentary*, *Perspectives*, *Film Culture*, even soft-core *Cavalier*) and often taking the form of longer position papers generously laced with antimiddlebrow vitriol. Yet there was also something else afoot here—a cultist, even auteurist celebration of neglected oppositional directors such as Anthony Mann, William Keighley, and Phil Karlson, unpretentious purveyors of rugged "male truth" in an otherwise anemic American cinema.

Was Farber selling out? Hardly—he implicitly pitched his own auteurist cultism as the real deal, an option simply too personal, too quirky to be readily co-opted by the mainstream. Rather than provide a pompous pantheon, he would prefer to display his superior cultist skills by continuing to reveal the niggling infiltration of unheralded technicians into the hidden corners of a text's surface. The liberty and vitality of bottom-up expression was still to be prized over any potentially stifling top-down formal arrangement, yet now the latter would be clearly identified with middlebrow values so pervasive as to have led to a general cheapening of the arts in America. If the fresh innovations of the nascent New York School had given way to the pillow painting of Rothko and Pollock, authentic jazz was now being softened into the palatable strains of Dave Brubeck and Stan Getz, the rough-hewn pulp novel succeeded by the hollow pretentiousness of Saul Bellow and John Cheever (Farber 1971d, 113). Perhaps worst of all, the glorious new medium of television spewed an endless stream of preachy liberal dramas and banal interview programs offering "middle-brow art talking about itself" (1959b, 27). The trend, Farber feared, threatened to precipitate "the worst era in the history of art."

> Not even the ponderously boring periods, similar to the one in which Titian and Tintoretto painted elephantine conceit and hemstitched complication into the huge dress-works affair called Venetian painting, can equal the present in-

ferno of American culture, which is so jammed with successful con men. One can only glance back in wonderment at those sinkings in each art form where the "shrewdster" gained a decisive entrance. In painting, it occurred in the late 1940's, when certain eruptions combined to bring about a glib turning in avant-garde painting. . . . (1971d, 123–24)

The situation was indeed critical. "Now that the middle class has found serious art," he warns, "it is almost impossible for a natural talent—good, bad, or in between—to make any headway" (124).

Part venomous diatribe, part nostalgic paean to the testosterone-drenched days of yore, "Underground Films: A Bit of Male Truth" (written for *Commentary* in 1957) probably stands as Farber's single best piece of criticism, and the clearest representation of the polemical slant of the position papers. Faced with a misguided interest in Art among Hollywood slicksters, and a trendy fashion for second-rate cultism among hipsters who flocked to a new De Sica and gushed over westerns but lacked even a basic sensitivity to cinematic nuance, Farber had to admit that as a vanguard maverick he had simply failed. His audience had been duped by the "fake underground films" of the late 1940s, "plushy thrillers with neo-Chandler scripts and a romantic style that seemed to pour the gore, histrionics, decor out of a giant catsup bottle." The new neocultist regard for Hollywood genre pictures was blind and frivolous, a chic pastime for those content to "play the garbage collector or make a night court of films" (1971i, 24). Would-be film aesthetes were hilariously undiscerning, equally reverent of the symbol-heavy, overbearing mannerism of Wilder, Mankiewicz, and Stevens and the smarmy pseudorealist liberalism of younger TV-trained hacks like Martin Ritt, John Frankenheimer, and Sidney Lumet.

As an elder statesman of refined pop culture taste, Farber fondly recalls the 1940s as a heyday of resistant moviemaking—a time when, untempted by commercial success, skilled directors could undercut the formulaic nature of their material by burrowing into a scene, subtly introducing nuance, detail, and texture while enhancing the film's authentically rough, virile effect. Such filmmakers—Raoul Walsh, Anthony Mann, John Farrow, William Keighley—did not simply manage to produce vital, unpretentious "second-gear celluloid" (12) within the confines of low budgets and genre formulas; they actually thrived under such conditions. "Stiff, vulgar, low-pulp material" forced William Wellman to display a "low-budget ingenuity, which creates flashes of ferocious brassiness, an authentic practical-joke violence . . . and a brainless hell-raising" (13). On the other hand, the temptations of "unlimited cash, studio freedom, an expansive story, message, heart, and a lot of prestige" had only tempted this director to commit unfortunate mishaps such as *The Public*

Enemy (1931) and *The Story of G.I. Joe* (1945). That these two "over-weighted mistakes" had even attained the "almond-paste-flavored eminence" (17) of MOMA's Film Library in turn revealed this institution's disconcerting taste for middlebrow obviousness. In this sense, MOMA's cultural guardians were no hipper than the typical film critic, whose "choice of best salami is a picture backed by studio build-up, agreement amongst his colleagues, a layout in *Life* mag (which makes it officially reasonable for an American award), and a list of ingredients that anyone's unsophisticated aunt in Oakland can spot as comprising a distinguished film" (14). Where was the fun in watching films that seemed to "bear the label of ART in every inch of their reelage" (15)? The pretentious middle-brow prizewinner, laden with "philosophical undertones, pan-fried domestic sights, risqué crevices, sporty actors and actresses, circuslike gymnastics, a bit of tragedy like the main fall at Niagara, has every reason to be successful. It has been made for that purpose" (14).

The same could certainly not be said for the marginal efforts of the underground director, relegated to murky cinemas and "prints that seem overgrown with jungle moss, sound tracks infected with hiccups." But for this artisan, and thus for his connoisseur audience too, suffering brought rewards—chiefly, the freedom to *avoid* the pitfalls of surface obviousness by hiding out in the *underground*, "sub-surface reaches" (15) of his films, whence he might pursue "private runways to the truth" (17). In fact, these subsurface reaches were not so deep: still very much an abstractionist, Farber meant not psychic subtext so much as the nooks and crannies of a film's complex terrain, faces and forms obscured within the seemingly banal textual surface. Yet these runways were nevertheless *so* private as to be strictly off-limits to all but the initiated. Those with merely an eye for thematic consistency would miss the real accomplishments of Farber's neglected technicians, for only a close scrutiny of rough texture could reveal

> the unheralded ripple of physical experience, the tiny morbidly life-worn detail which the visitor to a strange city finds springing out at every step. The Hawks film is as good on the mellifluous grace of the impudent American hard rock as can be found in any art work; the Mann films use American objects and terrain—guns, cliffs, boulders, an 1865 locomotive, telephone wires—with more cruel intimacy than any other film-maker. . . . (17)

In avoiding the "butter-slicing glibness that rots the Zinnemann films," underground directors explored the physicality of the most routine actions—Raoul Walsh, for instance, had his gangster traverse a saloon "with so much tight-roped ad-libbing and muscularity that he seems to be walking backward through the situation" (19). The YMCA scene in Lewis Allen's *Appointment with Danger* (1951) "emphasizes the wonderful fat-waisted, middle-aged physicality of people putting on tennis shoes and playing handball" (20). Instead of using shadows and perspective as stock artistic devices, underground directors would "play movement against space" (22), rendering narrative details as isolated abstractions. For the attuned connoisseur, the most lowbrow, seemingly functional cheapie could thus be shown to contain a wealth of formal complexity, perhaps expressed in "the way a dulled waitress sat on the edge of a hotel bed," or in "the weird elongated adobe in which ranch hands congregate before a Chisholm Trail drive" (21).

As usual, Farber was asserting genuine aesthetic discernment in the face of middlebrow mediocrity, while at the same time insisting on his own closer ties to authentic popular culture. But the threat of "muddlebrow" mock seriousness (1959c, 27) would soon push him to wild extremes of iconoclasm, horning him into the small haven of safety between the contradictions of vanguard ideology. Spotting the cultural enemy was easy—Michelangelo Antonioni aspired only to "pin the viewer to the wall and slug him with wet towels of artiness and significance" (1962–63, 13). But leading the audience out of bondage was another matter, as it suggested fundamental compromise on the critic's part. By keeping his cultist alternative inaccessible, closely tied to his own revelatory vision—and, indeed, to his revelatory prose style—Farber neatly avoided the problem of influence by ensuring that his insights would be difficult for the reader to activate as a means of constructing her own alternative culture.

In his own mind, any facile cultism, such as an updated directory of acceptable oppositional directors, would be doomed to embarrassing failure simply because it ignored the sheer complexities that made movies worth examining in the first place. During the 1960s, as the rival cultism of Andrew Sarris began to offer a connoisseurship of lists instead of details, Farber retreated even further into the hidden recesses of cinematic surfaces, to the fascinating minutiae perceptible in the underfed and over-stuffed alike. Why look for "subterranean inventiveness" (1959c, 27) merely at the level of direction, when—as Farber himself had long assumed—it might issue from any of a film's personnel? Because a movie was the product of a horde of workers "situated in different spots of the universe in relation to art, business and talent" (echoes of Tyler's "centrifugal collective"), its real fascination lay not in a "sum total of esthetic effects" but in the "underground channels created by each artist pursuing his path" (1959d, 27).

Farber typically pitched his enhanced discernment in oppositional terms—now it became a matter of "White Elephant Art vs. Termite Art." This was certainly not a simple matter of Bad films vs. Good films, or even vital films vs. lethargic films, but rather a more fluid distinction between films (and artworks) that squashed minute expression and those which allowed for it, intentionally or not. He could use "white elephant art" as a blanket term for domestic and imported middlebrow hokum while still searching for termite elements even in the most elephantine of epics. Though this did move Farber's approach a bit toward camp (finding the "real" film under the apparent film), his feet remained planted in cultism to the extent that insurgent termite material could still be traced back to a "fantastic technician" resolutely "building with suicidal force within a stale, corrupt, losing proposition" (1959d, 27).

Significantly, this increasing willingness to look beyond directors to termite technicians would also encourage Farber to explore the minute textures of performance. This was, and still is, highly unusual for film criticism. Most critics had rated performance, a few (Tyler, for one) had interpreted it, but none had seen in acting such a wealth of abstract surface detail or potential plethora of expressive material. Strictly speaking, Farber had mined this vein already in the 1940s, lauding the realistic depiction of human behavior in movies as varied as *Moontide* (1942), *Shadow of a Doubt* (1943), and *Going My Way* (1944). Now, however, the termite performance might serve as a chief source of spectatorial interest within an otherwise bland, lethargic production, suggesting in a gesture, action, or even glance an attention to real human vitality absent from a work's elephantine body. A movie's mistakes could seem "inconsequential beside the seemingly picayune contributions of a bit player" (1959d, 27)—Jackie Coogan in *Lonelyhearts* (1958), Walter Brennan in *Rio Bravo* (1959), an unknown black teenager in *The Sound and the Fury* (1959).

The importance of performance as an indication of underlying aesthetic interest within middlebrow cultural products became all the more obvious in the face of recent tendencies in film production. The success of the European art cinema and trendy Hollywood features of the early 1960s suggested a new approach to filmmaking—a Wellesian orchestration of cinematic effects so overwhelming as to stifle any expression of vitality issuing from a film's lower depths. "The strange evolution of movies in the last ten years," he noted in 1963, had led to the disappearance of

> those tiny, mysterious interactions between the actor and the scene that make up the memorable moments in any good film. These have nothing to do with the plot, "superb performance," or even the character being portrayed. They are moments of peripheral distraction, bemusement, fretfulness, mere flickerings of skeptical interest: Margaret Sheridan's congested whinny as a career woman sparring with Kenneth Tobey (Christian Nyby's *The Thing*); Bogart's prissy sign language to a bespectacled glamour girl through the bookstore window (Howard Hawks's *The Big Sleep*); or Richard Barthelmess's tiredly defiant dissolute slouch when he enters the *cabaña* in *Only Angels Have Wings*. . . .

Such tingling moments liberate the imagination of both actors and audience: they are simply curiosity flexing itself, spoofing, making connections to a new situation. (1971c, 145)

By contrast, the new filmmakers, hungry for fame, riches, and the prestige of a critic's award, pursued success at the expense of aesthetic liberation. Like the fashionable New York abstractionists of the 1940s, they chased middlebrow security by stifling their art, stuffing the performer into overdressed symphonies. In "one inert film after another," Farber bemoaned, "by the time the actor moves into position, the screen has been congealed in the manner of a painting by Pollock, every point filled with maximum pungency" (146). Personal tics, nuances of bodily and facial movement had been rigorously overmanaged, placed in the service of the larger theme or message. Whereas William Powell had once been permitted to "use his satchel underchin to pull the dialogue into the image, then punctuate with his nose the stops for each chin movement" (148), the actors in *Lawrence of Arabia* (1962) seemed burdened with heavy masks, the leading players in *Sundays and Cybele* (1962) reduced to "walking receptacles for the production crew" (147).

At worst, there was no escape. For the arty filmmaker, spontaneous performance threatened a film's careful erector-set construction and thus had to be squashed. Antonioni's performer became a "slight bulge in the glossy photography"; Truffaut's, a "mask painted over with sexual fatigue, inert agony, erosion, while his body skitters around weightlessly like a paper doll" (153). "Fellini-Bellini" so overloaded his movies with stylistic mannerisms and pointless decoration as to create a wholly artificial "Gauze Wonderland" (1971j, 167) in which nothing, and no one, could breathe. Even in America, the most talented performers could be straitjacketed, prevented by an overzealous auteur from tunneling to freedom. Martin Ritt had made sure Richard Burton was "squeezed into his role" (1971a, 173) in *The Spy Who Came in from the Cold* (1965); Marlon Brando had previously proven able to "grab attention from any Chevrolet or sequin gown that the lower technicians [threw] in his way" (1971b, 164), but now he struggled in vain to combat *The Chase*'s (1966) rigid theatricality.

A valiant few might, however, still slip through the knots. Refusing to become a prisoner, the rebel performer could stubbornly assert his freedom and vitality with a carefully nuanced termite performance, perhaps even by "obliterating one word to emphasize a raised syllable or accented laugh" (1971a, 174)—as Oskar Werner had managed in Ritt's *Spy*. Because classic films were "never more savage and uninhibited than in those moments when a whirring energy is created in back of the static mannered acting of some Great Star" (1971e, 180), it behooved the critic to discern worthy successors to Leonid Kinsky, Eric Blore, Edgar Kennedy, and other macho bit performers of little range but awesome explosiveness. As usual, fascinating termite work could be found in the unlikeliest of places— in Michael Kane's "forceful amalgam of silent cunning and subofficer deviousness as the "Exec" in *The Bedford Incident*" (1965), or in "Eleanor Bron's mugging, put-on acting that just skirts sickening cuteness as the fake Indian girl in *Help!* [1965]" (1971h, 186). Termites were on the loose even on television, in performances by Martin Balsam, Jack Warden, Jack Klugman, and even Dick Stark, who delivered a Remington Rand commercial with "sandpaper directness" (1959a, 27).

Farber's recommendations had always stemmed from a resolute antiestablishment stance, but their increasing particularity now suggested a seemingly eccentric passion for detail. In singling out one or two of a film's many minor performers, or in pinpointing peculiar microactions in the performance of a well-known actor, he was retreating into the obscure recesses of films. Larger plot mechanisms now seemed far less interesting, because choice moments were found not in a film's deliberately acted showcase scenes but in relatively minor passages, where performers could display minutiae of physical detail, enhancing character complexity and formal interest. Farber, like Otis Ferguson before him, had always assumed that the camera eye could not tolerate affectation; the best directors, now as then, recognized this and worked with the medium's natural strengths. The excitement of Robert Aldrich's *Flight of the Phoenix* (1966) stemmed not from its camerawork or plot, but from its

> baroque latticework, unimportant bits of action that seem to squeeze through the cracks of large scenes: The freakish way in which Hardy Kruger's Germanic gabble works over a sun-cracked lower lip; the job-type sensation of watching work procedures from the perspective of an envious, competitive colleague; Ian Bannen doing a monkeyish prancing and kidding around the German. . . . (1971h, 186)

Once Farber moves decisively into a cultist connoisseurship of physicality, even famous stars can be rehabilitated as aesthetically interesting, insofar as one knows where and how to look. In *Fail-Safe* (1964) Henry Fonda liberates himself from the saintly performances of his past by articulating his body movements as a formal element within a scene.

> Telephoning the Russian premier, desperate over the possibility of an atomic war . . . Fonda does a kind of needle-threading with nothing. He makes himself felt against an indirectly conveyed wall of pressure, seeping into the scene in stiff, delayed archness and jointed phrasing—a great concrete construction slowly cracking, becoming dislodged. It is one of the weirdest tension-builders

6. "A great, concrete construction slowly cracking." Henry Fonda in *Fail-Safe* (1964).

in film, and most of it is done with a constricted, inside-throat articulation and a robot movement so precise and dignified it is like watching a seventeen-foot pole vaulter get over the bar without wasting a motion or even using a pole. (1971f, 177)

Similarly, Elizabeth Taylor's "mushy" (178) performance in *Who's Afraid of Virginia Woolf?* (1966) nevertheless becomes fascinating when the actress manages to exploit her own physical presence as a cinematic force in its own right. As Taylor moves "from counter to fridge to sink, her hips become a hub around which the kitchen appears to be moving." Ultimately, Farber concludes, the film "picks up interest when people are treated as terrain," as "shifting scenery" (179).

To the casual *Cavalier* reader this line of criticism must have seemed a trifle esoteric, even bizarre. But in treating cinematic material as mass, line, and texture, Farber was returning to basics, regarding films as he would modern painting. In the process, he disregarded most of the casual niceties of reviewing, but that had always been his style. More important for us, however, is that in moving into territory extreme even for cultism, he was exploring the possibilities of a style of criticism which, though still steeped in vanguard resistance, was unlikely to catch on with an American counterculture. He certainly wouldn't have had it any other way: now able to discern the hidden complexities of a broad range of films, including those which he otherwise disdained, he could reassert his status as a resolutely vanguard tastemaker while eschewing the vulgar cultism of pantheons. "One day," he could write in 1966,

> somebody is going to make a film that is the equivalent of a Pollock painting, a movie that can be truly pigeonholed for effect, certified a one-person operation. Until this miracle occurs, the massive attempt in 1960s criticism to bring some order and shape into film history—creating a Louvre of great films and detailing the one genius responsible for each film—is doomed to failure because of the subversive nature of the medium: the flash-bomb vitality that one scene, actor, or technician injects across the grain of a film. (1971h, 184)

But the successful New York avant-garde also increasingly eschewed Farber and his critical obscurantism; there would certainly be little room for this level of cultist discernment within the 1960s Underground. From the edge of the scene, he could only watch as the oppositional tradition he had so proudly extended was reduced to chic tastemaking. An uninvited guest at the 1965 New York Film Festival, he complained bitterly about the new trend toward crude judgment and sweeping statement by film intellectuals:

> I've sat through about three of these [panels] and I've never heard a discussion of one actor yet, one scene. I never heard one director express any doubt of any story angle. In other words if you talk[ed] to Agee at any point or Ferguson, he almost never had an all over idea of the film. He would go straight into the film, he would be inside of it, he would talk to you about Lionel Barrymore's acting, how it worked for him, what was wrong with it. . . . Now we've been swimming over the surface. This evening I've taken down some of the words: "unbeliev-

able," "most exciting," "immense and fantastic," "glorious," "incredible," "very glorious." Now, that is the terminology both of the classroom and of the amateur. . . . (Quoted in Wellington 1966, 26)

Farber derides "swimming over the surface" of films because it suggests a shallow engagement with the material. But his own resistance to shallow engagement is significantly compromised by his commitment to a particular vanguard notion of artistic criticism as resistant engagement with mass culture via methods complex enough to ensure limited appeal. Thus while Farber's move into esoterica may have expressed a desire to reassert vanguard critical principles in an intellectual scene dominated by amateurs, this in itself hardly discounts the validity of the new, accessible avant-garde. Indeed, in the hands of Andrew Sarris, the easier cultism of the 1960s may have fulfilled vanguard ideals more fully than Farber ever had.

POWER AND PANTHEONS

Andrew Sarris's rival film cultism was nothing if not easier to emulate. A critic as sympathetic to Arnoldian pedagogy as to Wildean artistry, Sarris eagerly offered those similarly disaffected from the mainstream of middle-brow culture a means of entering the cultist coterie. As a result, another countercultural option soon took its place alongside hard bop, rock-and-roll, and Norman Mailer. For those interested in foreign films and American experimental shorts, an aggressive young journal named *Film Culture* had arisen on the scene. Published and edited by a Lithuanian expatriate poet named Jonas Mekas, *Film Culture* was founded in 1955 with the aim of lending depth, vigor, and artistic purpose to American film production and criticism. "Like all art"—Mekas declared in the debut issue— "cinema must strive towards the development of a culture of its own that will heighten not only the creative refinement of the artist but also—and pre-eminently—the receptive faculty of the public." Because art was to be championed over commerce, foreign films would be given significant coverage in *Film Culture*, and the "responsible filmmaker" (Mekas 1955b, 1) would be provided an opportunity to guide, and be guided by, the aesthetically attuned audience. In its first fifteen years of existence, the journal would be profoundly successful in fulfilling most of these aims, promoting and enriching a New York–based American film culture in the modernist and vanguard traditions. As we shall see, in the process its founder would gradually adopt an aesthetic stance so liberal as to provoke others—notably Parker Tyler—to accuse him of abandoning his commitment to basic standards. But Mekas was only paving the road to vanguard success: the very gestures that would eventually provoke Tyler to rhetorically ask, "Is Film Criticism Only Propaganda?" were also those which successfully promoted camp and cult attitudes within a broader public sphere.

Sarris was introduced to Mekas in late 1954 in a film class at Columbia University; at Mekas's behest, he soon became a *Film Culture* contributor and editor, and a few years later, a film critic at the *Village Voice*. By no means a renegade—he had been attending teacher's college and pursuing a master's degree in dramatic arts (Gunning 1992, 62–63)—Sarris brought to his criticism humanistic values and (initially at least) a thoroughly measured approach, championing films that presented nuanced expressions of thematic material through a marriage of sophisticated technique and appropriate style. His method courted the atomism of journalistic reviewing to the extent that it gauged the effectiveness of constituent cinematic elements (script, staging, camerawork, performance, and direction), but it also judged a movie on its ability to unite these elements into a coherent and intellectually satisfying whole. For an overwhelmingly successful film such as Bergman's *The Seventh Seal* (1957), the critic could delve into an extended discussion of the film's "many layers of meaning" (Sarris 1959, 51), then show how its intricacies were bolstered by effective acting, camera technique, and editing. With a dud like Daniel Mann's *The Rose Tattoo* (1955), Sarris was more concerned with explaining why the production seemed not integrated but "confused" (1969b, 19): Anna Magnani was strong but Burt Lancaster miscast, the subplots insipid, the tones disjunctive, the director "weak in developing a unified conception for his actors" (20) and thus unable to handle Tennessee Williams's difficult material.

Yet because Sarris's approach so stressed the subtle rendering of complex thematics (soon renamed "interior meaning") in foreign and domestic films alike, he ran a significant risk of seeming a middlebrow apologist. Whereas Farber had used the position papers to draw a line in the sand, clearly identifying cultural enemies at home and abroad, prior to 1962 Sarris seemed uncomfortable with dismissing films outright. For Farber, *Giant* (1956) was a "gapingly empty" (1971i, 22) middlebrow mess padded with an "endlessly masturbatory 'building' of excitement" (23). Sarris, characteristically, was far more measured: though the film suffered from the weak characterization and melodramatic falseness of Edna Ferber's novel, and though ultimately neither Ferber nor director George Stevens evinced sufficient sensitivity to their material, Stevens's excellent casting, logical editing, and appropriately epic design were still worthy of commendation (Sarris 1956). For Farber, Antonioni had nothing to offer but stinging wet towels of arty pretension, but Sarris could see in *L'Av-*

ventura an "intellectual muscle" appealing to "anyone who seeks something more from the cinema than the finger exercises of conventional films" (1969a, 35).

Support for foreign films was certainly acceptable at the *Village Voice* and especially *Film Culture*, where Mekas had initially hoped to promote an American independent cinema after the European model. Increasingly wary of middlebrow encroachment, however (*L'Avventura* would soon appear on John Simon's 1967 list of "all-time greats" [Simon, 22], alongside *The Seven Samurai* [1954], *Smiles of a Summer Night* [1955], *I Vitelloni* [1953], and *Kanal* [1956]), *Film Culture* gradually supplemented measured discernment of extant works with more clearly vanguard critical strategies. After 1961, Mekas (as we shall see more clearly in the next chapter) increasingly steered independents toward his newfound camp sensibilities, while Sarris, for his part, championed a retooled American version of Europe's "auteur theory," in the process spreading cultism to middlebrow's disgruntled fringes.

Interestingly, whereas European auteur criticism continues to be considered worthy of study by today's film scholars, its American counterpart is generally not taken seriously, regarded as a simplistic corruption of purer models or merely as a bad memory for those who have since espoused more exacting critical approaches. Yet Sarris's development of the auteur approach served a valuable, indeed crucial function in the development and eventual flourishing of American film cultism, because it provided the reader a means of enjoying some of the critic's own vanguard cultural authority. A popular avant-garde of moviegoers now had a model of resistance accessible enough to follow.

Caughie (1981, 62) notes that Luc Moullet had actually used the term "*auteur* theory" in 1959, three years before Sarris's "Notes on the Auteur Theory in 1962." However, the sheer audacity of the American critic's appropriation of *la politique des auteurs* (which at the *Cahiers du cinéma* had only ever suggested vanguard editorial *policy*) certainly helped make the latter piece something of a cultural watershed, leading off *Film Culture* 27 ahead of Farber's own "White Elephant Art vs. Termite Art." Ultimately, the advantages Sarris's auteur theory provided film criticism— principally, heightened access to cinema's "deepest meanings" (Sarris 1961, 73) via the artist-director's thematic and formal preoccupations— were less important than the critical shorthand it provided those searching for a usable alternative culture within the American cinema. While this "theory" carried the cultural cachet of scholarship, it was also simple enough for the reader to absorb, because at root it was merely a polemical assertion that at least the personalities of the most interesting movie directors manage to shine through their humdrum, generic material.

Sarris frequently cautioned against use of the theory as a "short-cut" critical method, suggesting for instance that

> with a "you-see-it-or-you-don't" attitude toward the reader, the particularly lazy *auteur* critic can save himself the drudgery of communication and explanation. Indeed, at their worst, *auteur* critiques are less meaningful than the straightforward plot reviews which pass for criticism in America. Without the necessary research and analysis, the *auteur* theory can degenerate into the kind of snobbish racket which is associated with the merchandising of paintings. (1962–63, 2)

Nevertheless, he seemed to understand that even for those prepared to engage in "research and analysis" (which for the film buff meant merely following one's subcultural instincts), a primary appeal of auteurism lay precisely in a freedom to take critical shortcuts. In aiming to "rescue individual achievements from an unjustifiable anonymity" (6), the method ultimately favored breadth over depth, in that the latter was unobtainable without the former. Focusing cultist interest in the director's "distinguishable personality" opened Sarris to reproach from rival film aficionados (notably Pauline Kael), but it also enabled him and his followers to flaunt the vast knowledge of movies required for critical sifting. Ford's intentions, personality, and worldview all inform *The Man Who Shot Liberty Valance* (1962), but they can be gleaned only through at least two viewings, plus "a minimal awareness of a career ranging over 122 films in nearly half a century" (1962a, 13) and a knowledge of the work of other auteurs such as Welles, Hitchcock, Murnau, Godard, and Kurosawa.

A model of vanguard provocation masquerading as aesthetic theory, Sarris's auteurism granted creative and hermeneutic authority to the film director only in the most limited sense, because in practice it was used to shore up the cultural authority of spectators who had seen enough films to be able to claim the artists in their midst. The "theory" itself was embarrassingly weak: because it was bolstered by oppositional taste and not logical proof, it was unable, for instance, to explain satisfactorily why the distinguishable personalities of minor or genre directors were aesthetically preferable to those of their pretentious middlebrow counterparts. (Kael: "The smell of a skunk is more distinguishable than the perfume of a rose; does that make it better?" [1965, 297].) Sarris's answer lay in the heightened "interior meaning" that arose from the "tension between a director's personality and his material" (1962–63, 7), but this explanation itself failed to distinguish the tension of a Hollywood auteur production from that of a middlebrow epic or European art film. True, Farber had suggested something similar when he noted that the virtues of Underground action movies "expand as the pictures take on the outer appearance of junk jewelry" and correspondingly shrink in "art-infected," big-budget prestige projects (Farber 1971i, 17)—but Farber had been openly defending an oppositional canon, not propounding a theory of cinema which might prove that "Alfred Hitchcock is artistically superior to Robert Bresson by every criterion of excellence" (Sarris 1962–63, 5), let alone that the American cinema is "the only cinema in the world worth exploring in depth beneath the frosting of a few great directors at the top" (6).

However unconvincing as theory, Sarris's early defense of his cultist canon nevertheless boosted his vanguard authority, making him a key player among American film intellectuals of the 1960s. More important still, it helped to justify his own recent move from careful valuation of middlebrow art films to vanguard oppositional tastemaking (à la Farber). This shift is already evident in 1961, when Sarris credits the French *Cahiers du cinéma* critics for helping to realign his own aesthetic biases. In "repudiating everything that most American critics held sacred," they had actually

> performed an invaluable service at a time when the fantastic decline of well-made cinema in Hollywood had completely demoralized even such lonely pastimes as the Directors' Game. 1956 was the last year when there was any correlation between "official" directors, "major" themes and what was then considered effective Anglo-American film-making. It was not an entirely satisfactory year even after the long drought of '54 and '55, but one could still go through the motions of making a respectable ten-best list without seeming hopelessly esoteric. (1961, 74)

From the perspective of 1961, many of those on that list—namely, middlebrow directors such as Stevens, Wyler, Wise, Kazan—now seemed embarrassing choices, as Hitchcock's *The Wrong Man* (1957) and Nicholas Ray's *Bigger Than Life* (1956) seemed embarrassing omissions. As a rebel tastemaker, Sarris was adopting the stance of native art critics twenty years earlier, advocating the development of a distinctly American film culture based on the European example. While denigrating America's long-standing "provincial isolation from world cinema" (78), he was careful to present himself as his own critic, with a homegrown perspective distinct from those of the *Cahiers* and *Sight and Sound*. If the former journal's "exaggerated regard" for American cinema itself seemed to betray a "disconcerting condescension toward Hollywood's primitive vitality" (74), the latter's preoccupation with leftist sentiment suggested an equally disturbing regard for facile content at the expense of holistic form. Sarris was left as a properly American cultural authority on the vast field of American movies, and he would pride himself on the sheer numbers he had viewed: "I have seen so many more movies than Dwight Macdonald and so many less than Bill Everson that I am torn between plunging on and pausing to consolidate what I have seen into a coherent theory" (1964–65, 13).

Evidently bruised by Kael's admonishments ("I now tend to avoid abstract arguments like the plague" [11]), he prudently chose to plunge on and spent much of the decade expanding the scope of his cultist appreciation of movies. In truth, the theory had already served its usefulness, allowing Sarris to wield his cultural authority through evolving canons and succinct judgments that readers could adopt, rework, and personalize, without having to become serious critics themselves. Perhaps such readers were not accessing the deepest meanings of the medium, but they could nonetheless be empowered through identification with a subcultural, cultist alternative lurking within a Hollywood cinema they had taken for granted. Unlike Farber, whose position papers of the 1950s developed an increasingly esoteric cultism of Underground depth, Sarris pursued oppositional tastemaking through a more accessible cultism of *breadth*. As his own position papers grew more encompassing, detailed analysis of individual works correspondingly shrank in importance: the movie became a constituent element of the director's oeuvre, the oeuvre a constituent element of the corpus of American cinema.[2]

The growing penchant for summary judgment and cultist cataloging that would culminate in *The American Cinema: Directors and Directions 1929–1968* (1968) is already well in evidence in 1961's "The Director's Game" (*Film Culture* 22–23), in many ways the watershed critical text that marks Sarris's rebirth as a cultist. Beginning with a list of forty-six American and British directors of forthcoming releases, the critic systematically plows through the names in an attempt to predict the probable artistic worth of their movies. This provides him with an opportunity to flaunt his knowledge of obscure auteurs and films but also presents him as an aesthetic authority able to summarize careers and artistic value in a few choice words or phrases. "Nonentities by any standard" (1961, 68) and unlikely cult objects, Byron Haskin, R. G. Springsteen, Harry Keller, Roger Corman, Rudy Mate, Bert I. Gordon, Robert Webb, and Ken Annakin can be eliminated immediately. (Corman and Gordon would have the last laugh.) Several British directors (John Lamont, Don Chaffey, Terry Bishop, and the like) can also be swiftly excised, here by virtue of their sheer obscurity in America. This clears the way for Sarris to proceed headlong into the field, wielding critical judgment like a razor-sharp scythe. The films of Daniel Mann, Walter Lang, Delmer Daves, and Joseph Pevney possess a "dreadful fascination" but leave an "aesthetic hangover" (69). Jerry Lewis is a "curiosity and quite possibly an acquired taste." Philip Dunne and Delbert Mann lack the "rudiments of pacing and structure" and thus are "generally duller than their material." Rouben Mamoulian and Mervyn LeRoy "have seen their brightest days and now belong to the historians if not necessarily to the ages" (69). John Franken-heimer and Seth Holt are "battling the sophomore jinx which afflicts both directors and baseball players" (70). The handful of directors remaining may offer a little more promise, but they are dealt with just as swiftly: Vincente Minnelli is "an unevenly glittering stylist of the second rank," Joseph Mankiewicz a director "handicapped by the failure of his tech-nique to equal his sensibility," Anthony Mann merely "an expert techni-cian without much depth" (72).

Those tempted to dismiss this as shallow and unproductive film criti-cism were missing the point, because Sarris's pronouncements actually functioned more as a rough guide to film appreciation, providing in the "directors' game" a model of cinema cultism available to all seeking alter-natives to middlebrow pretense within popular culture. Sarris well knew that the *Cahiers du cinéma* and Britain's *Movie* had already refined pan-theon building (and toppling) in Europe; now an American countercul-ture could reclaim its own movies, and vanguard taste, from a generation of European *cinéphiles*. The accompanying sacrifice of critical depth for breadth was thus necessitated by the urgency and enormity of the task at hand—a "systematic reappraisal of the American cinema" that could not end until "the last worthy director has been rescued from undeserved anonymity" (1963a, 1). If this meant dumping middlebrow art's commit-ment to social relevance, so be it. Rather than "standing up to be counted," Sarris suggested, "we might try sitting down to better concen-trate on the great art in our midst" (1962b, 70). This stance may seem reactionary to some, but in large part it was only a repudiation of radical politics for vanguard resistance disguised as Arnoldian discernment. The movies could be rescued from middlebrow tyranny, asserted as *the* rich American art form, only through a vigorous reassertion of oppositional snobbism.

In the process, however, vanguard snob taste would need to be broad-ened, movie cultism's narrow focus exploded outward. The "American Cinema" reassessed in Sarris's special spring 1963 issue of *Film Culture* is one defined extremely loosely, as the cinema created by auteurs who directed at least one English-language film. In so enlarging the *corpus* of American cinema to include Murnau, Ophuls, Renoir, Pabst, and Rossel-lini, Sarris and collaborator Eugene Archer were not simply elevating a "doctrine of directorial continuity" over "ethnographic considerations" (Sarris 1963a, 1); they were promoting the movies as worthy objects of both high and low cultism, Europhile aestheticism and American cultural populism. Long denigrated as nonartistic and homogenous, American cin-ema was certainly being redeemed. If the auteur theory's emphasis on personality had allowed Sarris to assert that even despite middlebrow encroachment, this cinema was as rich and subtle as the directors working within it, the loose definition of "American" enabled him to claim that it was actually remarkably diverse, too.

Participation in this new cultism was easy, in that it was now largely a matter of absorbing a large neglected body of cultural material (American film directors, whether notable or nonentities), and engaging with the critic's aesthetic ranking of that material. One could object to Sarris's placement of Frank Borzage in the "Second Line" of auteurs, or to Lubitsch's exclusion from the elite "Pantheon" of twelve—or even to the denigration of John Huston and Billy Wilder as "Fallen Idols"—without otherwise questioning the critic's guiding mission. Indeed, such objections were all part of the fun. Sarris repeatedly stressed that his hierarchy was personal and always subject to adjustment, his conclusions necessarily "tentative" (1966, 22). Because validating the auteur theory itself entailed continual revision in light of new or newly discovered movies, the end would "never be in sight" (1962–63, 8).

Thus while the sheer audacity of the "Directorial Chronologies" included in both the "American Cinema" issue and the *American Cinema* book that followed (Sarris 1968) seems remarkable from today's perspective, it also reflected this ongoing commitment to ranking and categorization as valuable and interactive ends in themselves. This "weighted critical valuation" (1963b, 52) of literally thousands of auteur films made between 1929 and 1962 (updated to 1967 in the book) is nakedly personal and often openly provocative: for 1938, Cukor's *Holiday* is ranked first, ahead of Hawks's *Bringing Up Baby*, while Ford's *Submarine Patrol* is ranked well above poor Wyler's *Jezebel*, which actually lingers at the bottom as a "False Reputation" alongside Norman Taurog's *Boys Town* and Henry King's *Alexander's Ragtime Band*. The revisions made between article and book are also substantial and display the seriousness with which Sarris regarded his enterprise. Von Stroheim leaves the Pantheon while Lubitsch, Keaton, and Lang enter, Anthony Mann moves up from "Esoterica" to the Second Line (renamed "The Far Side of Paradise"), and Tay Garnett rises from "Likeable but Elusive" to the Third Line (renamed "Expressive Esoterica"). Hitchcock's *Under Capricorn* now seems a much more significant film of 1949, moving from eighth position to second (behind Ford's *She Wore a Yellow Ribbon* and *Three Godfathers*, ahead of Ophuls's *Caught* and *The Reckless Moment*). Lengthy explanations were not required, simply because Sarris's cultism offered the critical *gesture* as adequate and effective cultural provocation. If cultural authority derived from broadly vanguard taste and access to the fullest possible body of American movies, such authority was open to all antimiddlebrow film buffs willing to learn the core hierarchies while remaining open to adjusting them in accordance with new discoveries ("I am ready to concede on Roy William Neill as a minor stylist" [1966, 22]).

For Manny Farber, by contrast, the "sickeningly frivolous" film buff audience (Farber 1971i, 24) was to be admonished for desecrating sacred ground. In its exclusivity and gruffness, Farber's criticism successfully alienated all but diehard followers. His cultism may also have been personal, but it was so steeped in the critic's own peculiar aesthetic biases, stubborn iconoclasm (Phil Karlson and William Keighley over Antonioni and Bergman), increasing passion for obscure detail, and quirky, often bizarre prose style ("the spectator watches two or three action films go by and leaves feeling as though he were a pirate discharged from a giant sponge" [15]) as to make emulation a rather difficult and perhaps unappealing proposition. Sarris's new cultism of breadth was considerably more inviting, not least because it rewarded the efforts of other buffs with a wide template of aesthetic achievement subject to continual revision. As we have seen, Farber responded to the growing cult audience by burrowing even more deeply into obscure corners of cinematic terrain, seeking even in actors' intricate microgestures hints of resistant termite activity. By contrast, when in 1965's "Acting Aweigh!" Sarris turns his attention to performance, it is in the spirit of another broad personal revaluation of cultural material. Because he intends simply to indicate his "own tastes in acting over the years from today's vantage point, and let others consider their own" (47), he can proceed directly to fourteen pages of ranked performances from 1929 to 1964, with the hope that interested readers will engage critically, and productively, with his weighted judgments.

Such engagement lay at the heart of the new cultism's appeal. When in 1964 Sarris admitted to some "professional misgivings" over the "growing power and influence of cult criticism," he had in mind cultism's increasing sway over filmmakers, not its popularity with counterculture spectators. Like Farber, he disdained artistic self-consciousness, fearing that it might turn cinema into "one year-long joyless film festival." Filmmakers lacked the requisite "critical detachment and distance" (1964–65, 11) to be serious, committed cultists; in refusing to provide raw material for cult appropriation, they also threatened to ruin the fun for everyone else.

For Sarris, cultism enabled the critic to pursue the difficult yet necessary job of sorting through the sheer mass of cinematic product. But ultimately his cultism also suggested that this mass should be assessed strictly on the critic's own idiosyncratic terms, and further that the *very act* of sorting empowered the critic and reader alike, by demonstrating that the vast field of commercial cinema could actually be assessed through a quick, authoritative gesture. In assuming that culture could be purchased by a public willing to buy the right magazines, see the right movies, and allow guidance from a discerning critic, Sarris was actually dipping into the

Arnoldian tradition; yet in daring to discover sweetness and light in the vulgar culture of the everyday, he revealed his underlying agenda as a subversive, quasi-parodic inversion of Arnoldian ideals. Sarris's Culture was still pitched as an alternative to a middlebrow norm infected by mass mediocrity—but Arnold's "best that is known and thought in this world" certainly did not include the contemporary equivalents of *Submarine Patrol* or *Under Capricorn*, nor would Arnold have been pleased to see his ideal of careful discernment reduced to oppositional rankings. But of course he could not have known that by the 1960s, the Wildean tradition of spectator-empowered cultural refashioning would become influential enough to allow a pantheon of reassessed culture to be successfully pitched as the genuine article. In suggesting that authentic popular art is not foisted upon us but actively chosen, ranked and/or dismissed in a quick, clean gesture, Sarris was, in his own way, insisting that aesthetic consumerism could be readily seized by rebellious members of the middle-brow public.

Vanguard Cultism and a New Sensibility

It is hard to overestimate the profound effect that the new cultism's vanguard inversion of Arnoldianism has exerted on our culture, through its open challenge to traditional standards of artistic value. Film criticism was not the only or even the most visible expression of these new sentiments: Warhol's art and persona also offered a radical aestheticizing of mass production, even a kind of parody of constructivist utility. But in retrospect, film criticism may have allowed the fullest expression of the pop ethos, in that it not simply justified popular taste as aesthetically cutting-edge but encouraged non-art-world members with similar tastes to assert themselves as artistic producers within an enormous new avant-garde. The movie critic was assuming a highly significant role within this culture and its "new sensibility," which for Susan Sontag meant its revolutionary, anti-Arnoldian conception of art as extension of life, as a "representation of (new) modes of vivacity" (1966b, 300)—art no longer opposed to science, no longer ranked as "high" and "low," no longer split as form/content. This was art as anything that expanded the consciousness and senses, suggesting that "the feeling (or sensation) given off by a Rauchenberg painting might be like that of a song by the Supremes. The brio and elegance of Budd Boetticher's *The Rise and Fall of Legs Diamond* or the singing style of Dionne Warwick can be appreciated as a complex and pleasurable event. They are experienced without condescension" (304).

Vanguard film criticism had for years been driven by this same desire to display such an appreciation for the complexities and pleasures of low culture. What the arrival of Sontag's new sensibility actually signaled, for better or worse, was that the battle had been substantially won, that even the lowest movies were now worthy of serious discussion (or at least serious ranking). Indeed, if all culture could be said to expand our intellectual or sensual awareness of the world, then aesthetic judgment was not simply irrelevant but potentially counterproductive. Sontag herself had been somewhat cautious on this point, insisting that the new sensibility suggested not a philistine "renunciation of all standards" but merely a more pluralistic set of standards appropriate to a "new, more open way of looking at the world" (304). Yet the nature, function, and value of these new vanguard standards proved remarkably hard to pin down. Sarris's central auteurist criterion, the distinguishable personality of the director as seen through his films, may have been appropriate for vanguard provocation, but its value as an aesthetic measure was certainly debatable, as Kael— in her pointed reminder about the distinguishable smell of skunks—had dutifully indicated.

Sarris's cultism had revealed the aesthetic pitfalls of the new sensibility even as it had helped to develop an expanded vanguard audience. While Sarris positioned himself as a tastemaker, an arbiter of aesthetic value, in eschewing credible aesthetic standards for vanguard polemics and utility, he freed cultism to flourish as a kind of oppositional fandom. Though his desire to rescue every last Hollywood movie from the slagheap of obscurity had been undertaken in the interest of fair reappraisal, the mere act of unearthing such movies was enough to grant them legitimacy, certainly for anyone wishing to assert her own gestured, vanguard reappraisal against Sarris's. Indeed, by ranking the disreputable amid or above the respectable, the critic actually helped to level distinctions between movies, forcing an adoption of taste criteria flexible enough to accommodate the sheer variety of releases that constitute the hierarchical lists. Thus while one may have disagreed with Sarris's revised rankings for 1955—Rossellini's *Strangers* on top, with four Phil Karlson efforts outranking *The Man with the Golden Arm*, Edgar Ulmer's *Murder Is My Beat* besting *East of Eden*, and *Marty* finishing up third from the bottom—one was nevertheless encouraged to place the sixty-two films and forty-two directors in contention on a playing field level enough to allow the relative (if wildly disparate) merits of *all* to emerge clearly.

Important, though, is that here Sarris's cultism, while certainly more catholic and accessible than the version offered by Farber, merges with camp—the new sensibility's governing ethos. When all manifestations of culture are granted potentially equal interest, so long as the appropriate aesthetic inquiry is initiated by the creative spectator/critic, aesthetic standards can be applied, strictly speaking, only to the mode of inquiry. In attacking middlebrow aesthetic judgment, vanguard criticism had ultimately made a work's value and interest a function more of the intellectual's creative skills than of the artist's. Again as in the 1940s, the empowerment of the vanguard critic/spectator at the expense of the artist was a pseudopopulist gesture of defiance directed toward culturally dominant aesthetic norms (Pollock's expressive abstraction, Kazan's liberal polemics), a retreat from marketable art making into a haven of safety and oppositional distinction. Yet this gesture now threatened to sweep away the specialness of artists altogether, with even the deliberate aesthetic gestures of filmmakers working within the American experimental tradition seeming to many like sorry manifestations of an outdated notion of modern radicalism. In truth, vanguard activity redefined as radical, aesthetic *perception* had made traditional art making superfluous, because now critics and spectators could construct aesthetic culture on their own, drawing on a vast field of valid, potentially useful movies.

THE ARTIST ECLIPSED?

When rival notions of vanguard activity clash, critics and artists actually become rival cultural producers. So it was in the modernist film culture of 1960s New York—a scene of turmoil and transformation marked by the ascent, as we have seen, of a new accessible cultism enabling spectators to more easily reclaim mass culture as their own. But as we shall see, camp criticism would enjoy its own revival too, also in a more accessible mode that stressed utility and gestural simplicity over willful obscurity. This would involve not so much a playful inversion of Arnold as outright dismissal, a move away from fixed aesthetic values toward something altogether more liberal, encompassing, producerly. The modernist film artist now had plenty of (unwelcome) company, as the American avantgarde soon become a haven of critical camp spectatorship, with truly remarkable, aesthetic films set alongside home movies and porno. This makes it doubly ironic that the battle for the soul of the avant-garde was waged so heavily at the level of discourse, and not art, leaving those who had the greatest stake in the continued support of their artistic community—the artists working within it—at the mercy of critics, the vanguard leaders of the future.

A further irony is that a central figure seeking to prevent the collapse of American modernism at the hands of the revitalized avant-garde was none other than Parker Tyler, the playful camp critic of the 1940s. That Tyler could have rejected camp values for a more traditional aesthetics suggests something of his changing tastes in cinema, but it also reflects his increasing faith in the ability of the film artist to provide ample aesthetic interest. With the emergence of Akira Kurosawa, Federico Fellini, Stan Brakhage, and John Cassavetes, creative transmutation seemed, frankly, unnecessary. Tyler's rearguard struggle to overturn vanguard precepts would ultimately be waged in vain, but its spirit does tell us much about the shift in values that allowed interest in artistic cinema to decline, while encouraging artistic interest in movies to flourish. As with cultism, camp, with key modifications, could be rendered friendlier and, ultimately, more empowering—though as Tyler himself was now painfully aware, the aesthetic cost might be considerable.

Chapter Six

HEAVY CULTURE AND UNDERGROUND CAMP

> We need critics who have the madness, the vision, the inflexi-
> bility, the self-centeredness of artists.
> *(Sheldon Renan)*[1]

A S AN ACCESSIBLE means of self-empowerment, Andrew Sarris's
movie cultism epitomized the new American avant-garde. Audi-
ence-centered, reader-friendly, and resolutely opposed to middlebrow pretense, it presented active spectatorship as a springboard to countercultural authority. Valuative discernment could become an aggressive,
significant gesture in and of itself, so long as one accepted distinguishable
personality as a sufficient condition for art. As a result, even lowbrow
fare such as Edgar Ulmer's *Murder Is My Beat* could become aesthetically
activated by cultist spectators looking for a means of asserting their own
distinction as cultural producers against both middlebrow's pretentious
modernism and lowbrow's passive consumerism.

Were such films artistic, by any serious standard of discrimination? Perhaps not—but serious discrimination was itself being rejected here, as the
province of middlebrow poseurs. (That *Marty* and *East of Eden* had been
considered Art by most made *Murder Is My Beat* all the more appealing.)
Preferring Ulmer over Stevens, on artistic grounds, allowed for a certain
cultural distinction within 1960s America, empowering the spectator to
wield a gesture of mastery over popular culture. Yet in its accompanying
rejection of dominant artist and work-centered notions of art for the utility of the avant-garde's aesthetic gesture, it profoundly challenged the
influence of traditional discernment within film appreciation, eventually
forcing highbrows to take sides in what became a battle over the very
nature of a medium's aesthetic value. In this chapter we will examine the
battle more closely, focusing on its climax in the New York Underground
of the 1960s—where a camp critic of old waged a one-man war against
the libertinism of the popularized vanguard perspective.

As America's preeminent erotic spectator of the 1940s, Parker Tyler
had initially embraced creative camp reception because the movies were
unable to control and dominate the aesthetic experience themselves—
hence the critic could rework them, introducing (or excavating) aesthetic
complexity and depth that had not at first seemed evident. But these mov-

ies were not themselves artworks (on this point he had been quite explicit), and his resistant camp refashioning had always been something of a game, a playful, quasi-satirical exploration carried on in the absence of genuine film artists.

By the mid-1950s, however, films had begun to seem too serious to be played with. With a preponderance of legitimately artistic films in the marketplace, Tyler could consider creative transmutation passé, unnecessary, perhaps even a little frivolous. Local experimental shorts and foreign features alike demonstrated that films might be mythically provocative without being aesthetically retrograde. Here were existing cinemas worthy of serious critical analysis and appraisal; why engage in the makeshift, fantasy film art of creative transmutation when the real thing was staring one in the face? Now questions such as "What is the artist trying to say, and with what formal techniques?" and "Is the result of aesthetic interest?" suddenly became relevant, and the critic could step out of the shoes of artist-creator to allow the filmmaker his or her own formal exploration and intellectual inquiry. By 1960—Tyler would later observe in hindsight—it had become clear that his early books had

> seemingly been sown in a field where a strange aftermath was currently blossoming. The canon promulgated as elite movie-going in the forties was becoming, two decades later, a brand of elite movie-making. The slant on which I had first concentrated was now taking hold with people who *made* films rather than with people who *looked at* them. (1967b, 12)

What Tyler had probed in criticism, filmmakers were now projecting on the screen, in effect producing their own critical Hollywood hallucinations, complete with somnambulistic characters and an acute sensitivity to the complexities of cultural mythos.

Yet even as Tyler honed his new appreciation for a different sort of film art, he saw—much to his horror—a new generation of vanguard highbrows willing to throw it all away for some juvenile fun. A spirit of eager capitulation seemed to have entranced those who should have known better: the same modern film scene that had produced the promising experimentalists was gravitating toward an "anything goes" attitude which so severely vaunted expressive liberty over controlled form as to render serious aesthetic judgment irrelevant. All expression was equally valid, exciting, groovy.

This was the new vanguard *camp*, which arose alongside the new cultism and likewise appeared easier, more accessible, more democratically empowering.[2] Under the aegis of promoter/critic/filmmaker Jonas Mekas, the New York Underground of the 1960s shifted the ethos of American experimentalism from modernism to avant-gardism, and its aesthetic focus from work to audience. Less important than the formal or hermeneutic sophistication of a particular film was its existence as an experience to be shared, praised, explored. Once a complex aesthetic procedure, camp was becoming a readily available mark of distinction for all those assertive and aware enough to champion aberrant, resistant taste for all "nonaesthetic" (i.e., nonmiddlebrow) cinema.

If camp had lost its edge, it had certainly gained an audience. The consequences for film art, however, seemed less certain, and Tyler now joined like-minded stalwarts such as Dwight Macdonald, Stanley Kauffmann, and John Simon in a valiant struggle against any descent into cultural relativism and obliteration of reliable aesthetic standards. Film was simply too young a medium, and too uncertain an art form, to be treated so disingenuously. What was needed was a rigorous adherence to standards, not a wholesale abandonment of them, and a return to the aesthetic activism of Arnold, and not Wilde. For Simon, the critic, "while waiting for the day when it will be possible to limit oneself to writing about serious films for serious publications," must undertake, "with every means at his command, to help bring about that day" (1967, 16). This meant championing the pictorial and intellectual sophistication of the most advanced films (*L'Avventura*, *Rules of the Game*, *The Seven Samurai*, *Children of Paradise*), skeptically scrutinizing the merits of the most faddish (*Last Year at Marienbad*, *Shoot the Piano Player*, *Alphaville*), and treating the rest with the respect or disdain they deserved. Not to make such critical distinctions was ultimately to deny the real power and complexity of art, and the cultural importance of artists—as opposed to creative spectators—working with the cinematic medium.

The new Underground tastemakers were thus standing in the way of aesthetic progress, irresponsibly hindering the development of the medium with their "indiscriminate encouragement of everything" (Macdonald 1967, 197) and their "party fun and games that become films" (Simon 1967, 18). But they were also implicitly deriding the values and efforts of the older generation of American modernists who had fought hard for film's recognition as a serious art form, forcing their predecessors to witness in this "too complete" (Macdonald 1967, 197) vanguard victory an explosion of the very principles they had held so dear. Hence the importance of Tyler's inevitable confrontation with Mekas and his scene: here we have not, as with Farber, the vanguard veteran quietly one-upping the young turk, but a heartfelt, ripping critique of the new vanguard stance delivered by a born-again critic who now felt obliged to lecture his wrongheaded spiritual successors on the dangerous excesses of their ways. True, Tyler's new respect for the film artist's critical creativity now risked allying him too closely with the hordes of middlebrow film buffs that the new vanguard cultism had arisen to repel. But for this active member of New York's art, poetry, and intellectual circles, sacrificing basic aesthetic values and a long-standing commitment to excellence on the altar of fashionable camp catholicism hardly seemed a viable alternative.[3]

FILMIC VIRTUE AND THE MORAL IMAGINATION

Tyler's film criticism of the 1950s and 1960s assumed that movies could be artworks, on their own terms. But by the same token, he could now hold them accountable for their own success and failure. Valuation thus became a core element of his approach: not only was he not afraid to point out faults; he considered this one of the critic's fundamental responsibilities. In shunning Wildean critical play, he was moving toward a distinctly Arnoldian notion of criticism as highbrow discrimination for a larger, chiefly middlebrow audience. As highbrow gatekeeper, he would evaluate individual works for merit while highlighting their relevance to the surrounding cultural sphere. Some films *did* matter; the critic's job was to point out why.

What made a film worthy of appraisal in the first place? In a nutshell, its treatment of complex human (psychic, mythic, ethical) concerns with appropriate gravity, through advanced poetic/symbolic form. Whereas Hollywood tended to literalize the film medium's "universal" (freely traversed) space/time, European surrealism and Eisensteinian montage had both offered the additional possibility of an *ideal* (i.e., figurative, symbolic) space in order to convey ideas or emotions in a more radical manner allied with modern painting and literature. Still, film's true aesthetic promise lay in its ability to interweave the two traditions, rendering man's emotions as "translucent" (exteriorized and interiorized) while eschewing theatrical presentation for "verbal-pictorial metaphor" (Tyler 1948b, 141).

Like the space of paintings by Ernst and Tchelitchew (and of Tyler's creatively transmuted Hollywood movies), the space of superior modernist films would form a symbolic landscape manifesting complexities of psychology and myth, exploring the productive realm between the unappealing extremes of naive realism and empty formalism. Though film was, at heart, a representational medium (and thus ill-suited to formal hermeticism), its reproductive capacities were ultimately superficial at best, as the unaided apparatus could never hope to capture reality's psychomythic depths, or to provide enlightening commentary on the human condition.

While these theoretical assumptions may not have been terribly new or original, even for America (contemporaries Erwin Panofsky and Maya Deren were elaborating similar positions around the same time),[4] they did provide firm support for Tyler's forays into aesthetic discrimination. If they justified his outright rejection of cinematic realism (embodied in the propagandistic notions of John Grierson and in the documentary-flavored narratives of the late 1940s),[5] they also made him increasingly receptive to the related stylings of local experimentalists.[6] Many of these independent artists—Maya Deren, Curtis Harrington, Gregory Markopoulos, Stan Brakhage—were actually making films that resembled Tyler's own Hollywood hallucinations. Nonrational, symbolically charged subtexts were now floating on the surfaces of openly psychomythic works. Deren's *Meshes of the Afternoon* (1943), Harrington's *Fragment of Seeking* (1946), and Brakhage's *Reflections on Black* (1955) even presented mysterious interior worlds peopled with somnambulistic protagonists.

It's really no wonder Tyler felt such a kinship with these films: their makers had emerged from the same aesthetic zeitgeist that had helped to shape his own surrealist perspective. He certainly wanted these artists to succeed—their sheer imaginative energy and unyielding opposition to the commercial industry made them the "purest and most single-minded force in the perpetuation of filmic imagination" (1949a, 99), even "Filmic Virtue incarnate" (1960f, 60). And while the public might find their movies strange and uncomfortable, here Tyler could act as Arnoldian mediator, introducing their charms and explaining their relevance to the readers of *Theatre Arts*:

> Experimental film asks you to accept a magical world, a world of illusion in which people move like sleep-walkers because they are not quite wide-awake and conscious, although they sometimes seem so. It asks you to accept this world as a matter of course; not as though it were something untrue, "a fairy tale," but as though the mental phenomena of a dream, which psychologically are the same as unconscious life, were *true*—as well as important. (1949a, 48)

Aesthetically, these filmmakers were working in relatively unexplored territory, testing the cinematic possibilities of "poetic" construction—which for Tyler suggested the complex interweaving of visual symbolism, dream content, and mythic influence that had long preoccupied his favorite artists (from Tchelitchew and Ernst in painting to Cocteau in film). Against this measure, a few of the American experimentalists fared quite well: Maya Deren's "creatively outstanding" visual poems, for instance, were "very personal and subjective-symbolic in scope but with a lively sense of film vision; she *thinks* in the cinematic medium" (1949b, 143). In stark opposition to mainstream cinema, Deren and the other top young filmmakers seemed to be eschewing adopted "prose narrative" for a more poetic and cinematic "film narrative" (144) affirming the dual (subjective-objective) nature of reality and using concrete facts "only as starting points, as elements of composition, for a total form *expressing* . . . a complete human experience" (1960h, 70–71).

7. "A world of illusion in which people move like sleepwalkers." *Meshes of the Afternoon* (Maya Deren, 1945). Courtesy of Anthology Film Archives.

Yet in the end, Tyler had to admit that most of these films were not in themselves Great Works. While the courage and integrity of the independents was certainly laudable, their aesthetic immaturity could not be completely overlooked. Thus though his discussions of Brakhage, Harrington, Markopoulos, Sidney Peterson, and Willard Maas (all in *Film Culture*) treat these filmmakers as young, talented artists whose work is usually interesting and occasionally masterful, Tyler's tone is always measured, tempered by an awareness of individual weaknesses and of the broader insufficiencies of the larger movement. Brakhage possessed a passionate nature and admirable tact, but he lacked Deren and Peterson's imaginative gifts (Tyler 1958). Maas's *Geography of the Body* (1943) was admirable as a "true poem of the nude . . . concerned with the mystery of the human identity" (1959, 53), but his other films were sometimes conventional and frequently solipsistic. The painterly optical experiments of Sidney Peterson were provocative but might also tempt a young movement to "*facile* emulation . . . as though the film were mainly Abstract Art operating in the domain of movement" (1960f, 61).

Even given Tyler's somewhat relaxed standards (owing to film poetry's importance as "a form of bravery, a form of pioneering" [1960c, 34]), experimentalism seemed in danger of becoming mired in a "kindergarten stage" (1960f, 56) of development. He well understood that these artists needed nurturing, especially by critics, but many were apparently having difficulty steeling themselves against the lure of material success. If unlike the abstract expressionist, who went out of his way to court fame and riches, the experimental filmmaker was necessarily "seeking a place in art through a medium of glamour" (1960c, 33), the accompanying temptations were just as dangerous—even more so, considering the movement's aesthetic immaturity. Harrington was already a casualty, having been enticed by producer Jerry Wald to join the commercial industry; Markopoulos had similarly been tempted to film *Serenity*, a feature shot in Greece and "financed by parties interested as much in Greece as in making a profit" (36).[7]

The inescapable truth was that America's independent film art, however noble and daring, still struggled within a country whose culture, and culture industry, were simply not used to conceiving of cinema in artistic terms. No wonder Tyler found more sophisticated examples of artistic cinema in foreign releases. An affection for European art films would certainly place the critic on more crowded turf than would a connoisseurship of American experimentalists. He might even be labeled a middlebrow apologist. Again, however, such criticisms came with the territory—for Tyler increasingly saw his mission as a matter of practicing superior discernment on behalf of the insufficiently cultured hordes. With uncritical cultism all the rage, even MOMA couldn't be trusted (as Farber had recently noted), having thrown caution to the wind in rooting its film library in an amusing "natural history" of costume and performance, rather than a more challenging history of the medium as *art*. Here the legitimate so hopelessly intermingled with the vulgar as to produce a collection useful only if one already knew "how to interpret it in correlation with internally aesthetic values" (1960e, 20).

Here Tyler's discernment came in, offering readers of publications as varied as *Kenyon Review*, *Forum*, *Art News*, and the *American Quarterly* a guide to the internal aesthetic values of the world's best films, while elevating the tastes of a rapidly growing audience for cinematic art. Reluctant to confront the deeper truths of humanity, or indeed their own lives, the film buff audience typically sought security in the historical splendor and/or romantic exoticism of *Open City* (1945), *Children of Paradise* (1945), *Hamlet* (1948), *Symphony Pastorale* (1946), and *Devil in the Flesh* (1946). No wonder Renoir's *Rules of the Game* (1939) had failed to excite this crowd—the film's pointed critique of the "ethics of wealthy middle-class, quasi-aristocratic, snob society" struck a little too close to home.

Apparently, we cannot expect of even the best film audience the purely personal moral culture which is developed in the individual by the creative type of artistic discernment. A treatment of ordinary social aspirations (money and a successful love-life) that is dry rather than flamboyant, intellectual rather than emotional, cannot but be distasteful to an audience whose enlightenment does not encompass collective or individual self-criticism, a rational intelligence in ethical matters, or foolproof artistic culture. (1950b, 694)

Foreign art films offered so much more—their advanced poetic form and heightened awareness of the human condition suggested cinema as the "probable savior of the classic human image in our age." The medium's representational bias was thus useful, up to a point, because it encouraged a figurative modernism that compared favorably with the social irresponsibility of nonobjectivism. In its failure to "report man in the fluid grip of his historic fate as man" the latter spoke of a desire for "absolute withdrawal of the individual from the world" (1960d, 144); like the pop and camp fashions to come, it simply refused to acknowledge the individual's special importance, and responsibilities, as a moral agent.

In 1948 Lionel Trilling had declared the European novel to be "for our time the most effective agent of the moral imagination" (1950, 209); now Tyler could envision a comparable role for foreign cinema. Like surrealism's own poetic antiabstractionism, the art film implicitly attacked the complacency into which the classical humanist tradition had fallen, all the while offering pictorial interest, intellectual insight, and ethical engagement. The essays compiled in *The Three Faces of the Film* (1960, rev. 1967) and *Sex Psyche Etcetera in the Film* (1969) downplay analysis of Hollywood's symbolic mythos[8] for formal, thematic, and ethical critiques of films that, like *Rashomon* (1950), boldly refuted conventional realism's "prosaic, unimaginative and reportorial view of the world" (Tyler 1961, 31), instead plunging into life's great mysteries. Whereas even Hollywood's artiest efforts (*Citizen Kane*) conceived mystery crudely, and literally, as a matter of unexplained surface details, Kurosawa offered an exploration of "existence itself [as] a mystery as conceived in the deepest psychological and aesthetic senses" (1960g, 37), presenting multiple perspectives of a single event (à la Picasso's *Guernica*) in an effort to restore order within a world of moral chaos.

Most important, these films were fundamentally *critical* in nature.[9] Like other legitimate artworks, and like Tyler's creative criticism of the 1940s, the best foreign films employed poetic (symbolic, allegorical) form as a means of investigating core human issues. The swarming news photographers of Federico Fellini's *La Dolce Vita* (1960) were "nightmarish apparitions from Bosch's 'Hell' " (1969a, 112)—quite appropriate for a film that excoriated contemporary lusts for sex and publicity, as grotesquely embodied in its climactic moral emblem, the dead monster-fish. In *L'Avventura* (1960), *La Notte* (1961), and *L'Eclisse* (1962), Michelangelo Antonioni—"one of the most intellectual film makers in history"—provided suites of "fluid, panoramic pictures"(1969c, 86) to convey the ennui of agoraphobic figures lost within a contemporary moral landscape poisoned by a fear of atomic annihilation.

Films might even provide critical insights into the nature of art and perception. *Dead of Night* (1945) actually interrogated the psychomythic import of the cinematic apparatus in a complex, allegorical manner not far removed from Tyler's own hallucinations of the 1940s: in lending an *"archetypal* form to the supernatural patterning of commercial movies," it revealed the processes "which unite film with the mechanism of dream and of supernatural hypothesis"(1960b, 75). *Blowup* and *Persona* (both 1966) offered implicit rebuttals to Siegfried Kracauer's wrongheaded theory of cinematic realism and Suzanne Langer's own notion of film as dream, instead presenting cinema as a productive interaction between outer reality and perceiving self. If *Blowup* highlighted the reality of "psychic consciousness, which cannot be photographed in an instant of vision or an infinity of instants"(1969b, 131), *Persona*'s rich text reaffirmed the importance of poetic shaping, demonstrating "the absurdity of the dream-mode theory of film unless there be some intellectual framework to sustain it as a creative entity" (127). In the end, Antonioni and Bergman were, like Tyler, asserting that the real cannot be captured objectively, that the realms of dream and reality are continuously transformed, each by the other.

Tyler was not renouncing erotic spectatorship per se, only ceding it to those advanced filmmakers who critically transformed their own worlds into art. His adopted role of Arnoldian tastemaker allowed him to step back, offering his own careful appraisals of the artist's efforts, while spreading the word to others. *Classics of the Foreign Film* (1962) even provided middlebrow aficionados a palatable overview of the best of world cinema, from 1919's *Cabinet of Dr. Caligari* to 1961's *La Notte*. Many of Tyler's choices were far from obvious—Detstvo Gorkovo's *Childhood of Maxim Gorky* and Michael Waszynsky's *The Dybbuk* (both 1938) stand alongside *The Bicycle Thief* (1949) and *Wild Strawberries* (1959)—because he deliberately selected films for their humanist and aesthetic import, not for their hipness. Now *Rules of the Game* might bear comparison with Mozart's *Don Giovanni*, Powell and Pressburger's *Stairway to Heaven* (1946) with the work of Dali and Tchelitchew. Duvivier's *Poil de Carotte* (1933) could be lauded for its "fine humane poetry" (1962a, 92), Vigo's *Zéro de conduite* (1933) for its "unforgettable marks of a humanity exalted by children" (89). If Tyler ultimately defers to these films, it is because he is simply not interested in having aesthetic fun with them. There is too much important critical work to be done, disseminating "the best that has been known and thought" for an eager but un-schooled public.

NOTHING AT STAKE? NEW WAVES AND A NEW GENERATION

Tyler obviously took his tastemaking seriously, and he was understand-ably aghast when, only a few years after the publication of *Classics of the Foreign Film*, he seemed to be the only one not keen on playing with movies. By the mid-1960s, he noticed that a new spirit of bandwagon jumping had overtaken the foreign film crowd, with careful discrimina-tion taking a backseat to chic frivolity. Increasingly, directors and fans alike seemed to prefer films that in essence camped on the world, treating art and even the human condition even less respectfully than Tyler had treated Hollywood movies in the 1940s. At least the surrealist game of sophisticated moviegoing, however satiric, had provided some "interest-ing speculations about society, about mankind's perennial, profuse and typically serio-comic ability to deceive itself" (1967b, 11). Now the French New Wave reduced the Hollywood hallucination to fashionable spoof, with everything depending on "correct points of reference to other films and film-types" (16–17). Camp spectatorship had been tapped by chic filmmakers as an "empiric formula to render the popular fantasy life in more select, enlightened, and adult terms" (14), offering in lieu of seri-ous, productive engagement with culture a retreat into vulgar fantasies of withdrawal—the reinvention of existence itself as a sort of mirage, or wild LSD trip.

This new camp was unrepentantly banal. Informed by comic-strip pop myths, Godard's *Alphaville* (1965) oversimplified the human predica-ment with its "fake intellectual satire for juvenile adults and adult juve-niles" (20). Whereas Cocteau's hallucinations, like Tyler's own, had pre-sented themselves as the *true* reality, enabling humans to "realize themselves and to come into full possession of life's meanings," film chic now contented itself with a "pseudo-reality that is palpably fictitious, im-plausible, and preposterous" (19). Inevitably, the movies demanded by the new foreign and experimental film cults were, beneath their flashy surfaces, aesthetically inconsequential and morally shallow.

> The impact of an art, whether comic or serious or somewhere between, must depend on the positive value of *what is involved*. "What, and how much, is at stake?" is a question every work of art or near-art must answer since the same question, consciously or unconsciously, is asked by every spectator, reader, or listener. The "smallness" of so much film art, held these days to be chic and

amusing, is due to its deliberately electing to put very little at stake in terms of both form and content. Is it not the point of [*Last Year at*] *Marienbad*'s satire that all its refined hocus-pocus about the resumption of an illicit love-affair is foolish and futile exactly because the initial erotic incident *had very little at stake?*

Most infuriating to Tyler, who had been highly impressed with Alain Resnais's *Hiroshima mon amour* (1959), was that *Last Year at Marienbad* (1961) didn't seem to take its own subjects and enigmas seriously—whatever its lucid truth, "it scarcely matter[ed] to anyone concerned" (18). The new camp of moral and aesthetic frivolity was using pop culture to retreat from—not engage with—life's deeper truths. This entailed nothing less than an abdication of artistic and critical responsibility, the camp filmmaker merely plundering the icon-laden surface of culture for his own amusement, the new camp critic eschewing cogent cultural analysis for an intoxicated celebration of all cinema as art. The new sensibility of the 1960s flew in the face of Tyler's long-standing commitment to aesthetic standards, and he spent much of the decade attempting to stand his ground against the growing tide of opportunism and trendy banality.

He focused much of his criticism against what he perceived as the wholesale corruption of American experimentalism into the fashionable, vanguard Underground at the hands of filmmaker/impresario Jonas Mekas.[10] Tyler's battle with the Underground, which would culminate in the 1969 publication of his scathing *Underground Film: A Critical History*, offered the critic an opportunity to stake out his own reactionary position within the expanded vanguard scene, while deriding the excesses of the once-virtuous movement as a capitulation to Establishment aesthetics. The threat posed by Mekas transcended matters of taste: at stake was not simply the health of artistic filmmaking but the very notion of the critic as aesthete. Mekas seemed frankly uninterested in careful valuation of experimental works; he would rather aggressively promote the movement's full array of products, regardless of artistic merit. In response, Tyler attempted to rescue the integrity of criticism and avant-gardism alike by injecting some measure of sound aesthetic judgment into the Underground's self-congratulatory discourse.

We have already encountered Mekas and *Film Culture* in the context of Andrew Sarris's new cultism, but the journal became best known for its promotion of independent modernist filmmakers such as Stan Brakhage, Kenneth Anger, Jack Smith, and Andy Warhol. If, during its first few years of existence, *Film Culture* had offered an eclectic array of conceptions of cinematic art, encompassing Hollywood features, documentary, foreign films, and experimental work, the arrival of a new generation of American experimentalists in the early 1960s occasioned an increasing emphasis on promotion of the new aesthetic as a valid counterpart to those which had arisen in contemporary Europe. Mekas's discussions of his New American Cinema, both in *Film Culture* and in his regular "Movie Journal" column in the *Village Voice*, melded romantic modernism with a more properly avant-gardist celebration of the transcendence of any and all constraints (aesthetic, social, political) placed on radical expression. Tyler had recognized the ethical virtues of experimental filmmaking too, but now Mekas seemed to elevate such virtue to a new level, perhaps even above aesthetic integrity. To Tyler, himself a frequent contributor to *Film Culture*, such a willful abandonment of reliable aesthetic guidelines would signal nothing less than total surrender to the whims and fashions of the new camp culture.

Interestingly, Mekas had initially pursued a critical approach clearly influenced in part by Tyler's recent turn to distanced discernment. In a 1957 *Film Culture* editorial he notes that "whereas the experiments of our commercial producers . . . are guided by an immoral impulse to extract more money,"

> it is good that at least some independent film-makers, however few they are, are trying to explore the true possibilities of the cinema, so that their individual statements can be effective not only as truth, but also as art. (1957, 1)

Yet Mekas was from the start equally attracted to the freedom/vitality paradigm still current in much American art criticism: in "The Experimental Film in America" (1955), he even sounds like Sam Kootz, harshly criticizing poetic/cineplastic work as unimaginative, complacent, and lacking masculine vigor. The article's notorious condemnation of a "conspiracy of homosexuality" (1955a, 17) among independents may seem ludicrous today, but it too reflects an implicit affinity for the rough-hewn macho stance characteristic of many postwar abstractionists, including Manny Farber.

In truth, Mekas's remarkable success in promoting a vanguard explosion stemmed in no small measure from his deftness in absorbing the ideas around him and reworking them for his own ends. If, as Sarris recently suggested, Mekas wasn't a critical journalist so much as an evangelist (Gunning 1992, 69), it is because he increasingly refused to subordinate vanguard pragmatics to rigorous discernment. Thus while he was initially keen to embrace choice European directors (even concluding "The Experimental Film in America" by fondly recalling the superior work of Cocteau), his interest in foreign films would move from their ambiguous depths and planned artistry toward their "vitality, freshness and originality" (Mekas 1959, 1).

The shift is probably most clearly manifested in 1960's "Cinema of the New Generation," in which Mekas explicitly lauds Britain's Free Cinema and France's *nouvelle vague* as admirable models for a New American Cinema that might meld realism and vitality in a manner reflective of the new energy of the times. Whereas Tyler derided the New Wave's fashionable formlessness, Mekas praised its contemporary spontaneity.[11] If for Tyler modernist filmmaking often failed to live up to the greatness of past works (Cocteau, again, providing the most frequent example), for Mekas the new cinemas of Europe and America were important precisely because they overthrew past traditions. Once the critic of "technical crudity" and "absence of artistic discipline" (1955a, 17) in alternative work, Mekas would now embrace haphazardness and immediacy in an attempt not merely to reproduce the New Wave attitude in America but to inject the very spirit of vanguard cultural revolution into its modernist cinema.[12]

With "Cinema of the New Generation," Mekas also moved decisively away from aesthetic discrimination toward an extreme vanguard polemic, demanding an overthrow of traditional forms and an abandonment of traditional concerns. Only five years earlier he had lamented that "if the struggle of the new film poets to make a dramatic affirmation of [moral] value could be plotted on a graph, the result would be a parabolic curve extending from the absolute zero of Maya Deren to the absolute zero of Stanley Brakhage" (1955a, 18). Now, such an affirmation seemed quaint and anachronistic, rooted in the stuffy conventions of the past:

> I would call a fool anybody who would demand of this generation works of art that contain clear and positive philosophies and esthetics. There will be nothing of that! This generation is too young, too alive for that. This decade will be marked by an intensified search and by the further loosening of sensibilities for the purpose of reaching still deeper into less contaminated depths of man's soul, trying desperately to escape the cliches of art and life.

The new aesthetic sprang from free and direct creation, the liberation of the self unencumbered by technical rules and formal niceties. Like the New American Painting, Mekas's New American Cinema flaunted liberated, vital expression as an end in itself. Guided by intuition, the new filmmaker would aim "desperately, as his colleague action painter . . . at art in its very flight, at a free, a spontaneous inspiration: art as an action and not as a status quo" (1960, 19).

This was 1960—the abstract expressionist bandwagon had long since left town and would soon be sold for scrap somewhere in Nebraska. But Mekas was hardly succumbing to the temptations of middlebrow; rather, he was playing off the cachet of the New York School in order to help lend recognition to these talented young filmmakers while validating a radical, fundamentally *anti*middlebrow notion of wildly liberated expression and completely unrestricted appreciation. The earlier quasi-surrealist, heavily symbolic films of Deren, Harrington, Anger, and Maas now seemed hopelessly dated, precisely because they were so carefully wrought, so artfully posed. For Tyler these works had been intriguing if immature stabs at aesthetic sophistication, but Mekas wasn't interested in encouraging further refinement—instead, he wanted to move on to "a film poetry free of obvious symbolism and artistic or literary influences, a poetry where the filmic syntax achieves a spontaneous fluidity and where the images are truly like words that appear and disappear and repeat themselves as they create clusters and blotches of visual meanings, impressions" (1972, 46–47). Far from respecting timeless highbrow aesthetics, the new film poet didn't "giv[e] a damn about Hollywood, art, critics, or anybody" (23). Even more important, anybody could join the ranks, producing work valuable for its sheer immediacy, simplicity, and radical accessibility. In 1960, it could seem that films would "soon be made as easily as written poems, and almost as cheaply. They will be made everywhere and by everybody" (20).

The vitality and freed sensibilities of the New Generation films were also increasingly reflected in Mekas's own loosened aesthetic judgments. He could revel in the idiocy and sloppiness of Taylor Mead's *The Flower Thief* (1960), praise the "free creative expression" (84) of an eight-year-old filmmaker, or herald Jack Smith's *Flaming Creatures* (1963) as a "most luxurious outpouring of imagination, of imagery, of poetry, of movie artistry—comparable only to the work of the greatest, like Von Sternberg" (83). Traditional aesthetic standards—the province of highbrow and middlebrow alike—could be jettisoned at will. "There is no such thing," Mekas insisted, "as a 'normal movement' or a 'normal image,' a 'good image' or a 'bad image' " (92).

> Didn't you know that, when you think about it, I have almost unlimited taste! I can enjoy the poetry of Brakhage, the silent movies of Griffith and Eisenstein, the movies of Hawks and Ulmer, the pornographic flicks of Hoboken, the films of Vanderbeek, the psychiatric movies shown at Cinema 16, the Westerns shown only on 42nd Street, and, depending on my mood, practically anything that moves on the screen? I had one of my most exciting evenings of cinema while watching somebody's home movies taken with an 8mm. camera on a trip across the country. (62)

Carefully weighed aesthetic evaluation was outmoded, prejudiced, blinkered. The new critic would instead reflect the spirit of the scene, agitate the culture, act as a "raving maniac of the cinema" (79) in order to help create the "right attitude for looking at movies" (96). In his "Movie Journal" column in the *Village Voice*, Mekas honed his antiestablishment stance, becoming a self-proclaimed prophet of the counterculture and ardent defender of self-liberation. The extreme looseness and breadth of his aesthetic—what he called his "almost unlimited taste"—now encouraged him to champion the vitality of all movies, regardless of origin or intent. Underground freedom was more than simply freedom from repressive moral standards. It was also freedom from taste conventions and aesthetic niceties, the freedom to appreciate without criticizing, to enjoy all culture, and on one's own terms. These were radical and unabashedly vanguard ideas. Mekas was brazenly liberating the artist and spectator, throwing out the old guidelines for effective art, throwing into question the very importance of valuative criticism.

THE PERILS OF PROPAGANDA

Tyler had a right to be miffed. In its extreme catholicism (Eisenstein, porno, home movies, psychiatric films) Mekas's critical attitude epitomized the Underground's new vanguard camp. Borrowing and exploding traditional cultism's careful aesthetic selection of conventionally nonaesthetic material while merging it with camp's aesthetic transmutation of nondescript moviemaking, the new stance flaunted a critical perspective that would see any and *all* films as potentially aesthetic, exciting, and beautiful, to anyone.

Mekas certainly wasn't the only critic to hold such views. Indeed, while *Film Culture* itself continued to serve as a forum for sophisticated discussion of artistic films and film artists, the growing middlebrow acceptance of aesthetic cinema occasioned a decisive, vanguard shift in film criticism, provoked by Mekas and other key members of the New Generation. Something of this sort had been brewing for many years—Amos Vogel's Cinema 16 screenings had touted an eclecticism of taste even back in the late 1940s—but the success of the Underground now provided the younger critics ideological and institutional support. Alongside the new camp critics, Tyler frequently seemed less elder statesman than hopelessly square father trying to comprehend the new fads and fashions. As the somewhat bewildered moderator of a 1966 New York Film Festival symposium on criticism (printed in *Film Culture* 42 as "What Are the New Critics Saying?") he tolerates a number of celebratory remarks from the likes of Sheldon Renan ("I think that only people who love films should be allowed to criticize them" ["What," 77]) and P. Adams Sitney ("I can see absolutely no reason for a man to sit down and presume to explain what's wrong with something" [82]) before lurching headlong into the fray:

> TYLER: I'd like to clarify one thing. What's the consensus of opinion on the platform: do you think it's ever necessary to point out what's wrong with something when it's on the whole very good? Do you think it's worth pointing out what minor faults it may have? . . .

RENAN: Sometimes you want to point out a fault and say, "This is a fault, but pay no attention to it, because it isn't important." Sometimes, you want to point out something to a film-maker . . .

TYLER: Oh, excuse me—faults are always important. An art can't have an unimportant fault.

RENAN: This preoccupation with perfection I find annoying and unimportant, because—

TYLER: You mean you shouldn't ever be aware of something that's faulty?

RENAN: Sure, but it seems faulty to you—it may not be faulty to the film-maker.

TYLER: Is it possible for a film to have a fault?

TOBY MUSSMAN: Sure.

TYLER: So I'm not being subjective, then? (82)

This was indeed a gap not simply of generations but of critical ethos. For Tyler, of course, pointing out aesthetic faults (*evaluating* the artwork) was one of the chief jobs of the critic. Yet for Mekas, Sitney, and Renan, because the critic functions as a sort of aesthetic visionary, someone who (in Sitney's words) "can teach us how to see" ("What," 76) through the artist's newfound perspective, anything that serves to cloud that perspective, to withhold the work—including a critic's negative judgment—becomes counterproductive.

Tyler had already expressed his frustration with this critical stance rather pointedly in "For *Shadows*, against *Pull My Daisy*," published in *Film Culture* 24 (Spring 1962). Here the veteran connoisseur faces his anti-intellectual, cliquish progeny head-on:

> I can hear some of my readers: Here's that Heavy Culture Man again! Right, man. And it's not going to let up so long as there's a drop of think in me. All my opportunities for joining literary cliques have been passed up or automatically short-circuited, opportunities that began appearing about 1927. . . . I daresay this beginning is more self-conscious than it ought to be, but observation of the milieu over many years has given me the impression that the grammatical first-person no longer denotes egocentrism so much as do certain transports of self-forgetfulness, where identification with others—in fact, with almost anything—requires a minimum of cerebral effort. . . . (1962b, 28–29)

For Tyler, the clique viewpoint had clouded the subculture's ability to distinguish genuine art from vulgar fashion; here he attempts to reinject some measure of considered aesthetic evaluation into the proceedings by contrasting two films that, as J. Hoberman has noted, had been Mekas's two key exemplars of revolutionary moviemaking. Indeed, Tyler's implicit attack was doubly barbed. Whereas Mekas had loudly denounced the "commercial," recut version of Cassavetes's *Shadows* (1960), instead championing Robert Frank and Alfred Leslie's *Pull My Daisy* (1958) as a replacement

8. "Sassy youth, moral anarchism." *Pull My Daisy* (Robert Frank, Alfred Leslie, 1958). Courtesy of Anthology Film Archives.

"avatar of the new cinema" (Hoberman 1992, 101), Tyler would now aggressively challenge the fashionable bias, praising Cassavetes's film (in either version) over the wildly overrated Beat extravaganza.

For Tyler, *Pull My Daisy* was fashionable, ill-formed, shallow, self-satisfied, and hopelessly ignorant of its own modernist antecedents, which it nevertheless managed to plunder mercilessly ("the grabbing is as big as the bag" [Tyler 1962b, 29]). In so trampling its legitimate artistic ancestry, the film reduced vanguard traditions to an assortment of clichés. "Never before today," he insisted, "has bohemian revolt been considered so ofay—and never before, consistently, has the outcast tramp-poet been so much a theatrical charade" (30). Beatism amounted to a chic pastiche of avant-gardism, a "wee, wee cult with a public-relations palate as visible as that of the Wolf when he impersonated Little Red Riding Hood's grandmother" (29). Most important, its complete lack of self-awareness suggested not artistic incompetence so much as a shameless, adolescent dismissal of all relevant critical standards. Beat culture's vacuous display of "sassy youth, moral anarchism, cadged wine and beer" (30) was apparently "to be enjoyed because it 'had to be,' and if not enjoyable, it's you who don't 'belong' " (29).

By contrast, the currently unfashionable *Shadows* stood as a worthy exemplar of the modernist tradition. Though the film had been appreciated for its surface resemblance to *Daisy* and the documentary tradition, Tyler could discern more credible connections with Sherwood Anderson, Eudora Welty, Chekhov, even Eliot's *Waste Land*. *Shadows* also courted modernist ambiguity, honoring psychological depth and the complexity of human relationships, and powerfully conveying the horror of racial prejudice. Cassavetes became, for Tyler, a paradigm of the thoughtful art-film director on a par with Bergman or Antonioni. A filmmaker of "power and insight," a "fresh and difficult sense of style, and the courage to reveal human depths raw with controversy" (32), he evinced an insight into humanity balanced by a keen aesthetic sense and a delicate touch.

Mekas's crowd had disowned Cassavetes when he appeared to spurn them by remaking the film. The loss, for Tyler, was entirely theirs—they had rejected a promising filmmaker and tremendous artwork in favor of fashionable, pseudovanguard posturing. Was the purpose of film criticism now merely to promote those ambitious, if indifferently talented, filmmakers who happened to garner the favor of the subculture's ruling class? Did the Underground merely play out a bizarre camp ritual, producing trash artifacts to be adored by the movement's resident tastemakers? The situation might not have seemed so sorry had America's own experimentalists not offered such promise in the immediate postwar years. But they had needed to be nourished and guided, not exploited and disingenuously praised. The fault lay in critical irresponsibility, in the abdication of the critic's duty to encourage growth and maturity of artistic expression. No one really cared whether these new films were any *good*, so long as they were outrageous enough to call attention to their devoted followers. In such a climate, criticism itself seemed to have been reduced to propaganda: if the new independent cinema eschewed aesthetic and moral standards and even technical competence in favor of complete freedom of expression and "absolute parody of absolutely everything" (1966, 34), the new film criticism encouraged the decline of values by replacing careful aesthetic discernment with mere "self-promotion, a variety of commercial advertising rigged up with gags, more or less refined and sophisticated" (29).

For Tyler, responsible film criticism had been discouraged by a number of tendencies, including a fetishizing of a "Good Old Days" of classic cinema and a decline in serious film commentary in favor of mere journalism. Most pernicious, though, had been the influence of the new Underground itself: its blissfully amateurish neodadaism tacitly reproduced Hollywood's own traditional emphasis on "energy without intelligence."

(At least, he could imply, his own film criticism of the 1940s had looked beyond such surface vitality to underlying complexities of psychology and myth.) In the course of its insistence on radicalism as an end in itself, it had "homogeniz[ed] all protest elements" using a sign language that possesses "no scale of values, no intelligible aims and therefore is beyond criticism." In such a climate, serious aesthetic analysis could seem positively old-fashioned.

> If, in the presence of fetich footage or related activities, one mentions some "principle" of art, one is apt to be rebutted by a partisan of the current independent modes that one simply isn't in step with "what's happening." If one refers to last year's sensations, these are no longer, perhaps, *au courant*—they may have been replaced by newer ones.

In sum, this seemed "the avant-garde attitude over-asserted to the point of lunacy"—a remark that nicely captures the essence and spirit of Tyler's concerns. The best modern art was, to him, not at all frivolous and self-absorbed; indeed, against modernism's serious and sophisticated moral deliberations, Mekas's specious vanguard "resistance" courted social irresponsibility, betraying art "into the hands of those to whom the dignity and the future of man, his glory and consciousness of godhead, the destiny of the great emotions and the great trials are all very incidental things" (33).

Here, however, Tyler was only partly right. In truth, Mekas's vanguard stance *was* radical. In being easy to emulate—and thus more accessible to the public—it was perhaps ultimately more radical than Tyler's high-flown transmutation had ever been. But Tyler could never accept, let alone adopt, the new attitude, because it so brazenly rejected the authority of outside critical judgment and taste. In seizing the freedom to declare, "I even enjoy *this*!" the new camp profited nicely from the dubious reputations, even dubious quality, of Underground movies. If many of these films were indeed no better than Hollywood's trashiest offerings, so what? At least this was the *Underground*'s trash. In asserting control over their own freedom of taste, the new vanguard activists proclaimed their liberation from the stranglehold of middlebrow and highbrow alike.

More to the point, the Underground had attempted to reinvent middlebrow's commercial art along vanguard lines. Like middlebrow taste, the new cultism and camp were accessible and, potentially, popular. If members of the scene appeared to court notoriety and material success, if many of its works seemed to have emerged from a drug-addled version of Monogram studios, so much the better—for here was the very flip side of middlebrow, popular art *reclaimed* from the Establishment. Thus while Tyler attempted to attack the Underground as quasi-commercial (as he had earlier done with abstract expressionism), attributing the "slick semi-success" of Pop Film to a "conspiracy among businessmen (including frustrated film makers)" (1967b, 35), the charge was no longer really relevant. Tyler was speaking from a different generation; he was even speaking a different language.

THE HEAVY CULTURE MAN, ABANDONED

Tyler's increasing irrelevance to the scene is most potently expressed in his blistering *Underground Film: A Critical History*. "Critical" is an understatement: its 240 pages of vitriol relentlessly assault the movement while pleading for a return to the aesthetic and moral commitment of those very traditions Mekas had fought so hard to transcend. But again Tyler insists on applying to the Underground standards of judgment it had largely rejected. Here he plays his trump card, spotting in Underground play a more insidious infantile regression.

Whereas the surrealists had based their art in a healthy self-liberation, the New Generation filmmakers seemed content to wallow in self-indulgence, producing a "wish-fulfillment psychology masquerading as a system of aesthetic values" (1969e, 25). Warhol's "rejection of the mature vocabulary of filmic effects" suggested to Tyler a child's "trancelike, arbitrary fixation on certain objects"; the "streamy-dreamy rhythm" of Brakhage's recent work seemed to emerge from the filmmaker's "crude infantile compulsion" (28). Itself something of a "great big toddler," the Underground film was actually

> noticeably underprivileged. The last, of course, is my own word; in the eyes of the Underground ideologists this attribute is construed as the expression of a natural privilege such as "poetic" talent. Strength in numbers is merely ancillary to such large benign theories. Shining epithets are integral with the ideological blarney of the movement, the Underground's unabashed lyricism of self-praise. In Mekas's prose it is like a fond papa's lullaby. (An interesting point is that while Mekas himself, by the clock, gets older and older, his ideas get younger and younger.) (30)

There is more to Tyler's child metaphor than mere denigration of the movement's self-indulgence. In appealing to his own psychomythic approach of the past, he implies that like the artless popular movies produced by the centrifugal collective, the grotesque pop extravaganzas spawned within the Underground warrant only critical transmutation, not deferential explication. At least the aesthetically immature avant-garde of Deren and Markopoulos had aspired to greater things; this new scene reveled in its own vulgarity, which was unforgivable.

In response, Tyler was fighting camp with camp, treating these films as no better (and perhaps worse) than Hollywood movies of the 1940s. Drawing on his skills as a vanguard maverick, he snubbed the new cinema by condescending to it, flaunting its lack of aesthetic power over him. The Underground's camp was ignorant and masturbatory, reveling in aesthetic freedom without accepting any accompanying responsibilities. In parading its own devotion to the nonaesthetic, it had played off old camp's affection for Hollywood while rejecting its intellectual insight and careful aesthetic refashioning. Like the new cultism, the new camp was spectator-friendly, available to all; with creative transmutation and deeper cultural insight so downplayed, hipness could itself emerge as a prime vanguard credential.

To Tyler this may have amounted to intellectual bankruptcy in the name of chic, but nevertheless it allowed the dissemination of a vanguard perspective within a larger (counter)cultural sphere. If the new camp and cultism hindered informed aesthetic distinctions among artists and works, they were also furthering core vanguard ideals, denigrating the aesthetic "autonomy" of middlebrow art in favor of universal artistic production. Its success in this regard made Tyler's defection a little ironic, because in the public's mind he would be forever associated with the amusing excesses of his Underground successors. In Gore Vidal's wildly parodic *Myra Breckinridge* (1968), Tyler was immortalized as the original pseudo-intellectual campist, a critic whose

> vision (films are the unconscious expressions of age-old human myths) is perhaps the only important critical insight this century has produced. Also, Tyler's close scrutiny of the films of the Forties makes him our age's central thinker, if only because *in the decade between 1935 and 1945, no irrelevant film was made in the United States*. During those years, the entire range of human (which is to say, American) legend was put on film, and any profound study of those extraordinary works is bound to make crystal-clear the human condition. For instance, to take an example at random, Johnny Weissmuller, the zahftic Tarzan, still provides the last word on the subject of soft man's relationship to hard environment . . . that glistening overweight body set against a limestone cliff at noon says the whole thing. (13)

If one spots beneath Vidal's burlesque a certain affection for (and recognition of) Tyler's pioneering efforts, it is because twenty years later, a thoroughly "popped" culture had warmed to the vanguard agenda.[13] For celebrated culture critic Marshall McLuhan, TV shows, newspaper layouts, even *MAD* magazine all invited active, participatory spectatorship in a manner that recalled the modernism of Picasso, Joyce, and ragtime jazz. What McLuhan called the "brand new world of allatonceness" (McLuhan and Fiore 1967, 63) was not simply a return to primordial roots and tribal communalism: it heralded the demise of passive consumerism and the birth, in effect, of a vanguard mass culture, a culture that eradicated high art as a form fundamentally distinct from *The Ed Sullivan Show* and tabloid headlines. Because McLuhan's theory so openly embraced the readerly qualities of heretofore overlooked media of everyday life, it made traditional aesthetic judgment seem an elitist distraction. Declaring the medium itself to be the "message" (McLuhan 1964) may have forced a reevaluation of (and new respect for) communication channels, but it also universalized aesthetic experience, flattening the hermeneutic and formal complexities of art into a heightened sensory involvement shared with TV commercials and computers.

Tyler saw the writing on the wall. "The medium is the message," he declared, was a slogan that "automatically silence[d] all that we know as criticism" (1972b, 166) by confusing technology with content and naively celebrating mass cultural myth. But by this point, few were still listening to Tyler. Younger spectators were too busy honing their own resistant spectatorship, rejecting Hollywood's patronizing "youthpix" of the late 1960s and early 1970s[14] while instead creating cults around *Night of the Living Dead* (1968), *El Topo* (1970), *Pink Flamingos* (1973), *Eraserhead* (1978), and of course *The Rocky Horror Picture Show* (1975). Sizable audiences were now willing to go out of their way to support dissident moviegoing as a countercultural activity, attending midnight screenings as close-knit communities of spectators reveling in their own selective, oppositional consumerism.[15]

In New York the way had been paved by *Pull My Daisy*, *Flaming Creatures*, and *The Chelsea Girls* (1965–66), but now the phenomenon had spread across the country. Consider *Harold and Maude*—a film that opened in December 1971 to abysmal press ("all the fun and gaiety of a burning orphanage," moaned *Variety* ["Harold" 1971]) but managed to hang on by word of mouth for two years in Detroit, and over three at the Westgate theater in suburban Minneapolis, largely *because* the studio had invested little or no publicity in the film. Encouraged, Paramount revived *Harold and Maude*, carefully marketing it as a cultist gem (starting with test-runs at New York's counterculture Thalia and Elgin). By 1974, the film had reopened across the country to critical acclaim; it soon became a certifiable hit.

Harold and Maude may or may not have been a sophisticated work of art, by Tyler's standards. But the question itself had been rendered moot by the film's diehard followers—who, perceiving that the movie's specialness would otherwise not be recognized within the culture, had engaged in openly vanguard praxis, keeping *their* chosen taste object in the marketplace against the wishes of others.[16] Whereas Tyler's aesthetic discrimination of the 1950s and 1960s had sought to uplift middlebrow taste judgment above mere consumerism by supplying timeless pictorial and ethical values delivered with his own critical authority, the new popular avant-garde strove to overturn middlebrow judgment entirely. This was not a matter of carefully discerning "the best that is known and thought," but of totally redefining "popular art" on individual and subcultural terms.[17]

A New Beginning

Once the exclusive property of highbrows, vanguard principles had entered the mainstream of American culture as popular art's populist Resistance. This horrified Tyler, but only insofar as it threatened Culture itself; though a highbrow, he had long abandoned his own commitment to the avant-garde, even risking much of his distinction from middlebrow for the sake of cultural elevation. But not all his highbrow brethren were willing to make similar sacrifices, even for the sake of Art. Yet where was there to go? Certainly the choices were severely limited. With the sheer success of the vanguard agenda among the counterculture audience, not only was Tyler's discernment untenable; so was popular camp/cult engagement.[18] Highbrows, it seemed, had been pushed to the wall. Was the avant-garde lost for good?

Hardly. As we shall see more clearly in the next chapter, many highbrows boldly sought to reclaim the avant-garde for themselves, decisively pulling it back into difficult territory by again limiting access to vanguard strategies of spectatorship. The new cultism's shorthand assessment and Underground camp's wild catholicism needed reining in—remystifying—in order to highlight the special skills and insights of intellectual critics. Sarris's auteur theory and Mekas's "almost unlimited taste" had been presented as radical gestures in themselves. They refused conventional taste boundaries in order to transcend both middlebrow aesthetics *and* the old critical avant-garde's detailed aesthetic rehabilitation of low culture. The pop avant-garde had brazenly seized spectatorship, but in a gestural manner easily emulated by counterculture followers: resistance became simply a question of opening oneself to the aesthetic pleasures of all cinema. In rescuing this gesture *back* from the counterculture, highbrow intellectuals would restrict access to it by asserting their own privileged awareness and understanding of aesthetic principles. Instead of informed taste judgments, which were now a dime a dozen, the highbrow critic might rely on the currency and difficulty of her own aesthetic approaches, which could be applied to high, low, and middlebrow films in a manner disrespectful to the niceties of taste.

Thus though the new vanguard intellectual could still profess an interest in a broad array of movies, the critical procedures that revealed the aesthetic complexities of such films became more intricate, involved, harder for the average spectator to grasp. The disparity between critical complexity and apparent textual transparency would become especially pronounced after 1969, when political imperatives sparked a renewed highbrow focus on lowbrow movies. As the critic's skill in applying an analytical method increasingly supplanted quirks of taste as a defining mark of distinction, the cultural authority of the highbrow critic again grew enormously vis-à-vis his middlebrow brethren. By the 1970s, that authority could be further validated by the academy, whose walls provided an additional institutional distinction while protecting highbrows from the pop avant-garde.

Even in the late 1960s, we see early manifestations of the new highbrow approach within the art world, which briefly provided the necessary cover for film critics seeking to distance themselves from the vagaries of fashion. Here they could hone a distinct, encompassing method that asserted their independence and intellect while respecting the integrity of each film studied. Armed with appropriate methodologies, even a pugnacious vanguard veteran could now use his tenure at a major art magazine to reassert his presence on the cutting edge.

Chapter Seven

RETREAT INTO THEORY

> It's a monumentally unimaginative movie: Kubrick, with his
> $750,000 centrifuge, and in love with gigantic hardware and
> control panels, is the Belasco of science fiction.
> *(Pauline Kael, on* 2001: A Space Odyssey*)*[1]

> The critical performance around this film, object, Structure,
> revolving as it has about the historical, anecdotal, sociologi-
> cal, concerned as it is with the texture of incident is, of
> course, the clear projection of aging minds and bodies. Its
> hostile dismissal constitutes, rather like its timid
> defense, an expression of fatigue.
> *(Annette Michelson, on* 2001: A Space Odyssey*)*[2]

THE RISE of a popular, accessible critical/spectatorial avant-garde in 1960s America made the empowering aesthetic gesture—and by extension, personal film art—available to all those seeking an alternative to the marketable excesses of Great Cinemah. The growing irrelevance of highbrow vanguard critics in a middlebrow vanguard culture was confirmed by the rapid ascent of Pauline Kael, a critic whose spirited rejection of Sarris's cultism and Mekas's camp Underground alike helped to conceal her own skillful mainstreaming of both traditions. Kael's fierce independence could make her seem courageously free-spirited and sensibly conservative at the same time, but her refusal to follow any party line only helped to clear space for her celebration of the uniqueness and pragmatism of her own cosmopolitan taste. This taste would in turn help to redefine middlebrow options for the 1970s: while ostensibly individualistic, populist, and antihighbrow, it nonetheless implicitly reaffirmed the vanguard power of consumers to seize their own film culture from the high and low cinemas offered them.

Kael's own position papers established her persona of wizened skeptic eager to repudiate any critical position that smacked of trendiness. In "Circles and Squares: Joys and Sarris" (*Film Quarterly*, 1963), she has little difficulty (and a great deal of fun) decimating auteurism simply by calling Sarris's bluff and evaluating his naked polemics as serious theory.

What really troubles Kael, however, isn't so much Sarris's weak argumentation as his penchant for trash: the theory is really "an aesthetics which is fundamentally anti-art" (1965, 311) and serves mainly to sustain the "intellectual diddling" (304) of perpetually adolescent male critics who prefer silly macho movies to a culture of "poseurs and phonies and sensitive-feminine types" (319).

For Kael, the critic could achieve her ultimate goal—the "formation and reformation of public taste" (1959, 192)—only by resolutely refusing the vagaries of intellectual fads: Tyler's myth criticism, Farber's cultism, Siegfried Kracauer's realism, and Mekas's radically liberated taste would all come under fire as absurdly limited perspectives. She prided herself on her own iconoclasm: like Farber, she might reject George Stevens's middlebrow prestige films as "heavy, expensive pictures full of obese nuances" (198), while like Tyler, she could laud Cocteau as a worthy, neglected alternative. In the end, slamming popular junk was just too easy and too limiting—sober judgment might also reveal art-house favorites Fellini and Godard to be undisciplined (if not uninteresting) poseurs more interested in the idea of being serious artists than in taking the time to make serious art (1966, 30), and even the most noble experimental film to be a "squiggly little mess of abstract patterns or a symbolic drama full of knives, keys and figures receding in the night" (1959, 209).[3]

Though she may have seemed an antivanguard reactionary, Kael was actually reconceiving vanguard individualism in terms more palatable to the middlebrow mainstream. Her willingness to slaughter sacred cows in the interest of fair and open judgment might have allied her with the likes of connoisseurist Parker Tyler, had it not assumed a cultural playing field far more level than Tyler would have permitted. In truth, by the late 1960s Kael had thoroughly bought into the "new sensibility," aligning high and low against the ever-vulgar middle. Her celebrated "Trash, Art and the Movies" (*Harper's*, 1969), indeed, seems very much a reworking of Farber's earlier "White Elephant Art vs. Termite Art," asserting that

> Movie art is not the opposite of what we have always enjoyed in movies, it is not to be found in a return to that official high culture, it is what we have always found in good movies only more so. It's the subversive gesture carried further, the moments of excitement sustained longer and extended into new meanings. At best, the movie is totally informed by the kind of pleasure we have been taking from bits and pieces of movies.

Now the crazy vitality of one small scene could make even the most terrible picture worthwhile, reminding us that Art is first and foremost about enjoyment, not boredom or pedagogy. Middlebrow gentility—the "approved culture of the schoolroom" (1970, 106)—drained the life out of material by preaching moral lessons and by "using 'artistic techniques' to give trash the look of art." Even *The Thomas Crown Affair* was far more entertaining than Richard Lester's *Petulia* (both 1968), the silly pretitle sequence in *You Only Live Twice* (1967) more fun than the entirety of Kubrick's ponderous *2001: A Space Odyssey* (1968): "all that 'art' may be what prevents pictures like these from being *enjoyable* trash; they're not honestly crummy, they're very fancy and they take their crummy ideas seriously" (117).

Kael may not have been breaking new ground here, but her irreverent discernment garnered the sort of popular influence Farber could not have imagined. The unprecedented success of *I Lost It at the Movies* (1965) and its immediate successors, *Kiss Kiss Bang Bang* (1968) and *Going Steady* (1970), established Kael's preeminent tastemaking authority and solidified her reputation as a critic distanced from faddish extremes and beholden to no one. Yet her willingness to see "art" as something actively seized from culture, and "artistic cinema" as productive aesthetic engagement *with* cinema, nevertheless belied her reactionary posturing, revealing the extent to which middlebrow culture had itself absorbed the avant-garde's lessons. Sensible open-mindedness had made the vanguard extremes seem superfluous, even a little silly.

Concerned highbrow intellectuals may be forgiven for having feared the worst. In blurring its own distinction from middlebrow, hadn't the avant-garde actually allowed itself to be co-opted by the enemy? Not really—after all, it was the avant-garde's very achievement that threatened the vanguard highbrow's privileged cultural authority. Nevertheless, for highbrows to reposition movie art—and themselves—on the cutting edge, a difficult new aesthetic would need to be brought in to replace the thoroughly middlebrow free/vital expressivism of old. Luckily, two related modernist aesthetics had recently appeared on the horizon; even better, both boldly opposed the expressive excesses of cosmic abstractionism while defending their own staunch *in*accessibility in highly intellectual terms. One was American, the other European; one curiously mum, the other stridently political. Together, they would allow select highbrows to reclaim the cultural margins by presenting "cultural mastery" as a much more complex and difficult prospect than the Underground had suggested.

The key attraction of American minimalism and European materialism was that both aesthetics defended themselves as a return to basics—to material essences, even. For the American highbrow, Underground catholicism could thus be combated with a superior knowledge of the medium itself. The question became: how did a given movie relate to what cinema was (or should be), *essentially*? Here potentially all films could become relevant, with "unlimited" vanguard taste now disguised beneath a shroud of specialized knowledge and theoretical objectivity. Objectivity was what now distinguished the serious critic from the casual aficionado: for those critics taken with the politicized, Brechtian version of minimalism offered by European materialist theory, it even helped to enhance a persona of serious social agent, highly relevant to the explosive times.

While the successful importation of the materialist aesthetic would, indeed, make America's own minimalism of Robert Morris and Donald Judd seem by comparison positively (and positivistically) retrograde, the sheer success that European materialism has since enjoyed within the American academy should not blind us to the importance of homegrown minimalism, which in retrospect played a significant role in vanguard retrenchment. For a time, minimalism provided an important enclave for select highbrows seeking to stake out their own territory in a post-Underground climate: it offered a stepping-stone between the world of artists, from which vanguard film criticism had arisen, and the world of academics, where it would become comfortably entrenched. It also enabled Manny Farber to end his critical career the way he started it, as an uncompromising visionary.

Terrain and Funk

Minimalism was as well suited to creative film criticism in the late 1960s as abstract expressionism had been in the 1940s. Here again was an exciting development in American aesthetics, as visceral in its reaction to expressionist romanticism as Pollock's and Motherwell's abstractionism had been to staid provincial realism. New York School artworks had captured and reexpressed the psychic, mythic, and emotional depths of their makers. Minimalist art of the mid-1960s simply *was*. It just sat (or hung) there, stubbornly silent, apparently expressing nothing more than its own self-evident presence. The work could be as maddeningly straightforward as a set of six steel boxes mounted on a gallery wall, or a thirty-three-foot-long row of bricks laid out on a floor.

Now, even the worst B-movie had never been quite as self-evident as a row of bricks. But because movies could still be maddeningly straightforward, the vanguard film critic might take a crucial lesson from his art-world brethren: if you looked closely enough, you were bound to find something interesting. If at second glance the work seemed to offer nothing more than it did at first glance, the third, ninth, or sixteenth glance might still reveal a wealth of hidden details within the surrounding flat regularities, or at least insights into one's own pained apprehension of space and time.

In broadest terms, art-world critics had solved the problem of minimalist objecthood (the radical refusal of content, especially psychological) by redirecting attention from naked form itself, to the perception thereof. Minimalist art could be interrogated phenomenologically; it could be *about* its own perceptual and cognitive difficulty. In the end, the work wasn't really an object at all but a catalyst for complex, liberated apprehension. Simplicity of form only turned the attuned spectator outward, toward the work's aesthetic transformation of a perceptual environment—and inward, toward the nuances of detail and texture hidden within the seemingly banal facade. For Lawrence Alloway, minimalism had finally abolished invention as a fundamental criterion of quality art making, forcing the critic to look not for "unity within variety" but for "variety within conspicuous unity" (1968, 56).[4]

Conspicuous unity? Again the movies suggest an obvious analogy. We will recall that as a vanguard film critic, Manny Farber had been seeking out variety within the unity of Hollywood product for years—first locating on the neglected fringes his own cultist underground of masculine movies far more vigorous than the lethargic middlebrowism of Pollock, Rothko, Kazan, and Stevens, then gradually moving his attention much closer, to the microlevel termite activities and textural details hidden within the bland surfaces of individual films. Hardy Kruger's lower lip, Burt Lancaster's hands, and Henry Fonda's "supremely convex body" could become tangible details removed from larger narrative or symbolic significance, existing for their own sake, as self-sufficient elements within the surrounding work. The camera's ability to capture physical reality allowed most films to display human features such as shoulders, hips, and mouths on a par with props and sets. All became objects in space, elements of the film's shifting "terrain."

Farber's involvement with painting had always influenced his film criticism—his oppositional appeal to interpretive standards of freedom and vitality had, after all, stemmed from his involvement in New York modernism of the 1940s. Yet he had never really allowed himself to become a blanket supporter of art movements, always preferring an eclectic cultist connoisseurship of select works and microelements. In the 1940s he had favored the likes of Robert DeNiro and Kimber Smith; in the 1950s and early 1960s he would rather discuss Jack Levine and Nathan Oliveira, or even neglected past masters such as Louis Eilshemius, than the overpublicized abstract expressionist and pop celebrities.[5] By the mid-1960s, however, Farber would begin to break with tradition, embracing the more appealing minimalist aesthetic within his own art[6] while pushing the quasi-minimalist obsessiveness of his recent film criticism to eccentric extremes. Perhaps most important, minimalism would allow Farber to push his own level of discernment decisively beyond oppositional genres, films, even directors—and thus beyond the constant jostling of Sarris's new cultist hipsters—by justifying his enhanced attention to interesting formal ele-

9. The beauties of banalized emptiness. *Persona* (1966).

ments as likely to appear in a film by Richard Lester or Ingmar Bergman as in one by Howard Hawks or Raoul Walsh.

Farber's criticism at *Artforum* (whose staff he joined in late 1966) certainly reflects this new eclecticism. He could now see roughness and "funk" (Farber 1968a, 66) in both Norman Mailer's *Beyond the Law* and Lester's *How I Won the War* (1967),[7] and a remarkable "syntactic invention" in both Mike Nichols's *The Graduate* (1967) and Bergman's *Persona* (1966). In the past he had loathed the European art cinema's middlebrow stuffiness and termite-squashing rigidity, but now its fragmentation and formal exploration actually made it quite interesting. *Persona*'s "march of bare, stringent compositions" (1968c, 68) suggested a film that had "almost accidentally arrived at the beauties, handsomeness, of banalized emptiness." Like many of the new directors, Bergman subordinated plot, making his films "slower face-to-face constructions," works that explored the shape and texture of countenance as formal variables.

> When this pensive, larger-than-life profile, back of the head, or full face, fills the screen with a kind of distilled purity, the image becomes purified abstract composition, a diagram, and any soul-searching is secondary. The movie, in a

mysterious fashion, diverts at this moment from the clutter and multiplicity of storytelling, naturalism, to a minimal condition. The screen is reduced to a refined one-against-one balance, and the movie's excitement has shifted strictly into a matter of shape against shape, tone against tone. (1968f, 72)

As Tyler had discovered in the 1950s, cinema now seemed to be aping the critic's own vanguard approach: as Farber had isolated obscure shots and gestures within more conventional movies, now films were regularly abandoning narrative progression for direct presentation of peripheral material, even textures. *Easy Rider* was marred by "draggy, romantic material" but saved by its visual presentation of "the quiet, the damp green countryside, and a spectacular last shot zooming up from a curving road and burning cycle" (1969c, 81). Bresson's *Une Femme douce* (1969) seemed a "geometric ballet of doors opening and closing, people exiting and entering . . . of objects or people moving into and out of the stationary camera" (1969d, 86).

Farber's refined aesthetic could accommodate his continuing interest in vitality and aesthetic freedom by presenting films as loose clusters of isolated fragments whose torpidity could be seen to be at once formally interesting and vitally real. If only a few months earlier he had given a mixed appraisal of Godard's *La Chinoise* (1967), discerning a "hollow shaft between the Hot Shot imagery and cunning rhetorical jam-up" (1968e, 65), by late 1968 he is ready to hail this director as an innovative minimalist—a "new species creator, related directly to Robert Morris in sculpture, in that there is an abhorrence of lethargy and being pinned down in a work, alongside a strong devotion to Medium" (1968g, 58). His films amplified the fragmentary structure of the most interesting new work, stopping regularly to confront the spectator with isolated, monotonous scenes, while eschewing the repressive control of Hollywood scripting and direction. His insistent reductivism even suggested emptiness for its own sake—"boredom and its adjuncts" took a Godard film "to its real home: pure abstraction" (60).

A logical extension of vital, reductive torpidity could be found, not surprisingly, in the narrative films of Andy Warhol. Haphazard and seemingly obsessed with incidentals, they almost fully abandoned narrative progression in favor of prolonged presentation of isolated images, without stifling the volcanic vitality of performers such as "hippopotamus of sin" Brigid Polk, who in * * * * (1967) "explodes the screen outwards by giant abandon and cravenness" (1968f, 73). The tortured psychosymbolism of Deren, Anger, and Markopoulos had been anathema to Farber, but the new experimentalists' rough-hewn Underground cinema of the 1960s proved far more appealing, even resembling in many respects his own "underground films" of old. Those movies, he had claimed, had drawn connoisseurs to "murky, congested theaters" offering a "nightmarish atmosphere of shabby transience, prints that seem overgrown with jungle moss, sound tracks infected with hiccups" (1971i, 15). The new Warhol-Kuchar Underground was really not all that different, offering fans a similarly rewarding foray into the cultural margins of "disenchantment, sordidness, feverish wastage."

> The theaters of the Underground—often five or six docile customers in an improbable place that looks like a bombed-out air shelter or the downstairs ladies room at the old Paramount—offer a weirdly satisfying experience. For two dollars the spectator gets five bedraggled two-reelers, and, after a sojourn with incompetence, chaos, nouveau-culture taste, he leaves this land's end theater feeling unaccountably spry. (1968b, 63)

In addition, many of the new Underground films were actually aesthetically challenging, even important. The experimentalists of old would never have thought to produce a work as raw and austere as *Wavelength* (1967).[8] Here was a film in which plot had been rigorously marginalized, in which the camera saw "every wall-person-light detail as equally important," fully reducing all cinematic elements to terrain. In Michael Snow, Farber found a director equally committed to formal/phenomenological concerns ("If a room could speak about itself, this would be the way it would go" [1969a, 71]), and to the importance of vigorous, virile energy. His panning film ↔ (a.k.a. *Back and Forth* [1969]) stared at an "asymmetrical space so undistinguished that it's hard to believe the whole movie is confined to it," yet still caused the spectator to "experience all the grueling action and gut effort of a basketball game" (1970a, 81). Snow's films were rigorously modern without being precious or prissy; they evinced the sort of masculine authority and intensity Farber had previously associated with hard-boiled auteurs, without sacrificing one iota of formal integrity.

Yet Farber was hardly turning his eye exclusively to modernism. Indeed, his new encompassing approach also allowed him to return to the auteurism he had neglected in his progression toward microanalysis. In the late 1960s, he again regularly discussed specific auteurs, both young and old, though now all were assessed from the vantage point of the new perspective. If Peckinpah's *The Wild Bunch* featured an awesome eye for physical and human detail and a "sensuous feel for textures" (1969c, 81), ultimately the director had pushed too hard, turning the film into a "bloated composition" (80). Few movies were better than Hawks's *Scarface* (1932) when it came to "nailing down singularity in a body or face, the effect of a strong outline cutting out impossibly singular shapes" (1969b, 79). Walsh, "the great traffic cop of movies," worked a style "based on traveling over routes which are sometimes accomplished by bodily movement, the passage that a gaze takes, suggested or actually shown, and the movement of a line of dialogue, the route indicated by a gesture" (1971g, 79).

Realism and formalism, phenomenology and self-evidence were all in play here, as they were in minimalist art-world discourse. Farber had, of course, put his own inimitable spin on the approach, carving out a singular niche in film criticism of the period. It is crucial, however, that we realize how flexible the new stance enabled him to be: *The End of Summer* (1961), *The Damned* (1969), *Au hasard Balthasar* (1966), and *Charlie Bubbles* (1968) may not in the end have been equally good, but they could all be shown to be equally fascinating, handling the physicality of space and performance in varied and often perverse ways. Termites were still very much on the loose here—where the film failed, a lingering camera or an arresting actor could still provide spellbinding moments. George Segal's "slurring ability to swim in abasement" (1970c, 87) could make *Loving* engrossing, while Liv Ullmann opened up Bergman's otherwise unbearable *Hour of the Wolf* "like a sharp knife going through old cheese" (1968d, 75).

The emphasis Farber placed on the relationship between critical spectator and isolated effect helped to distinguish his approach from the earlier mise-en-scène criticism of *Movie* and the *Cahiers du cinéma*. Even when discussing an auteur, he was careful to emphasize his heightened connoisseurship of distinguishing moments, often those which (happily) eluded the director's control. On the crowded playing field of middle and highbrow film criticism, he established his own curious identity as the nonintellectual intellectual, the gruff, iconoclastic (yet aesthetically hip) highbrow open to all films, but rigorously committed to the integrity of his position.

> Space is the most dramatic stylistic entity—from Giotto to Noland, from *Intolerance* to *Weekend*. How an artist deploys his space, seldom discussed in film criticism but already a tiresome word of the moment in other art, is anathema to newspaper editors, who believe readers die like flies at the sight of esthetic terminology. (1970b, 89)

It was precisely Farber's deployment of such "esthetic terminology" that grounded his continued eclecticism, enabling his best films of 1969 to include Godard's *Le Gai Savoir*, Ken Jacobs's *Tom, Tom, the Piper's Son*, Jean-Marie Straub and Danièle Huillet's *Chronik der Anna Magdalena Bach*, and Sembene's *Black Girl*, but also *The Wild Bunch*, *Easy Rider*, and even *They Shoot Horses, Don't They?* The seeming eccentricity of his method, as manifested in both his passion for physical details and his catholic tastes, had certainly served to distinguish him from the middlebrow pack of pseudointellects who also purported to care for the Art of film. Minimalist phenomenology allowed him to stress his own privileged *experience* of films, and to imply that a similarly cultured response could be learned (in time) by loyal *Artforum* readers. Further, by working such a variety of films of varying quality through the same aesthetic grid, he confirmed his increasing affinity for highbrow camp. While he would never lose his interest in—or respect for—gifted filmmakers, he nonetheless now implied that the source of cinema's value lay at least as much in the transforming perception of the beholder as in the caliber of aesthetic decisions made by the artist. When *Charlie Bubbles*, *Loving*, and *Back and Forth* are all of comparable formal interest, comparative discernment has given way to the critic's creative exploration of a medium.

HAPTIC DISORIENTATION AND THE NEW ACTION FILM

This move from a more film-centered to medium-centered approach is characteristic of the highbrow intellectual retreat from the excesses of popular cultism and camp. If Sarris and Mekas had made the seizing of popular spectatorship easy and accessible, a matter of acquiring a hip taste for movies, vanguard leadership was now being rescued by those with a deeper understanding of the underlying aesthetics of the *cinema*. This is one reason why film theory became highly attractive to American highbrow film critics during this period: as an aesthetic grounded in fundamental attributes of the medium, a film theory naturalizes aesthetic production and response, thus enhancing the highbrow's critical authority over, and distinction from, theoretically ignorant middlebrows. Theory can also be brought in to bolster a vanguard critic's oppositional tastemaking, as Farber had demonstrated in the 1940s, and Sarris in the 1960s. Even Parker Tyler, who had not needed theory per se in the 1940s because his surrealism was such a fully elaborated aesthetic, ended his career with his own modernist "world theory of film" intended to save cinema from realists, McLuhanites, and pop frivolity.[9]

Farber himself was now a little more hesitant about making theoretical claims than he had been in the 1940s; unlike Tyler, he now had no ax to grind, no overriding polemic to support.[10] For younger highbrows jockeying for position as tastemaking critics, however, theory could still be quite useful, making an oppositional aesthetic seem both intellectually sophisticated and culturally legitimate. When Farber's *Artforum* colleague Annette Michelson tackles *2001: A Space Odyssey* (1968), for instance, she sets her own quasi-minimalist interpretation on more clearly theoretical ground. In boldly assailing the "bewildered and apprehensive community (tribe? species?) of critics" who have disparaged Kubrick's film, she suggests that they have indeed missed something big. For here is

10. "Knowledge through perception as action." *2001: A Space Odyssey* (1968).

nothing less than the *ultimate* film—"here is a film like any other, like all others, only more so. . . . If one were concerned with an 'ontology' of cinema, this film would be a place in which to look for it" (1969, 56). *2001*'s slim plot could have thrown only audience members blind to the film's real interest: its formal exploration of cinematic phenomenology, of the "structural potentialities of haptic disorientation as agent of cognition."

> It proposes . . . nothing of more radical interest than its own physicality, its "formal statement" on the nature of movement in its space; it "suggests" nothing so urgent and absorbing as an evidence of the senses, its discourse on knowledge through perception as action, and ultimately, on the nature of the medium as "action film," as mode and model of cognition. (57)

The film medium itself, Michelson argues, characteristically heightens the spectator's "perception of being physical to the level of apperception: one becomes conscious of the modes of consciousness." This in itself makes *2001* a quasi-minimalist work (and hence worth discussing in *Artforum*), but the film actually goes much further, elevating such concerns to the point where it reveals itself to be in some sense essentially cinematic, a work that is fundamentally *about* our experience of film as a medium. For Kubrick's *Space Odyssey* actively solicits,

> in its overwhelming immediacy, the *relocation of the terrain upon which things happen*. And they happen, ultimately, not only on the screen but somewhere between screen and spectator. It is the area defined and constantly traversed by our active restructuring and reconstitution, through an experience of "outer"

space, of the "inner" space of the body. Kubrick's film, its action generating a kind of cross-current of perception and cognitive restructuring, visibly reaches, as it were, for another arena, redefining the content of cinema, its "shape of content." (59)

In appealing to theory, Michelson thus makes Kubrick's film seem rather sophisticated, without pandering to the hip cosmological discourse surrounding the work. Yet in the process, she also raises the vexing problem of agency. Simply put—to what extent is Kubrick still responsible for this film's "shape of content"? By tying *2001*'s phenomenological concerns to its proximity to the essence of the medium, Michelson renders the artist's role somewhat uncertain. Nevertheless, she still dutifully credits the director with the film's "maieutic" obsessions: Kubrick's "imagination, exploring the possibilities of scale, movement, direction as synthesized in a style, works towards our understanding" (61), proposing nothing less than a reenactment of the child's initiation (à la Piaget) into Euclidian Space. It is a little difficult to imagine the film's being conceived this way, though—did Kubrick really design the sequence in which the airline hostess walks upside down and retrieves a floating pen in order to foreground "the corporeal *a-prioris* which compose our sensory motor apparatus" (60)?

The problem is that Michelson has happened upon a vanguard critical strategy without adjusting her own assumptions and methods accordingly. In positing the film as *essentially* cinematic ("here is a film like any other . . . only more so") and the cinematic medium as essentially phenomenological, she has subtly allowed Kubrick's film to be discussed as an artwork, regardless of the auteur's guiding hand. Like Tyler's erotic spectatorship of the 1940s, Michelson's perspective actually eliminates the absolute need for the originating artist as an agent putting aesthetic forces into play; while as an art critic, Michelson may still want to credit the director, as a theorist she has no real need to do so. Her own authority as a highbrow intellectual will suffice.

Vanguard critics have relied on theory to the extent that it can enable aesthetic qualities to be ascribed to potentially any film, by suggesting that the medium itself is rooted in a legitimate aesthetic—be it realist, formalist, phenomenological, or materialist. One can be as choosy as one likes: "classical" film theorists such as Arnheim and Eisenstein had certainly striven to legitimize the cinema as art, but they were modernists with a mission and a canon, and had thus been quite particular as to what films might *count* as valid artworks.[11] Michelson was certainly familiar with classical theory (and especially fond of Eisenstein's phenomenology of cognition, with which she hoped to overturn Bazin's phenomenology of perception),[12] yet as a theoretically inclined critic of the late 1960s, she pursued a mission that was ultimately less driven by modernist aestheticism than by the vanguard ethos of aggressive aesthetic reclamation.[13] She sought not simply to analyze *2001* in highbrow terms but to wrest the film from the clutches of undiscerning middlebrows.

THE APPEAL OF EUROPEAN MATERIALISM

Here, then, was a refined version of vanguard criticism and a modified notion of the highbrow critic-as-artist, scouring the cultural scene for films to aestheticize in an oppositional or innovative manner. Michelson was one of a new breed of American highbrows who seized the opportunity to redistinguish their own elevated discernment by reinventing vanguard reception. Yet as Michelson herself would discover, application of the new minimalist aesthetic would ultimately be inadequate for the job— as minimalism had arisen as an extreme reaction to abstract expressionism, its discourse had been so obscure as to appeal to only a small coterie of art-world aficionados. Who listened to the art world anymore? Stuffy, snobby art critics would never be taken seriously as new vanguard leaders, not when the popular success of the new cultism and camp had made real engagement a benchmark of vanguard success.

If minimalism's stubborn art-world ties limited its suitability as a vehicle for renewed insurgence, a radically politicized version of minimalism would do the trick, enabling American highbrows to reclaim vanguard authority on broader socioaesthetic grounds while providing the cachet of European highbrow authenticity so useful to the American avant-garde in the past. In modifying European materialist film theory into a viable academic discourse, American highbrows would be able to point up the bourgeois complacency of sellout Underground hipsters and silent minimalists alike, while again lending legitimacy to artistic ventures beyond the middlebrow norm. Most important, though, the anti-illusionist materialist aesthetic also cleared the way for the victorious reinstatement of the highbrow critic-as-artist, by justifying the subordination of art making (and the artist proper) to more clearly theoretical work. The politicized French film critics of the late 1960s thoroughly adopted a vanguard agenda, and not simply in resurrecting radical filmmakers of the 1920s: in seeking to reassert their own centrality to political action, they opposed the bourgeois middle by uniting both high and low ends against it, as Dwight Macdonald had earlier advised. They asserted themselves as attuned experts on the film medium, able to discern bourgeois complicity, and the mechanisms of mass oppression, in the form and apparatus of cinema itself. Film's material essences had been disguised under a veil of sweet lies aimed at the proletarian public; an honest, revolutionary cinema, by contrast, would openly flaunt the material means of its own production.

Hence many materialists hoped that the radical filmmaking of like-minded Soviets such as Eisenstein and Vertov might come in handy, providing inspiration and direction for current work. Yet they also quickly realized that the agency of the most committed artist could still prove problematic, blocking (and compromising) the critic's own vanguard agenda. At the newly revamped *Cahiers du cinéma*, for instance, critics interested in resurrecting Eisenstein remained too enveloped within their own modernist biases to put the Soviet filmmaker/theorist's complex films and ideas to much revolutionary use.[14] For this they were roundly chastised by rival journal *Cinéthique*'s Marcelin Pleynet, who suggested that Eisenstein's "huge, and extraordinarily rich body of writing" (1977, 242) had swayed the *Cahiers* toward ahistorical aestheticism and uncritical adulation, whereas the urgency of the times demanded an excoriation of the theorist's Hegelian idealism and bourgeois values. In fact, *Cinéthique* ended up eschewing Eisenstein's work for the narrower materialism of Dziga Vertov—an ardent vanguard polemicist whose focus on the ideological implications of representation itself could also make Brecht's apparatus-centered notions of resistance seem equally relevant to the cause.[15]

Materialist pragmatism placed such a high value on theory's utility because the critic herself was now asserted as a key vanguard agent of aesthetic *and* political change. In this climate, encouraging radical art making proper could seem premature, until the art medium itself had first been reconceived by the vanguard critic attuned to the ideological implications of the artist's very materials. To Jean Thibaudeau's suggestion (*Cinéthique* 3, 1969) that cinema be used radically, as an educational tool to spread class consciousness within French neighborhoods and trade unions, Pleynet responds

> Don't you think that before wondering about "their militant function," filmmakers would do well to look into the ideology produced by the apparatus (the camera) which determines the cinema? The cinematographic apparatus is a strictly ideological apparatus; it disseminates bourgeois ideology before anything else. Before a film is produced, the technical construction of the camera already produces bourgeois ideology. (Quoted in Leblanc 1978, 155)

By this account Godard's *La Chinoise* is no better than a Rohmer film—the former, indeed, is "entirely invested by bourgeois ideology." Because the film camera itself is designed to adhere to principles of quattrocento perspective, it is bound to reproduce "in its full authority the code of specular vision as it was defined by Renaissance humanism." This clearly complicates the role of criticism but also offers the theoretically informed critic a heightened, productive role in relation to cinema. The critic is, indeed, obliged to guide the radical filmmaker whose work becomes an illustration of an ideal more fully worked out on paper. If, as Pleynet insists, "only when a phenomenon of this kind has been thought, only when the determinations of the apparatus (the camera) that structures reality by its inscription have been considered, only then could the cinema objectively examine its relation to ideology" (156), it is clearly the critic/ theorist who is meant to do most of the thinking.

By firmly divorcing theory from any hints of bourgeois modernist aestheticism, the narrower *Cinéthique* stance helped to refine examples provided by the Soviets, surrealists, situationists, and Brecht into an openly politicized vanguard film criticism. Now, aesthetics were supplemented with theories from other fields—Marxism, of course, but also Saussurian linguistics, Althusserian structuralism, and Lacanian psychoanalysis—brought in to help ground and nuance the notion of passive, uncritical spectatorship. But at heart the larger project was still fundamentally aesthetic, rooted in the same assumption that informed Dziga Vertov's talk of "film-vodka" and Tyler's discussion of the hypnotic "daylight dream"—that aesthetically retrograde mass culture could be substantially overhauled by the vanguard intellectual's seized spectatorship.

What had initially been a critical option could, however, now be elevated to a political imperative. Given the complicity of the apparatus itself, common commercial movies were as aesthetically interesting as art films. They were certainly more *important* than art films, given their heightened role in spreading dominant ideology. American middlebrow directors such as Hitchcock and Welles could be rescued for vanguard interest by being lumped with the fascinating lowbrows (Hawks, Ford) who toiled within—but perhaps secretly resisted—the Hollywood system. But again, their actual agency as film directors was no longer really needed. Knowledge of their achievements may still have afforded some cult distinction left over from the heyday of auteurism, but their presence kept interfering with the real job at hand—as in the *Cahiers du cinéma*'s landmark analysis of "John Ford's *Young Mr. Lincoln*," where the authors visibly squirm as they try valiantly to credit some of the film's subversive radicalism to an old master.

The real job at hand was, as usual, to reconstruct an aesthetic cinema out of cultural detritus—and here, too, many artists can spoil the fun. If, as Barthes would suggest, the author had drowned in discourse, camp criticism of movies had assumed this for years, picking effectively anonymous texts to open up, revealing a wealth of aesthetic complexity lurking within.[16] Not surprisingly, the specific nature of this complexity typically conformed less to the filmmaker's designs than to the critic's own aesthetic ideals: the symbolic and metaphoric richness that Tyler exposed in the likes of *The Brave Little Tailor*, *Mildred Pierce*, and *Gung Ho!* did not simply elevate these movies above the middlebrow tripe passing for hep art but allied them implicitly with Ernst's *Robing of the Bride*, Cocteau's *Blood of a Poet*, and Deren's *Meshes of the Afternoon*. The new European materialists were thoroughly politicized, but they were also camp critics steeped in the very aesthetic conventions of a middlebrow art cinema they sought to supplant. Is it any wonder they would find in films like *Young Mr. Lincoln* (1939) and *The Big Sleep* (1946) enough symbolic excesses and formal intricacy to make even these humble, authentic artifacts seem as rich as—and more politically relevant than—the humanistic masterpieces of Bergman and Fellini?[17]

Indeed, the ability to downplay those self-conscious film artists who had moved from highbrow to middlebrow in the previous decade was quite advantageous for this newly politicized avant-garde. First, it allowed critics to distance themselves from the depoliticized traditions of the past—especially *Cahiers* auteurism of the 1950s and early 1960s, which had favored arty Europeans as much as Hollywood mavericks. In addition, subordinating those filmmakers who liked to load their films with intellectual meanings also helped to allow critics themselves to become camp producers/liberators of those meanings, by focusing on films in which intellectual complexity had to be mined from the murky substrata whence it mesmerized the casual spectator.

Marginal and vanguard film artists fared better, but their authority too was tightly contained by the new approach—here, by its not letting them say very much. If a truly radical film practice could only follow prior radical theoretical practice (as Pleynet had suggested), the independent filmmaker would of necessity assume a fundamentally secondary role, implementing plans carefully devised by the critic. When regarded strictly as engaged materialist praxis, radical filmmaking could seem only ill-equipped and limited, hardly as rich or provocative as the critical-theoretical work that inspired and paralleled it. The aestheticized popular text's psychoanalytic substrata, formal patterns of dominance/submission, and deployment of the "suture" and/or male gaze could reveal it to be rich, ambiguous, and multifaceted, even appreciated in different ways by the popular and the highbrow spectator. The materialist vanguard film, by comparison, was designed to be a flat illustration; if it showed what an ideal, postrevolutionary cinema might look like, it also offered the critic little to discuss that had not been more eloquently set out in theory itself.

This is why American minimalist filmmaking provided an inadequate model for materialist film practice. Spare, rough, antinarrative, with a strong emphasis on the medium itself, Snow's *Wavelength* might have seemed radical enough at first glance,[18] but in the end it simply proved too autonomous, too beholden to modernist assumptions of artistic expression and contained form. Britain's alternative was the politicized, reflexive "structural/materialist" cinema of Malcolm LeGrice, Peter Gidal, and David Crosswaite. Advocating "form *as* content," these filmmakers (following Pleynet) found even Godard and Straub-Huillet too conventional and too elaborate for their tastes. The structural/materialists had been highly influenced by the Brechtian/Vertovian anti-illusionism favored at *Studio International* and especially *Screen*, which had reprinted many *Cinéthique* pieces in translation; they saw their work not simply as radicalized film practice but as a new moment in vanguard cinema, a return of sorts to the glories of 1920s abstractionism and a dialectical leap forward from the self-absorbed, artist-centered mysticism of the American Underground. For LeGrice, the cinema of cosmic abstractionist Jordan Belson epitomized the worst excesses of decadent formalism, veering dangerously away from the essential nature and purpose of his material.

> The language of the modern art tradition to which he relates is one which is based on the physical and existential. This relates to a philosophy which since Hegel has increasingly banished transcendental concepts and other-worldly religious heavens, seeing life and experience as, however varied in state, essentially finite and physical. Belson's work seems an attempt to reinstate the transcendental, a purpose at odds with the concrete basis of the aesthetic tradition to which he belongs. (LeGrice 1977, 84)

Like the other Underground filmmakers, Belson offered only a pernicious, false radicalism that seemed to be oppositional but ultimately bolstered the illusion of an autonomous, self-directed (and not materially contingent) subject as subtly as any mass text.

Even more troubling, however, was that Belson—like his middlebrow brethren Antonioni and Fellini—also claimed to be an autonomous *artist*. This was actually a bigger problem, because it challenged the new vanguard notion that filmmaking should be subordinate to (and an illustration of) critical practice. Structural/materialism's new moment of the avant-garde was one in which the nontheoretical artist was scorned, and the theoretical artist knew her place. Indeed, the new materialist aesthetic was so explicitly *critical* (of dominant social and aesthetic codes) that it was able to elevate the authority of the cultural critic over that of the artist (radical or otherwise) in a manner compatible with the American vanguard criticism we have already examined. No wonder the materialist example offered hope to American highbrows seeking to reassert their vanguard credentials.

In America, as we have seen, the highbrow film avant-garde's proximity to the art world had given rise to a particular dynamic, a complex set of relationships—between filmmaking and criticism, engagement and removal, cultism/camp and more "objective" discernment—through which this avant-garde negotiated its place in postwar culture. The importation of the materialist aesthetic in the late 1960s simplified things considerably, asserting highbrow vanguard criticism's dominance over film and art making through a set of political imperatives. Identifying America's preminimalist experimental cinema with autonomous, decadent modernism and suggesting a model of vanguard practice that required a knowledge of materialist aesthetics and pertinent social theory, the new approach would make the avant-garde seem more relevant than ever while decisively removing it from the reactionary grip of New York's insular art world.

A (Brief) Reprieve for the Film Artist

The avant-garde's liberation from the art world also helped to squelch, or at least muffle, highbrow critical support for autonomous artist-filmmakers. For American highbrows with strong allegiances to the art world, embracing materialism might thus prove rather difficult, as it entailed acceptance of the artist's new subservience to theory. Here again, Annette Michelson provides us with a particularly fruitful example of a critic with divided loyalties to two opposing, and finally incompatible, notions of artistic cinema: that she found it difficult to resolve the tensions between them actually makes her critical writing of the late 1960s and 1970s worth examining in a little more detail. In briefly sketching her development as a critic, we can highlight not simply the attractions of the new vanguard approach but also its considerable implications for our understanding of the relationship between critic and artist.

Already in 1966, the Sorbonne-educated Michelson had (within the pages of *Film Culture* no less) boldly critiqued the Anger/Brakhage tradition of American experimentalism along vaguely materialist lines, setting its self-absorption and false moral heroics against the altogether more revolutionary, even utopian modernism of Resnais and Godard. In adapting Hollywood conventions to their advanced film practice, the best contemporary European filmmakers were actually reviving a noble aesthetic tradition that had flourished in early Soviet art and cinema of the 1920s (notably in the work of Eisenstein), only to abandon its "totality of aspiration" under Stalinism. Thenceforth,

> the process of dissociation, the split between formal and political aspects of radical or revolutionary efforts was created, irremediably so—at least through our time. The result was either reaction, or a sublimation of the revolutionary

aspiration into a purely formal radicalism. The vestiges of the politically revolutionary experience and tradition are henceforth expressed in the form of nostalgia and frustration. (1966, 39)

Important, however, is the fact that Michelson does not want to jettison American experimental cinema wholesale, only to redirect attention to its radical potential, in terms of both content and form. Similarly, while she hopes for a new vanguard culture on the Soviet model, she still maintains a high regard for the artist's role within that culture. This profound faith in art making, and artist-centered radicalism, helps to explain Michelson's subsequent lauding of *2001* at *Artforum*: she insisted on embracing film theory only in the broadest sense, rooting her analyses of specific films in larger assumptions about the nature and proclivities of the medium, while trying not to seem tied to a narrow agenda, or indeed to an assumption of artistic subordination. Thus, unlike her British counterparts, she openly acclaimed the sufficiently radical aspirations of American minimalist filmmakers such as Michael Snow. (By 1971, hers would become the critical model most often applied—even by filmmakers—to the works of Michael Snow, Ernie Gehr, and Hollis Frampton.)[19] However, other artistic filmmakers could warrant discussion as well—even the once retrograde Stan Brakhage, whom in January 1973 Michelson audaciously placed alongside Sergei Eisenstein himself for an entire *Artforum* issue:

> One has . . . the sense of these two men as Masters, as artists who invent strategies, vocabularies, syntactical and grammatical forms of film, as men whose innovative functions and special intensity of energy are radical, defining the possibilities of the medium itself for their contemporaries. One sees, as well, that they share a common function, through a conjunction of *praxis* and *theoria*, to define those possibilities and to determine the arenas of discourse and of action. In so doing, they force the very best of their contemporaries to define themselves, in work and discourse, in relation to them. (1973, 30–31)

This gesture was bound to raise eyebrows; doubtless it was meant to. Paul Willemen, writing in Britain's *Studio International*, was frankly outraged: Brakhage wasn't a radical but a reactionary, "enthusiastically acting out the role bourgeois society imposes on anyone who wishes to regard himself as an artist." Michelson's likening of his work to Eisenstein's thus seemed rather expedient, a brazen sidestepping of "a whole series of potentially embarrassing questions" enabling her to "claim that Brakhage's aesthetics developed from Eisenstein's (thus indicating progress), while in fact Brakhage totally embraces a position that Eisenstein was never able completely to shake off (i.e. Brakhage = regression)" (Willemen 1973, 252).

Actually, Willemen's zeal to label *Artforum* retrograde had allowed him to misrepresent Michelson's position, at least as expressed in her own contribution, "Camera Lucida / Camera Obscura." Here she situates Brakhage and Eisenstein at opposite ends of a continuum (and her paradigm) of modernist practice in order to highlight not simply commonalities but also important differences between the two filmmakers. Each is a visionary intellectual who, in the face of repressive authority, had expressed a "will to define his function in the culture of his time" (Michelson 1973, 31). Yet the Soviet's heightened political awareness had also allowed him to develop a fully "externalized" style, which had led to "films conceived as moments in the development of historical consciousness as well as that of filmic consciousness" (33).

Specifically, Eisenstein's most fully realized montage sequences, like Michael Snow's films (and indeed *2001*), invite a reflexive, self-aware perception and cognition through formal manipulation. Sometimes space and time are extended, as when Kerensky ascends the endless staircase in *October* (1928); elsewhere, they are more radically disjointed, as in the same film's "Raising of the Bridge" sequence.

> As action is subjected to the extensive analytic reordering, when a multiplicity of angles and positions of movements and aspects alters the temporal flow of the event and of the surrounding narrative structure, the disjunctive relations of its constituents are proclaimed, soliciting a particular kind of attention, and the making of inferences as to spatial and temporal order, adjustments of perception. (34)

Brakhage's work, on the other hand, though similar in many respects, does not invite the same sort of reflexive perception. His assault on filmic space and time through manipulation of speed, anamorphosis, superimposition, inversion, focus, and leader may mark him as a modernist formal innovator, yet because his art "devours memory and expectation in the presentation of presentness," it refuses classification as Intellectual cinema and effectively renders itself "inaccessible to analysis" (37).

The scant scholarly attention paid to Brakhage's work since 1973—certainly relative to his importance as an American artist—makes Michelson's assessment somewhat prophetic. Because his films belong to an earlier, prepoliticized moment in radical filmmaking, they will clearly not seem illustrative of (or subordinate to) materialist criticism or theory. In fact, they may seem somewhat arrogant, refusing easy incorporation into any broad, encompassing critical grid, demanding precisely what vanguard film criticism increasingly refused to grant—humility in the face of extramaterialist mystery. They simply refuse to be dominated. Instead, they threaten to dominate the critic.

Michelson's tentative gesture of inclusion, then, reflects a critic torn between a politicized European critical agenda and the noteworthy film art of an American Master. If she cannot resolve this tension herself (at least here, in 1973), her colleagues give it their best shot through the rest of the special *Artforum* issue, rescuing Brakhage by bending him ever so slightly toward materialism, and Eisenstein ever so slightly toward mysticism. In "The Third Meaning" (reprinted from the July 1970 *Cahiers*), Roland Barthes posits an indescribable "obtuse meaning" (1973, 47) that exceeds the denotation and political symbolism of Eisenstein's films, suggesting that even a staunch materialist can sometimes seem beyond criticism. For Phoebe Cohen, Brakhage's *Scenes from under Childhood* (1967–70) has its material side, too: the film attempts not simply to depict "the memory process itself, to recreate the moment when the distant past surfaces into consciousness in the present" (1973, 51), but to make the viewer aware, through flicker, of "the sensuous power of pure color appearing by itself on the screen" (51–52). Perhaps most remarkable of all is the final piece, in which Fred Camper attempts to locate in *The Riddle of Lumen* a radically new form of conceptual organization. In this film, he claims, we move from "perceptual connections which unite the images in the mind's eye" toward

> connections which are more abstract, made somewhat outside the space in which the images are perceived, and thus leave the images with a kind of separateness and purity of their own, as we move from a connection based on simple juxtaposition of rectangles made more complex by an additional area of light to a connection which is really something made by the mind rather than the eye. (1973, 69)

Thus if Paul Willemen had exaggerated Michelson's political naïveté, he had accurately gauged the thrust of the *Artforum* issue: Brakhage was being rehabilitated here, clearly. Michelson's bending of her critical approach to the point where it might accept Brakhage may have been intellectually and politically risky, but as we have already seen in the case of Manny Farber, it might also demonstrate the breadth and depth of a highbrow's aesthetic faculties. More important, though, it reveals a critic still stubbornly committed to promoting major American artists, no matter how unfashionable this might seem from the standpoint of the new aesthetic.

As Michelson more fully embraced European materialism, however, the nature of her commitment to American film artists shifted significantly. After 1973, romantic film artists such as Brakhage would find little purchase in her criticism; by 1976, when she cofounded the art/culture journal *October* with Rosalind Krauss and Jeremy Gilbert-Rolfe, her attention had turned resolutely toward materialist praxis, with the filmmaker's assumed function modified accordingly. Her conception of Radical Aspiration was now much narrower than it had been back in 1966, with a film artist's warranting promotion only if clearly attuned to the overarching importance of theory. In choosing to call their journal *October*, Michelson and her coeditors stress they are celebrating not so much a modernist master as "that moment in our century when revolutionary practice, theoretical enquiry and artistic innovation were joined in a manner exemplary and unique."

> This movement, that moment, were memorialized in a work that is itself a celebration of the manner in which aesthetic innovation may be a vector in the process of social change. . . . *October* was the summa of the silent Soviet film, which transformed the nature of an art paradigmatic for our century. It was a penultimate stage in that revolutionary project which was to be modified by the Silence of totalitarian censure and its conscription of Sound. *October* was, as we now know, propadeutic for the realization of Eisenstein's two utopian projects, *Capital* and *Ulysses*, in which the innovations of intellectual montage were to be developed to their fullest dialectical potential. (Gilbert-Rolfe, Krauss, and Michelson 1976, 3)

It is certainly significant here that neither *Capital* nor *Ulysses* was a film. They were *plans* for films that could never be realized, as the radical aspirations of their conceiver had been decisively squashed by the forces of social and aesthetic oppression.[20] At this point, however, theoretical planning was enough. As the central criterion for relevant art making at *October*, it marked the difference between vanguard praxis and modernist autonomy. Hence the film artists favored by Michelson and her fellow editors were, like the Soviet aesthetic radicals (Eisenstein and Vertov, but also Tatlin, Meyerhold, and El Lissitsky), practitioners wise to the value of theory. Theoretical pieces by Hollis Frampton ("Notes on Composing in Film," "Mind over Matter"), John Epstein ("Magnification"), and Pier Paolo Pasolini ("Observations on the Long Take") could now take their place alongside feature scripts by Yvonne Rainer (*Film about a Woman Who . . .* , *Journeys from Berlin/1971* [1980]) and stills from James Benning's *Grand Opera* (1978). Other filmmakers—Maya Deren, Michael Snow, and even select classical Japanese directors—could also be rescued for discussion, but only if revealed to be theoretically minded and politically oriented.[21]

Now it was simply not enough for an artist to be formally radical, or even concerned with reflecting the phenomenology of perception. For instance, Snow's films had long elicited Michelson's interest and support, but to warrant continued attention as a vanguard maverick, he would be refashioned as an artist actively critiquing repressive cinematic codes, and providing ideal models of spectatorial liberation on the European model.

While working within the "scopophilic and fetishistic" (1979, 115) tradition of the American avant-garde,[22] Snow is now seen to reject Brakhage's "hallucinated gaze," but also the equally transcendental "cognitive" gaze (116) of the late-1960s avant-garde (exemplified here by Ken Jacobs's *Tom, Tom, the Piper's Son* [1970]), for something altogether more progressive, and subversive.

In retrospect, Michelson surmises, *Wavelength* had been such a hit (even winning over the regressive Manny Farber) because it *appeared* to offer spectators a resounding confirmation of their transcendental subjectivity through its foregrounding of Renaissance perspective. (Here Michelson liberally quotes Jean-Louis Baudry, but we may recall that Pleynet too had made a similar argument in 1969.) However, Snow's film was hardly as ideologically complicit as it seemed; for this artist

> was not content to reestablish "the referential norm"; he subjected it—and in this he is, indeed, the follower of Cézanne he claims to be—to constant analytic transformation. Thus the slight, constant movement of the camera within its sustained propulsion forward, the light flares and filters which punctuate that movement, the changes of stock and the final shot which intensifies, in superimposition, the flatness of the photograph on which the camera comes to rest. The depth and integrity of the perspective construction is at every point subjected to the questioning and qualification imposed by the deployment of anomalies as differences within the spatiotemporal continuum. (118)

Snow's *The Central Region* (1971)—in which the artist set up a programmed gyroscopic camera on the Canadian tundra—goes even further, not simply critiquing the disembodied, all-powerful eye of dominant cinema's transcendental subject, but also revealing Snow's relevance to later European film theory. In asserting the spectator's union with the camera itself (Snow: "The film seems to come from the machine towards the spectator. . . . Here, it is as if you were the cameraman"), the filmmaker has in effect presented an intensification of "what Christian Metz has described as the primary cinematic voyeurism, unauthorized, and reenacted, through framing, as a direct recapitulation of the child's vision of the primal scene" (123).

Through criticism, the film has again become an illustration of theory—not quite a piece of theory in its own right, but an artwork whose integrity becomes identified with its manifestation of particular theoretical precepts. True enough, Michelson is not really engaging in *classic* camp criticism here; unlike many of her highbrow compeers, she still clings to a notion of the special talents of film artists and refuses to treat *Wavelength* and *The Central Region* with the mixture of populist affection and highbrow disdain that had marked camp's seized spectatorship since Tyler's Hollywood hallucinations of the 1940s. Yet she is still clearly trans-

11. Analytic transformation of the referential norm. *Wavelength* (Michael Snow, 1967). Courtesy of Anthology Film Archives.

forming Snow's films so that they may conform with the theoretical sophistication demanded by the now-dominant aesthetic. If "anything" will suit camp's purpose, vanguard treatment, it seems, can now be applied even to radical modernism—at once subordinating the artist to theory while (ironically) rescuing for him *some* kind of role, however diminished, within film art.

THE AVANT-GARDE IN THE ACADEMY

The avant-garde's training of cultured spectators had indeed become institutionalized by the mid-1970s, when vanguard intellectuals found themselves teaching at American universities. (Michelson's own long-standing affiliation with New York University had begun years earlier; Manny Farber began teaching at UC San Diego in 1970.) Now they might finally have isolated themselves from the rival popular avant-garde of *Harold and Maude* and *El Topo*, but even in college hallways they still encountered remnants of the middlebrow pseudo-avant-garde they had tried so hard to distance themselves from, in the form of groovy English professors who had dared to pepper their curricula with liberal shakes of Fellini, Bergman, and Welles. In response, vanguard intellectuals continued to pursue their own resistant course, showing students how to empower themselves as critical, resistant spectators. Magazines and journals had allowed them to do this by example, but now in the classroom, elements of the critical process—movies, pieces of criticism and especially theory—could be displayed and discussed outright, made available to individuals who might not otherwise have been aware of, or receptive to, the avant-garde's agenda.

In entering the academy, the avant-garde would also resoundingly win its battle for autonomy within American highbrow art. But as we have seen, it did so largely by resolutely seizing its own power to define art—specifically, film art—on its own terms. Happening upon a cultural form that seemed artistically barren, the American avant-garde used the movies to showcase a new art of creative spectatorship, one able to revision the people's cultural detritus as aesthetically rich, and certainly more valuable and interesting than the commodified kitsch passed off on unsuspecting middlebrows. Defined in opposition to popular notions of art making and artists, this new art was progressive insofar as it sought to put resistant artistic power back in the hands of the public, encouraging consumers to refuse what they were being fed and instead create something new—new art, new canons—out of the materials at hand. But in its assumption of a Wildean elite whose function it was to provide instruction (by example, or literally in the classroom) in the means of creative resistance to mass culture, it revealed its true roots within highbrow aesthetics.

The highbrow intellectual avant-garde of the 1970s and 1980s sought to efface those roots completely; borrowing from Europe a radical materialist aesthetic that itself denied all ties to traditional autonomous art, it was finally able to reject American modernism, even traces of Underground excess, and assume the mantle of authentic vanguard production.[23] In rejecting modernist autonomy, however, it repudiated not simply the middlebrow canon of Great Works but also many basic assumptions that most other fine-art studies continued to hold about the value and function of artists and artworks within their fields. The submovements that have driven academic film criticism since the 1970s—structuralism, poststructuralism, psychoanalysis, postmodernism, cultural studies, even cognitive narratology—have not simply directed focus away from traditional artist studies, aesthetic analysis, and canon review; they have made these activities seem naive and retrograde. Instead, these otherwise disparate approaches all offer their own parallel visions of the active, productive spectator, often set against (straw) bogeymen of past subjugations.

As Parker Tyler's erotic spectatorship had implicitly offered an alternative to the worker's passive "daylight dream," so European materialists positioned their liberated spectators against the hypnotic passivity imposed by Hollywood deception and/or the ideologically complicit apparatus itself. Thus the *Cahiers*'s analysis of *Young Mr. Lincoln* explicitly countered Hollywood's hypnotic ideological project, Colin MacCabe's "Realism and the Cinema: Notes on Some Brechtian Theses" exposed the deceptive "classic realist text" (MacCabe 1974), and Laura Mulvey's discussion of visual pleasure (Mulvey 1975) sought to unearth the masculine subjectivity at the core of dominant narrative address. Yet in their own way, the revisionist positions that have appeared in materialism's wake have largely followed suit, only replacing passive spectators with intellectual models of passive spectatorship in order to continue to offer more liberated visions of viewer activity. After attacking MacCabe's simplistic, illusionistic notion of filmic narration, David Bordwell quickly offers his own notion of the active, cognitive spectator: a film "does not 'position' anybody" but rather "cues the spectator to execute a definable variety of *operations*" (1985, 29). Cultural theorist John Fiske rejects the Althusserian model of ideological dominance but then constructs his own theory of "excorporation" ("the process by which the subordinate make their own culture out of the resources and commodities provided by the dominant system" [1989, 15]). Jim Collins demolishes a monolithic, modernist notion of culture as Grand Hotel (as a "totalizable system that somehow orchestrates all cultural production and reception according to one master system" [1989, xiii]), erecting in its place a more modest but also more empowering culture of decentered environments, destabilized discourses, and dispersed audiences.

The theoretical obsession with empowered reception has helped to shift the locus of academic highbrow criticism decisively away from the value of the artist's forms, ideas, and intents. The sender-receiver model of communication—one that matches middlebrow assumptions about artistic effect—has been thoroughly discredited, replaced with a vision of the triumphant creative receiver. The sender, for her part, has been put in shackles or run out of town. However, highbrows have really not abandoned the art of film, or even valuative judgment. (By rejecting "autonomous" aesthetics, the highbrow academic can pretend to leave Art to middlebrow buff magazines such as *Film Comment* and *Sight and Sound*.) Still, the terms of aesthetic discussion have certainly changed: for highbrows, the art of film now lies largely in the art of seized spectatorship, and the evaluation/canonization of texts is now based on the text's suitability as illustration for theories of spectatorial power (either as object of creative resistance/dominance, or model of an empowering cinema).

THE REWARDS OF PROGRESS

If I am less interested, finally, in the strengths and weaknesses of various academic theories of cinematic spectatorship than in the aesthetic/vanguard contexts from which this tendency arose, it is because I merely wish to point out that criticism does not exist in a social or ideological vacuum. Critical approaches are not self-evidently correct; because they are necessarily guided by self-interest, the "road not taken" is not necessarily the wrong path. The avant-garde itself is not, of course, ideologically neutral—it is imbued with ideology. For instance, as Hadjinicolaou (1982) points out, it is driven by the ideological notion of social and aesthetic progress, as manifested in a linear, determinist, evolutionist/revolutionist conception of history, whose movements are to be anticipated by the unique, progressive artworks produced by an aesthetic elite.

Since the 1940s, vanguard American film criticism has similarly been driven by "progress": progress beyond modernist autonomy, beyond traditional notions of aesthetic spectatorship, beyond accepted roles for criticism, beyond the stifling dead end of middlebrow art. Many film (and now, television) scholars like to think of their field as progressive, too, a hotbed of activity in advance of both social progress and the comparatively traditional, even antiquated perspectives of neighboring fields in humanities, arts, and social sciences. Those English professors with middlebrow tastes for Bergman and Fellini were left behind by the academic field that developed beside them, insofar as they conceived the role of criticism itself in ways incompatible with the vanguard agenda. The quasi-middlebrow approach we have associated with Tyler's humanist art-cinema bias of the 1950s and 1960s consistently deferred to artistic authority, allowing the aesthetic text to be intellectually rich, even mysterious, and the artist to have the upper hand in her relationship with the critic. Tyler assumed that the critic might lead us toward the work, but that he could never assume to master it—if it could be so mastered, it would hardly warrant discussion in the first place.

Camp had no need for the artist; cultism had reduced her to a signpost in a larger cultural terrain to be conquered for creative criticism. All along, the vanguard critic had rejected discernment of aesthetic cinematic works as a reasonable path, because his aims were more pragmatic. Movies weren't artworks, anyway—and thank goodness, because that freed the critic to lend the authentic/popular film the aesthetic integrity, even fashionable aesthetics, of the recognized artwork. Farber and Tyler had sought gripping vitality and complex surrealist symbolism in routine entertainments, because both critics were at war with the middlebrow tide that appeared to be sucking the energy and depth from American modernism. European and American materialists sought symbolic and formal richness in popular movies when the middlebrow excesses of art filmmakers and pop camp/cultists alike had threatened to close off cinema for highbrow appreciation; they contained the threat of artistic filmmaking by favoring a radical antimiddlebrow notion of art cinema as anonymous model assembly.

In seizing the right to be artists too, vanguard critics—and those of us who have learned from them—have substantially stifled the authority of artistic films and film artists. In their reluctance to position themselves as traditional artistic spectators, highbrows find themselves increasingly unwilling to make aesthetic judgment calls based on anything other than transmutational utility. And with postmodernism and cultural studies, popular vanguard strategies have been reabsorbed together under the academic vanguard umbrella, with the popular utility of an-aesthetic texts asserted as the proper focus of criticism—because no other types of texts or spectatorship seem relevant. While pretending to drop aesthetics entirely, highbrows have now located aesthetic value so far afield from a discernible, integral artwork that both artist and work are in effect rendered peripheral, relics from another, simpler age.

These developments have profound implications—obviously for the study of film, but also for the analysis of artistic culture, and more generally for the role of highbrow discourse in our society. I hope to have raised such concerns implicitly throughout this book, but now I shall address them directly.

Conclusion

Love, Death, and the Limits of Artistic Criticism

> One of the most tangible, if dubious, myths of the century is
> that the movies are a mass art—i.e., as both art and commod-
> ity, "the movies belong to everybody". . . . As epidemically
> oppressive this idea is mainly responsible for the severe lag of
> film criticism as a respectable and effective entity. For serious
> critics, the movies function on the one hand as a set of sym-
> bolic texts for socio-psychological-mythical interpretation
> with aesthetic overtones, and on the other as a supposed labo-
> ratory where it is possible to show the Film has inexhaustible
> ways to produce what theoretically has every right to be
> termed "art," but which *is* art only because it must be in
> order to save "everybody's" face.
>
> *(Parker Tyler)*

INDUSTRIAL and ephemeral, craft and commodity, the movies are
a mess of contradictions. This is precisely what has made them so
interesting, but also so problematic—at least from the vantage point
of aesthetic discernment and analysis. In a sense, we have considered the
movies a "mass art" by default: they are part of mass culture, and we
have wanted desperately to treat them as artworks. The means we have
devised for doing so evince this desperation—and the highbrow anxieties
that spawn it—by brazenly overturning middlebrow hierarchies and unearthing symbolic richness in the most ordinary films. Today's highbrow
film critic does not presume to evaluate; he merely explicates and interprets. He does not put down movies; he recognizes and respects their
hermeneutic complexity and aesthetic legitimacy.

He may also assume—rightly or wrongly—that sober discrimination is
simply not appropriate for movies, because it would decimate the field
and leave him with little to discuss. Indeed, the influential critical traditions we have examined in this book can take movies "seriously" only
after they have been dismissed as autonomous works in their own right,
through the relocation of the site of aesthetic production to the mind of
the critical spectator. The serious critic can now assume difficult judgment
questions to be "beside the point," best left for those common journalists
still beholden to readers who insist on getting their money's worth. Van-

guard criticism does not allow the bar to be lowered so much as thrown away—or, rather, disavowed—by those who have cultivated a preference for the aesthetically incomplete, fractured, uncontrolled. Cultism, after all, makes a virtue of ordinariness, camp of obviousness; both approaches are meant to maximize the value and interest of naive art, not to reward skilled artists whose work offers the critic the threat of competition.

Vanguard film criticism has always pitched itself against the very possibility of popular movie art, assuming that Hollywood's "centrifugal collective" militates against formal unity and integrity, and that business interests, marketing campaigns, and popular fashion foreclose any real possibility of judicious gatekeeping within the commercial realm. Collapsing issues of value into issues of utility has allowed highbrows to avoid embarrassing forays into middlebrow turf by radically reclaiming the popular field for themselves, as raw material to be remade into something more interesting, and more personal. Seized spectatorship becomes a means to an end, a manner by which individuals can stake a claim to artistic authority within a commodified cultural marketplace; when we reconstruct the culture that constructs us, we hope to transcend consumption by aestheticizing it. Those dim middlebrows who still refuse to see any conflict between commodification and aesthetics may have given Andy Lloyd Webber his knighthood, but they are the hidden pariahs of our increasingly vanguard culture, derided equally for their weakness in the face of faux art and for their apparent inability to master the empowering artistic gesture.

The sheltered highbrows who have not yet bought the vanguard platform—still preferring dusty libraries to pop pleasures—fare only marginally better. At best they are offered the fate of hoary British writer Giles De'Ath (pun intended) in Richard Kwietniowski's 1996 film *Love and Death on Long Island*. A sort of postmodern Kaspar Hauser–meets–Gustave von Aschenbach, De'Ath (John Hurt) has lived his repressed existence in dark, stuffy studies and gentlemen's clubs, quite unaware of the outside world of faxes, car alarms, boxed milk, and cheeseburgers. But when he accidentally wanders into the wrong multiplex theater and encounters not "E. M. Forster's *Eternal Moment*" but Huck Murphy's *Hotpants College II*, he is instantly smitten with the sublime image of teen heartthrob Ronnie Bostock (Jason Priestley), and his life changes forever. Suddenly overcome with cultist hysteria, he enters the world of consumerist fandom, buying a television and VCR in order to lovingly scan Ronnie's visage in the likes of *Skid Marks* and *Tex Mex*, and scouring *Sugar* magazine for "Bostie"'s pop tastes (he likes pizza, Reeboks, and Axl Rose).

Hardly content merely to fetishize termites from afar, however, De'Ath actually journeys to America to meet Bostie in person. Here the film takes a decidedly optimistic, postmodern turn, suggesting that while Giles's actual courting of Ronnie may be ill-advised, even pathetic, the metaphoric cultural cross-pollination implied by their brief friendship can only benefit all concerned. Giles is literally rejuvenated by the vitality of pop culture (as he moves from the dark, enclosed interiors of London to the open vistas of the Long Island shore), while Ronnie is able to elevate the level of his work by sneaking Walt Whitman into a burial scene in *Hotpants College III*. The film's final handshake—a symbolic flashback to Giles and Ronnie's first meeting—recalls nothing so much as the end of Fritz Lang's *Metropolis*, with the aligning of high and low, head and heart, suggesting a bright future for the unified culture of the (no longer quite so) "new sensibility."

In this bright future, cultural liberation can be seen only in a wholly positive light, as an expression of personal (even sexual) liberation. Hence the middlebrows whom cultists typically define their taste *against* simply do not exist in *Love and Death*'s diegetic world, because to acknowledge their presence would necessitate questioning the larger ideology of emancipation upon which the film, and postmodern culture, rely so heavily. It is enough for Giles—the caricatured Arnoldian highbrow—simply to let his hair down, to relax and enjoy himself, to admit that cheeseburgers and pizza are tasty indeed, and that trashy teenpix offer valuable aesthetic experiences in their own right. His increasingly inclusionary, nonjudgmental critical perspective becomes a direct manifestation of a personal growth and renewed vitality with which we *must* empathize, if we are not to feel decidedly misanthropic.

Such are the values of our postmodern/vanguard culture, with its encompassing ethos of democratized artistry and empowered consumerism. The fruits of seized spectatorship lie all around us—in video cultism, comic book subcultures, independent music scenes/zines, sound sampling, channel and Internet surfing, interactive media, memorabilia collection, retro styles, even the Spice Girls. Within such a climate academic critics might seem a trifle superfluous (having successfully shown others the way), but the explosion of "cultural studies" in the 1980s and 1990s reveals that academics have worked hard to demonstrate their continued relevance by sharpening their own analyses of the resistant seizing of popular culture. In the process, scholars such as Lawrence Grossberg, George Lipsitz, Angela McRobbie, Peter Stallybrass, and Sarah Thornton have certainly pursued approaches far removed from those of the materialists, emphasizing careful sociopolitical analysis over camp interpretation and replacing mesmerized zombies with conscious, active spectators. But in continuing to focus on what Grossberg (1997) calls "the empowerment of everyday life," many continue to see the academic highbrow's role as that of the disenfranchised lowbrow's advocate and ally. Cultural studies' nagging populism (Gitlin 1997, McGuigan 1992) belies its underlying debt to the vanguard tradition of Meyer Levin and Otis Ferguson; if we now see less of a desire among highbrows to *make* art out of the people's culture, it is because they are more inclined to believe in the ability of people to create their own resistant art (meaningful culture) out of the materials at hand. In the end, highbrow interest in pop culture is still very much driven by the vanguard fascination with microlevel resistance to perceived high and middlebrow hegemony, which the academic now reveals not simply in subversive psychoanalytic and poststructuralist readings of popular texts but in discussions of postcolonial auteurs, *Star Trek* fans, mosh pits, body piercing, porno arcades, and cyber-liberation.[1]

Vanguard ideals have in fact been so profoundly influential within both popular and academic spheres as to have definitively transformed the way we think about art. In providing a means by which to appreciate mass culture, vanguard critics such as Manny Farber and Parker Tyler enabled us to reconcile our affection for movies, television, and consumerism with our regard for the authority of high culture precepts. In mocking or reversing normative middlebrow taste distinctions, they opened hitherto discarded artifacts for serious consideration and minute analysis. Challenging the notion that aesthetic value is fixed and inherent, they suggested quite the opposite—that it is variable, contextual, even spectator-centered. Here they were fulfilling the vanguard agenda, reclaiming art as a pragmatic, transformative activity. Art was something you as a modern spectator did with the world around you; the artwork might look like nonart at first glance, but that was only because its underlying aesthetic qualities had not been revealed. (To borrow the terms of Nelson Goodman [1978], the question "What is art?" could now become "*When* is art?") These pioneering film critics thus provided crucial models through which the disempowered might be emancipated from the tyranny of commercial and establishment aesthetics, and admitted into the world of personal, gestural art making.

If these models have given us innovative and frequently fascinating perspectives on movies, it is because they were designed to bring movies in line with familiar norms of aesthetic interest and value. The admirable "artistry" of Farber and Tyler's cultist/camp criticism betrays an underlying commitment to such norms, and to related ideologies. Both critics, we must remember, wielded their resistant affection for pop culture as a gesture of opposition to the encroachment of unauthentic commercial/middlebrow art, including marketable film art. Their apparent populism helped to obscure the fact that they were actually trying to advance a *rival* notion of "popular art," turning to movies for misshapen material through which to reassert their own creativity while keeping the riffraff at bay.

Their remarkable success here, however, unwittingly exposed troubling contradictions at the heart of vanguard ideology: by allowing others to simplify these procedures for the resistant fringes of the middlebrow public, they fulfilled the avant-garde's agenda yet compromised its staunch marginality. For while the avant-gardist may cherish the *idea* of popular aesthetic emancipation, in practice such emancipation will only leave him behind. He thus remains doomed to respond to his own success by retreating into obscurity and complaining of co-optation. Indeed, the counterculture's own promotion of cultism and camp was soon met with a spirited remystification of vanguard activity by highbrow intellectuals intent on subsuming the difficult new aesthetics of minimalism and European materialism within methodologies marginal enough to shake free all fashionable hangers-on. From the sanctity of the academy and art world, the highbrow avant-garde would now be able to reappropriate more popular vanguard activities through theory, recasting them as postmodern and deconstructive while officially entrenching modernism's reputation as autonomous and retrograde.[2]

Cultism and camp are fundamentally aesthetic procedures steeped in highbrow taste, and directed toward the assertion of highbrow distinction—by highbrows themselves, or by those who wish to appropriate such distinction within the middlebrow arena. Yet what makes them somewhat problematic, ultimately, is that as *vanguard* procedures, they carefully veil their aesthetic biases behind an overriding pragmatism and seek to naturalize contextual aesthetic value in the elevated sensibilities of the vanguard critic. The critic's own tastes—for surrealist symbolism, abstractionist vitality, minimalist/materialist self-evidence—are not questioned but assumed to be inherently justified and above all useful for getting to the job of artistic reconstitution. Unlike critics of inherent aesthetic value, who at least must confront and gauge the aesthetic assumptions of artists under scrutiny, vanguard critics draw on—but rarely question—their own aesthetic biases, which are used to help create the value of the objects they appropriate. When Manny Farber says he "can't see any difference between writing about a porno movie and an Academy Award movie" because "both are difficult objects" (in Thompson 1977, 44), he is almost certainly going to keep the *terms* of that aesthetic difficulty closely guarded, so as to highlight his own talent in spotting/producing it at various points in the cultural spectrum. But this also allows him to evade critical strategies employed to analyze and evaluate gestural artistic expression in traditional media—even in his own paintings. In short, the liberated spectator's integration of artist and critic functions has allowed him to create within aesthetic norms but also within a vacuum of judgment, while using cinema (or any mass cultural product) in order to reassert his own artistic autonomy as an end in itself.

Middlebrow culture has been so intensely feared by the avant-garde precisely because it raises the specter of inherent aesthetic value successfully marketed to the masses and therefore threatens the critic's prized authority and creativity. Granted, the culture industries themselves are not reliable arbiters of inherent value and can only hope to ensure a film's lasting cultural impact contextually, through hype and appeals to nostalgia. (*Don't you remember how great this movie seemed when you were sixteen?*) But the avant-garde's own attempt to make movies "last" by empowering spectators to seize such cultural authority for themselves is equally flawed, as it typically sidesteps the question of inherent value altogether without necessarily escaping the reach of market influence. (The cultist says, *Gosh, I remember how great this movie seemed when I was sixteen!*) In fact, both studios and vanguard critics recast cinematic value as contextual because both seek only to maximize the movies' utility: if the studio cloaks a bad film in the energy and splendor of a marketing campaign, the critic shrouds it in an oppositional or ironic perspective designed to make a virtue of its limitations.

Popular movies make terrific vanguard material because most can be assumed to be without much inherent value in the first place; this is why more difficult, seemingly autonomous films have always posed a problem for cultist/camp use. Farber, we may recall, rejected the American experimentalists of the 1940s outright. Sarris's auteur theory may have pretended to favor inherent value by rescuing the unheralded artists in our midst, but the true value of these artists' works could be activated only by a critic able to see each auteur film within the broader context of an oeuvre, and within the restrictive context of studio pressures. Parker Tyler's own exploration of inherent value in the 1950s and 1960s put him on a collision course with a camp avant-garde that itself encouraged haphazard, trashy, technically sloppy Underground films. Even the materialist critics of the 1970s and 1980s made sure radical filmmaking was safely subordinated to the terms of critical/theoretical praxis. If we now assume that (as a recent film textbook puts it) "film criticism does not mean criticizing a movie in the sense of pointing out its flaws or failed ambitions," but rather coming to terms with the "multidimensional meanings of a given film" (Prince 1997, 320), it is because we seem far less concerned with a film's fulfillment of aesthetic aims desired by its maker than with the critic's fulfillment of aesthetic aims imposed on the text from without. Because avant-gardism salvages from cultural detritus a gesture of aesthetic insubordination, it can only regard films coded as "artistic" at best with suspicion, and at worst with contempt.

As a result, film criticism's functions and importance have continued to shift dramatically over the past decades, with the notion of highbrow critic as elevated yet accessible connoisseur of film artistry—slogging through new releases in order to highlight the rare gems—in precipitous decline. If the vanguard perspective has enabled us to embrace today's hype-culture (albeit resistantly), it has also made the fierce independence coveted by middlebrow tastemakers of the past (John Simon, Stanley Kauffmann, Pauline Kael, Parker Tyler) seem hopelessly old-fashioned. This is unfortunate, because in retrospect such tastemakers played a crucial role in our culture, articulating models and standards of discernment within a public and popular medium, initiating and developing cultural dialogues on the nature of movie art, and on the values of particular films. In bridging aesthetics and consumerism, highbrow and middlebrow, these critics at least managed to remain open to the expansive field of feature film production while maintaining respect for inherent aesthetic value; in facing the difficult issue of "movie art" head-on, they openly confronted the problem of aesthetic sophistication within an industrial and commercial form.

In refusing to follow suit, the academics who have more or less replaced these connoisseurs as arbiters of highbrow movie art have bolstered their own artistic credibility while leaving middlebrow culture to its own devices. The price paid may be more than we care to admit. We may be faintly amused when a popular cable network labels *Back to the Future*, *A River Runs through It* and *A Fish Called Wanda* "the new classics," and faintly disgusted when the American Film Institute includes *Star Wars*, *E.T.*, *Tootsie*, and *Forrest Gump* (but neither *Greed* nor *Sunrise*) in a 1998 list of the hundred best American films of all time. But our embracing of vanguard ideals has given us sparse means, and little incentive, for earnest dissent. Perhaps these movies *are* Great Works, after all. How would we know otherwise?

In the end, the most unfashionable critical stance examined here—Tyler's quasi-Arnoldian discernment of the 1960s—may warrant careful reassessment at least as much as do the vanguard approaches that have come to dominate film criticism. Tyler's open courting of middlebrow values seems retrograde to us, but his assumed notion of "critical responsibility" was hardly more elitist than our own. Indeed, his insurgence in the 1960s Underground itself reflected not so much bitterness as passionate concern for the fate of his culture, which could not be entrusted to fashionmongers or company men. And while his core aesthetic values—thematic richness, ethical integrity, formal sophistication, spiritual resonance—were certainly ideologically loaded, and not nearly as absolute as he had assumed, they served not to riff on low culture's offerings but to nurture a more sophisticated cinema amid commercial apparatuses indifferent to such matters.

Like his distinguished predecessors—Henry James, Edmund Wilson, Lionel Trilling, Edgar Allan Poe—Tyler was assuming the role of an independent American cultural critic eager to engage aesthetic nuance and value within the larger public sphere, even writing as a highbrow journalist in order to meet middlebrows halfway.[3] Unlike his predecessors, however, he was seeking to advance one of the most public of arts, and one of the most fragile. Cinema's cost, labor-intensiveness, and institutional dependence problematize the completion and distribution of any feature film, let alone a nuanced, unified, and relatively uncompromised work. This may explain the appeal of the vanguard tradition, with its desire to make the artistic best of a tenuous situation, but it should also suggest the dire need for critics able to transcend the reviewer's sorry status of "underpaid cheerleader" for the culture industry (Hoberman 1998, 89) while equally resisting the academic role of vanguard artist-in-residence. Critics are needed, quite simply, to help build and maintain a constituency for film art. Here the Arnoldian ideal of critical disinterestedness—seeing the movie itself as it "really is"—might serve as a useful corrective to the impulse for oppositional fandom, encouraging sensitive response and honest, tough appraisal instead of patronizing affection and relaxed standards.

Contextualizing (and rethinking) their aversion to judicious judgment would afford highbrow film scholars the opportunity to confront some of their prized distinction from middlebrow journalists. More important, it would encourage an acknowledgment and interrogation of those stubbornly modernist aesthetic biases which underlie their appreciation of movies yet also discourage analysis and promotion of elusive and difficult works not illustrative of theory. Vanguard film criticism has undeniably provided receptive highbrows (and, now, many others) an important means of creative enrichment and cultural distinction. But the cost has not been insubstantial: in warping key conceptions of aesthetic value and critic-artist relations, cultism and camp have risked consigning an entire medium to the scrap heap of cultural detritus.[4] In privileging the marginal or derided, in claiming formal or symbolic intricacy where none exists, we prove again and again that we are more inventive and more profound than the guardians of the culture industry, that *we* ultimately exercise (aesthetic) control over the consumption of their trash. But we do so at the expense of engaging the larger possibilities of movie art, and the larger obligations of criticism.

NOTES

CHAPTER ONE
THE SPECTATOR AS CRITIC AS ARTIST

1. A note on terminology: throughout this book, I have endeavored to use "vanguard" as an adjectival form of "avant-garde," which is used as a noun. (Hence I refer to "*vanguard* spectatorship," but to "the *avant-garde* of the 1920s.") Occasionally I also use the word "avant-gardist" as a contraction of "vanguard artist." (Direct quotations, of course, are excepted throughout.)

2. Needless to say, the notion of critic as purveyor of good taste, as a guide to superior works and ideas, finds very few champions. Those who advocate a comparable program (even in calling for the reassertion of a canon of "classic" literary works) have met a distinctly chilly reception, especially within the academic community—witness the controversy surrounding Harold Bloom's recent attacks on the fashions of literary pedagogy, most notably in *The Western Canon* (1994).

3. Indeed, the notion of the active, critical spectator has become so endemic to media criticism that many scholars will doubtless be wondering what all this fuss is about. Film criticism is now so driven toward creative engagement that critical innovations typically pit themselves against insufficiently emancipatory approaches of old. In a recent study of film reception, Janet Staiger clearly distances herself from the auteur tradition of film criticism, insisting that textual meanings neither are "immanent" nor relate to "authorial intention" (1992, 24); yet she does so in order to clear the way for her own notion of active spectators as "complex historical individuals capable of acting within the contradictions of their own construction as selves and as reading selves" (48). Elsewhere, much current work in cultural studies positions its own spectator-activated theories of meaning and pleasure in reaction to text- and apparatus-dominated film theories of the 1970s. When, for instance, Jenkins (1992) avers that ardent fans "actively assert their mastery over the mass-produced texts which provide the raw materials for their own cultural productions and the basis for their social interactions" (23–24), he is seeking to debunk any theory that would deny spectators the ability to "become active participants in the construction and circulation of textual meanings" (24). Yet again the gulf separating Jenkins's approach from the theories of old is largely another rhetorical construct: the theories he wishes to supplant had, crucially, also argued strenuously for liberated spectatorship, though they assumed that liberation was hard-won, achieved through rigorous subversion via the mentor-critic's complex theoretical models.

4. I hope that readers familiar with Ross's *No Respect: Intellectuals and Popular Culture* (1989) will find my own study complementary, and any overlaps productive. Despite rough similarities of terrain (highbrows' use of the "popular" for their own cultural profit), time span, and terminology (camp, middlebrow, avant-garde), Ross is ultimately concerned less with aesthetics or the rescued "art" of pop culture itself than with the ongoing redefinition of American intellectualism in relation to sociopolitical traditions, and to those structures of domination/subordination through which categories of taste become "categories of cultural

power which play upon every suggestive trace of difference in order to tap the sources of indignity, on the one hand, and *hauteur*, on the other" (5). Intellectualism for Ross thus becomes closely tied to *containment*: intellectuals dip into yet contain pop culture, just as intellectuals themselves are contained within the increasingly corporate culture of American "liberal pluralism." By contrast, my own "intellectual history" is much more a history of aesthetic norms and artistic practices, with a focus not on power dynamics separating economic and cultural capital, or intellectual and popular, but on those questions of aesthetic taste, form, and value raised by vanguard criticism.

5. For incisive (though dissenting) discussions of the theory of the avant-garde, see Calinescu (1987, 95–148), Poggioli (1968), and Russell (1985, 3–38). Detailed analysis of prewar vanguard style can be found in Freeman (1989) and Perloff (1986), while the history of these early movements is still best served by Shattuck (1968).

6. As Russell (1985) notes, because antiautonomous avant-gardists are not fully willing to

> give up their presumption that aesthetic behavior is autonomous of the social realm, the formal innovations of avant-garde works can tend to be as self reflexive and idealistic as any of the creations of the modernists. Torn between the conflicting demands of the purely aesthetic and the social in their effort to radically change the form and functions of art in modern culture, the works of avant-garde writers and artists struggle to contain within themselves opposing tendencies and allegiances: between reason and the irrational; revolutionary praxis and utopic desire; present reality and the imagined future; negation and creation. (33–34)

This dual, activist/aestheticist nature of vanguard activity has also made for considerable confusion among historians and critics of the avant-garde, who have found artistic engagement with life praxis difficult to define and interpret within textual form, yet impossible to discuss *without* appealing to form in some way. (An automatically written text is, after all, still a formed "work" as well, as is Duchamp's urinal, which was deliberately chosen and inverted.) Several critics have attempted to avoid the problem—and to rescue the avant-garde's political integrity—by splitting the avant-garde into parallel but occasionally intertwining aestheticist and politicized movements: see Poggioli (1968); Calinescu (1987, 112–16); and Wollen (1982), who makes the argument in relation to avant-garde cinema. Others (Eysteinsson [1990], Karl [1988]) have gone the opposite route, seeking to rehabilitate modernist radicalism by refusing to grant the avant-garde special status at all.

7. More recently, American modernist autonomy has been assaulted by critics eager to clear space for their own culturally engaged, quasi-vanguard notion of *post*modernism. Huyssen (1986), McGowan (1991), and Hutcheon (1988) all downplay American modernism's radical textuality in favor of its perceived hermeticism in order to offer a postmodern alternative that might fulfill the prewar avant-garde's promise of (in Hutcheon's words) a "possible subversion and democratization of high art, of aestheticist hermeticism, and of nostalgia politics." Eager to present postmodernism as a cleaned-up, updated avant-gardism, Hutcheon even claims that postmodernism eschews not simply the avant-garde's revolutionary utopianism but its "focus on the individual subject, personal speech, and

the specific text," qualities that Bürger clearly identifies not with avant-gardism at all but with bourgeois art. Instead, Hutcheon's postmodernism displays "an interest in culture, in collective discourse, and in semiotic codes or aesthetic conventions" (Hutcheon 1988, 218)—all of which are inescapably vanguard traits, as dada collage, constructivist photomontage, and Duchamp's *L.H.O.O.Q.* should remind us.

8. This is at least partly due to Bürger's influence. While he suggests that aestheticism's rejection of the "means-end rationality of the bourgeois everyday" was a key influence on the avant-garde, he insists that aestheticism only "made the distance from the praxis of life the content of works"; it was left for the avant-garde to "organize a new life praxis from a basis in art" (1984, 49).

9. Wilde (through Gilbert) even insists, in a flash of deconstructive proto-poststructuralism, that "there is no such thing as Shakespeare's Hamlet. There are as many Hamlets as there are melancholies" (1981, 94).

10. He lauds decorative art as "the art to live with. . . . Mere color, unspoiled by meaning, and unallied with definite form, can speak to the soul in a thousand different ways" (Wilde 1981, 124).

11. Cultism as I have defined it may seem to some analogous to ardent fandom, as recently examined by scholars such as Jenkins (1992). Certainly there is some crossover here—many ardent fans are cultists, and vice versa. But fans are not true cultists unless they pose their fandom as a *resistant* activity, one that keeps them one step ahead of those forces which would try to market their resistant taste back to them. That such activity has grown enormously since the 1950s is one of the key arguments of this study; when Jenkins dissects the resistant tastes and desires of many *Star Trek* fans, he examines a phenomenon certainly tied to popular spectatorship, but also pushed by the growth of marginal, vanguard behavior into a larger cultural arena.

12. Though it is still quite common to call America's postwar experimental cinema *avant-garde*, I will need to qualify use of this term significantly for this study. Certainly if we define avant-gardism à la Bürger, the films of Stan Brakhage, Maya Deren, Gregory Markopoulos, and even Michael Snow would not seem to qualify—instead seeming far closer to the autonomous modernism Bürger loathes. Perhaps this cinema's peculiar, uneasy relation to both traditional art forms and dominant mass media has encouraged adoption of the more radical "avant-garde" moniker, but the label can be defended only with some difficulty. (A particularly cogent attempt can be found in James [1989].) As I will point out in subsequent chapters, because the work of filmmakers—even marginal, independent filmmakers—can actually challenge the authority of vanguard critics as radical agents, such critics have been careful to qualify their support for this work, subsuming it to a more properly vanguard agenda.

CHAPTER TWO
MOVIES TO THE RESCUE: AMERICAN MODERNISM AND THE
MIDDLEBROW CHALLENGE

1. The same sentiment that gave rise to vanguard film criticism in the 1940s continued to influence the ongoing vanguard critique of postwar art through the 1970s and 1980s. For Cockroft (1974), the movement Irving Sandler had recently

heralded as the "Triumph of American Painting" was instead a CIA-funded "Weapon of the Cold War"; for Shapiro and Shapiro (1985), it served as the "quasi-official art" (144) of the 1950s. Abstract expressionism's nominal radicalism, it is assumed, enabled it to become a boom aesthetic for a boom economy, an apolitical style for a conformist, reactionary climate, and the foundation for the "dead and stuffed" (Bell 1991, 164) official high culture of today.

2. Becker (1982) notes that the opposition between art and craft is never absolute, with different groups designating the same activity as both, and artists acknowledging the importance of craft skill to their work. Nevertheless, the defense of art as nonfunctional, unique, and somehow expressive of the artist's creative gifts implicitly highlights at least its desired transcendence of mere craft.

3. European modernism had certainly played a vital role in the Greenwich Village art scenes of the 1910s and 1920s; Alfred Barr's MOMA staunchly resisted the antimodernist tide of the 1930s by regularly featuring European work in exhibitions such as *Cézanne, Gaugin, Seurat, van Gogh* (1929), *Modern Works of Art* (1934), and *Cubism and Abstract Art* (1936). Many Villagers had been extremely receptive to psychoanalysis and psychoanalytic aesthetics since Macmillan's publication of *On the Interpretation of Dreams* in 1913; in 1937, John Graham would offer his own heavily influential refinement of Freudian and Jungian ideas in his *Systems and Dialectics of Art.*

New York modernism of the 1910s is ably covered by Watson (1991); Ware (1935) remains a useful, fascinating examination of the 1920s scene. MOMA's role in promoting European modernism is treated by Marquis (1989) and the Museum of Modern Art (1984).

4. The enormous impact of the surrealists on the New York art world of the 1940s and 1950s has been more fully covered elsewhere. Most recently, Tashjian (1995) offers an extensive history of surrealist influence, including informative discussions of Parker Tyler's work at *View,* which I have tried not to duplicate here.

5. For many in the New York scene, this new notion of the artist as metaphysical mystic cum social critic would be very appealing, as it offered an alternative not simply to the provincialist's studied craftsmanship but also to the traditional image of the American modernist artist as social sponger or determined elitist.

6. As a result, *transition* pioneered the close, careful analysis of surrealist work and championed the formal linguistic experimentation of others such as Stein and Joyce (whose *Finnegans Wake* was published in installments as "Work in Progress"). Jung, whose writings, far more than those of Freud, favored the role of the poet, became Jolas's favored source and a frequent *transition* contributor. For Jolas, conscious artistry was an essential, if not sufficient, component of aesthetic creation. Ideally the artist would meld the conscious, unconscious, and mythic realms, as in the "paramyth," which he described as "a kind of epic wonder tale giving an organic synthesis of the individual and the universal unconscious, the dream, the daydream, the mystic vision" (quoted in Hoffman, Allen, and Ulrich 1947, 179).

7. No doubt the acceptability of Jolas's views in America was also influenced in no small measure by the changing role of psychoanalysis in modernist literature: by the 1940s the spiritualism and primitivism of D. H. Lawrence, for instance,

had gained favor with members of the *Phoenix* group, which included Derek Savage and Henry Miller.

Miller developed his own variant on Lawrentian aesthetics in 1930s articles such as "The Enormous Womb" (*Booster* 4, no. 21 [1937–38]) where the unconscious becomes melded with the organic/biological and mystical. The analysis of a painting by Hans Reichel prompts Miller—a later *View* contributor—to blend surrealism and romanticism in a manner that presages much of Tyler's subsequent criticism:

> This cosmological eye is sunk deep within his body. Everything he looks at and seizes must be brought deep into the entrails where there reigns an absolute night where also the tender little mouths with which he absorbs his vision eat away until only the quintessence remains. Here in the warm bowels, the metamorphosis takes place. In the absolute night, in the black pain hidden away in the backbone, the substance of things is dissolved until only the essence shines forth. (Quoted in Hoffman, Allen, and Ulrich 1947, 187)

8. For a lengthier discussion of *View*'s politics and place within the New York art world of the 1940s, see Neiman (1991) and Tashjian (1995).

9. Rosenberg and Fliegel ([1965] 1990) provide numerous anonymous statements from American "vanguard" artists that suggest the extent to which the liberty/vitality paradigm would pervade the working assumptions of younger members of the movement. For example:

> I've several times referred to vitality. That's important, and vitality doesn't always mean jumping around and looking vital. I can only speak for myself. I happen to have a lot of energy and am often very spontaneous. Physically I like to be on the go and my mind also races at times. There's an excitement and thrill in painting. I mean, if you are in the middle of a picture or if you stand back and look at a picture you made, you feel thrilled by it and your heart pounds. This is very real. (336)

10. Philipson (1963) provides a cogent discussion of Jung's theories of art making.

11. Ashton (1979, 211), for instance, notes that Mark Rothko's top sale price rose from $150 in 1946 to $1,000 just three years later. A comprehensive analysis of the cultural ascendancy of abstract expressionism can be found in Crane (1987).

12. Coverage of the new work in the *Nation*, *Partisan Review*, and *Harper's* was by no means wholly critical; even *Life*'s indulgent mockery of Jackson Pollock in August 1949 is noteworthy not simply for its reflection of contemporary middle-class values but as an indication of the increasing acceptance of Pollock's persona within a larger cultural sphere.

13. The *Tiger's Eye* was first published in October 1947. *Possibilities* survived for only one issue, published in the winter of 1947–48. *Instead* probably dates from as early as 1943; its impact, however, was most strongly felt in 1948. For more information, see Gibson (1990).

14. Even French sociologist Pierre Bourdieu, whose theory of taste carefully accounts for social, ideological, and class determinants, nevertheless discusses middlebrow in a tone not so far removed from Macdonald's: such art is typically frivolous (avoiding serious social and political matters), fixated on flashy style,

and "characterized by tried and proven techniques and an oscillation between plagiarism and parody most often linked with either indifference or conservatism" (1993, 128). That these qualities also characterize high bourgeois art suggests for Bourdieu why middlebrow must be branded as illegitimate—but the fact that Bourdieu eagerly derides both suggests something of his own implicit aesthetic biases, which have certainly been informed by vanguard precepts.

15. The prohibitive costs of film production and the lack of a social network of artists comparable to that developed among WPA painters had prevented the emergence of a strong modernist film movement in New York before 1943. Even the American *ciné-club* circuit of the 1920s had showcased foreign imports from France and Germany; Mary Ellen Bute, Ralph Steiner, Paul Strand, and the Rochester-based team of Dr. James S. Watson and Melville Webber were among the few American experimentalists to receive substantial exposure prior to America's entry into World War II. Further, because much American interest in experimental work had been grounded in leftist sentiments and sparked by the politically charged films of Eisenstein and Pudovkin, the enthusiasm of those such as Strand, Steiner, and Lewis Jacobs, and the impact of the Film and Photo Leagues, declined markedly as the disillusionment of American leftist intellectuals grew during the late 1930s. For a thorough examination of American modernist filmmaking of the 1920s and 1930s, see Horak (1998).

CHAPTER THREE
LIFE ON THE EDGE: MANNY FARBER AND CULT CRITICISM

1. Bart (1950, 516).

2. Terrace's own recollections of her years with Farber (Richards 1979, 109–67) make for fascinating reading; Farber discusses his own background, tastes, and critical approaches in Thompson (1977). For a complete chronology of Farber's career, see La Jolla Museum of Contemporary Art (1978, 63–66).

3. Farber may have been pleased with a 1956 *Arts* review of an exhibition of his own paintings at New York's DeNagy gallery. Martica Sawin praises the "zeal and gusto with which Farber launches his attack on the canvas." "The paint," she suggests, "is laid on with a vigor and a bravura most truly deserving of the designation 'action painting,' for the work is principally a record of the compulsive energy which created it" (Sawin 1956, 61).

4. An informative and detailed account of Seldes's career as a critic can be found in Kammen (1996).

5. The very heritage of European cubism, so often appealed to by Greenberg in defense of the New York School (see, for instance, his 1949 "The Role of Nature in Modernist Painting," in Greenberg 1986), was for Farber another hindrance to free expression. Greenberg's prominent role as promoter of abstract expressionism helps to explain his strong commitment to the new art through the 1950s; though he too had confronted the development of local work into oversized, minimal canvases, his response (in pieces such as "The Crisis of the Easel Picture" [1948], in Greenberg 1986) was to praise the work as vital, contemporary, and worthy of the legacy of European cubism. Indeed, in his sustained defense of the New York School through the 1940s and 1950s, Greenberg reveals

an equally strong commitment to the interpretive standards of freedom, vitality, and internationalism, though without the antiestablishment kick that would drive Farber away from fashionable American modernism and toward the detritus of pop culture.

6. For a broad assortment of Ferguson's writings on jazz, radio, and theater, see Chamberlain and Wilson (1982).

7. Farber, who actually replaced Ferguson at the *New Republic*, must have been chastened by reader Carol Seeley's critical poem (1943, 184): after advising Farber that "Hollywood's not black and white," she concludes with

> Ask Uncle Otis for a lesson.
> He understood the pop expression.

8. For Bazin, the middlebrow excesses of wartime French cinema could be countered by a comparable celebration of vital, popular—yet nevertheless artistic— works by neglected filmmakers. A humanist intellectual *and* ardent supporter of cultural forms (nightclubs, movies, the circus) held in contempt by contemporary intellectuals, Bazin, like Ferguson and Farber, positioned himself as a tastemaker for the masses (Andrew 1978). The contradictions inherent in such a stance are distilled in Bazin's 1943 defense of a "happy snobbism that must sometimes be seen as a militant form of taste" (1981, 44). If, for Farber, Otis Ferguson had been the voice of the "underground audience" of the 1930s, Bazin was seeking to adopt a similar role in 1940s France. Significantly, Bazin's solution to the problem of adapting absolute aesthetic standards to the context of popular culture would also be similar to that offered by Ferguson and Farber: films would be judged according to their ability to replicate the behavioral subtleties of common people and the incidental details of everyday life.

The antiestablishment film critic might thus defend everyday, humanistic realism against overblown style and pretension. For Ferguson it had been *Dead End* and *Snow White* over *The Wizard of Oz* and *Kane*; for Bazin, Paul Mesnier's *Patricia* and Jean Stelli's enormously successful melodrama *Le Voile bleu* seemed anemic next to Carné's *Les Visiteurs du soir*, Bresson's *Les Anges du péché*, and Jean Delannoy's *L'Éternal retour*, films that transcended the "ambient idiocy" (31) of conventional cinema and suggested a return to the aesthetic glories of the 1920s.

9. So far as we know, Bazin did not view war documentaries until after the Liberation in 1944, at which time he promoted them enthusiastically in the pages of *Parisien Libéré*. Yet these films still played a pivotal role in the sophistication of his personal aesthetic, certainly confirming Roger Leenhardt's notion of film's primordial realism (Andrew 1978).

10. Greenberg: "Repin predigests art for the spectator and spares him effort, provides him with a short cut to the pleasure of art that detours what is necesarily difficult in genuine art" (1990, 345).

11. To Farber, Deren's films seemed "Freudian-toned, lesbianish, freezing, arty, eclectic, conventional and safe" (1946d, 555), the epitome of fashionable, mannered modernism. The understandably irate responses from Deren and her friends are collected in Clark, Hodson, and Neiman (1988, 410–17).

12. In his review of *Agee on Film*, Farber juggles an awkward deference to his *Nation* predecessor with a biting critique of his "blindness to chic artiness" (1958,

15). While Agee's style could be "exciting in its pea-soup density," his opinions were ultimately those of a liberal middle-class journalist who served an "undemanding audience that welcomed style and knew hardly anything about the inside of movies." His heavily cultured appreciation had stuck "close to what the middlebrow wants to hear" (14), mistaking overwrought Importance for genuine complexity. "If Agee had struggled more with the actual material of the popular nonartist," Farber suggests, "it is inconceivable that he could have missed the vapidity of so much 'good' film art" (15).

13. Farber might also be productively viewed in relation to a tradition of "antiestablishment" art criticism dating from at least the mid–nineteenth century, when rebellious critics began to use their columns to "outline new canons, creating discourses that came to be adopted not only by specialists and lay publics but even by the artists for whom they illuminated the meanings of their innovations" (Zolberg 1990, 203).

CHAPTER FOUR
HALLUCINATING HOLLYWOOD: PARKER TYLER AND CAMP SPECTATORSHIP

1. By contrast, *Nation* critic James Agee, whom Farber regarded as a middlebrow apologist, felt compelled to give the film its due. He agonized over it for two weeks, trying to reconcile enormous admiration for its direction and cinematography with dissatisfaction over its "patness" and "timidity" (1958, 230) in dealing with the realities of infidelity and banking ethics. Though he didn't doubt it would be possible to dismiss *Years* as "one long pious piece of deceit and self-deceit, embarrassed by hot flashes of talent, conscience, truthfulness and dignity," he confessed that he felt "a hundred times more liking and admiration for the film than distaste or disappointment" (231).

2. Indeed, a decade later Farber would shift again, damning the film as a "horse-drawn truckload of liberal schmaltz" (1971i, 15).

3. Here Robert Warshow was more equivocal. He attacked *Years* on ideological grounds, arguing that its "optimistic picture of American life" was meant only to neutralize real problems by showing that they can be "solved by the operation of 'simple' and 'American' virtues," and through fulfillment of middle-class responsibilities, namely, to "be patient and work hard (not to ask too much of life) and to face the future cheerfully" (1970a, 155). Yet because he sees a conspiracy at work here, he is willing to hold individuals responsible for the complex deceit. The filmmakers have exercised "unusual care" (156) in hiding their work; they are actually attempting to reinforce dominant American myths, carefully constructing an artificial realism designed to "control the explosive possibilities" (158) of the movie's subject by naturalizing its ideologically conservative vision of capitalism.

Warshow is openly challenging the authority of the filmmakers by defiantly positioning his own resistant spectatorship against them. But he is not a vanguard critic in the truest sense, because he is not interested in accepting aesthetic responsibility for the film; because he still acknowledges the equal authority of the filmmakers, the match can result only in a draw, at best.

4. I am responding in part to commentators' recent attempts to move toward a more restrictive notion of "camp" in order to reclaim its resistant spirit. Meyer (1994), for instance, feels that camp's vanguard edge may be preserved only through an aggressive reappropriation of the term to designate a specifically *queer* vanguard practice "engaged directly by the queer to produce social visibility in the praxis of everyday life" (5). The depoliticized appropriation of camp by straight culture in the 1960s (its absorption into what Ross [1989] calls "Pop camp") is felt to have implied a symbolic erasure of the queer, coupled with the inadvertent entrance of queer discourse and queer aura into polite society. For Meyer, the struggle to reclaim camp is at once political and historiographic in nature, and writers who employ the term without acknowledging its essentially gay identity are implicitly making a reactionary pitch for the status quo.

Again, however, I would suggest that vanguard zeal itself sometimes obscures problematic contexts and impinging ideologies. Camp, like cultism, is ultimately bigger than sexuality and sexual identity, and identifying it as an *essentially* queer activity may limit our ability to recognize its importance and influence as much a broader strategy of vanguard cultural resistance. For instance, in positing Oscar Wilde's "Critic as Artist" as a crucial model of vanguard criticism, I am clearly acknowledging Wilde's role as a pioneering exponent of cultism and camp alike; it is also obvious that his sexuality influenced the development of his personal and critical styles. Yet if Wilde's camp is essentially queer, what do we do with his debt to Arnold, Pater, Ruskin, Newman, Whistler, Art for Art's Sake, and French aestheticism? Camp's oppositional aesthetic has been flexible enough to accommodate a variety of individuals or groups seeking to distinguish themselves from the "mass" by asserting personal control over the cultural meanings around them. Thus while Parker Tyler was himself gay, I focus primarily on his significance as a vanguard/camp intellectual whose strong aesthetic biases fundamentally impacted on his adoption and deployment of a camp critical approach.

Above all, I wish to retrieve "camp" as a term to describe a larger *aesthetic* phenomenon, one whose close ties to vanguard practice should make us sensitive to any taste biases and highbrow interests underlying current theoretical defenses of camp practice.

5. Alternatively—as Robertson (1996) suggests—female performers can use camp to perform their own symbolic identity, as in the cases of Mae West, Joan Crawford, and (more recently) pop singer Madonna.

6. At an extreme, the aesthetic makeover can seem very strange indeed, as when filmmaker John Waters reminisces about formative films of his youth:

> In between acts at some of the strip houses, they routinely showed "nudist camp" pictures, and I was profoundly influenced. Since every other type of bad film is now the rage, I wish they'd revive this much-ignored great genre. The *Isle of Levant*, *The Garden of Eden*, *Naked Island*, *Nature Camp Diary*, *Mr. Peek-a-Boo's Playmate*—all classics of a sort. Happy, healthy idiots on pogo sticks with air-brushed crotches was my idea of sexy. . . . Come on, Museum of Modern Art Film Department, stop snoozing on the job! (1986, 69)

Hopelessly generic, aggressively nonaesthetic, and unable to regulate their own erotic subtexts, nudist camp films seem well suited to camp reappropriation. For

Waters, controlled artistry is anathema to aesthetic appreciation; elsewhere, he lists as embarrassing "guilty pleasures" art house fodder such as *Interiors* and *Why Does Herr R. Run Amok?* Nudie films can become alternative, highly personal "classics" because Waters easily dominates their meanings, peeling away the thin, halfhearted veneer of reportage, playfully asserting his affection for, but also superiority to, those "sexy" images of "happy, healthy idiots on pogo sticks with air-brushed crotches."

7. The obvious exception here is the intentional camp of *Beat the Devil*, *Pink Flamingos*, and TV's *Batman*, wherein the work willingly forfeits its own dignity in order to invite a distanced, liberated play with its textual meanings; yet because it is always clear that the game is now rigged, with the artist still controlling spectator response, such works will always seem less pure, authentic, and satisfying than their "naive" counterparts.

8. In retrospect, Sontag's biggest misstep in "Notes on Camp" is her inability to see the camp sensibility as fundamentally involving such hermeneutic play—instead, it becomes just the opposite, an aestheticist sensitivity to "pure artifice" (1966a, 283), which she assumes requires the absence of all meaning. Because Sontag associates meaning with content (something contained *within* a work), as opposed to style (which resides on the work's outer surface), she excludes the possibility of surface meanings altogether and even suggests that camp is essentially "apolitical" (279), which it certainly is not.

9. By this Dali meant that as a spectator he actively sought to reinterpret the world through a state of delirium, producing irrational knowledge founded only on desire, then rendering that knowledge concrete through photography, painting, or even critical interpretation. Max Ernst had explored similar territory in his development of *frottage*, a procedure of pencil rubbing that, in abstracting the original objects treated (leaves, thread, floorboards, even abstract painting) freed them to be revisioned by the artist-spectator's desires. He suggests that here, as in critical paranoia and automatic writing, the artist, "by widening in this way the active part of the mind's hallucinatory faculties," could actually "assist *as spectator* at the birth of all [his] works (quoted in Chipp 1968, 431), witnessing but also facilitating its development by way of his liberated vision.

10. For a useful discussion of European surrealist film criticism, see Hammond (1978).

11. The poetry boom of the 1910s was still being felt a decade later. Between 1920 and 1929, at least 120 "little magazines" sprang up in the United States, with more than 30 operating out of New York City (Hoffman, Allen, and Ulrich 1947, 258–94).

12. These included André Gide, Marianne Moore—even Marcel Proust, whose *Remembrance of Things Past* is assailed as "despicable, and superfluous for four-fifths of the time" (Tyler and Ford 1930, 25).

13. A far more comprehensive account of *Blues*, Jolas, and *View* in the context of American surrealism can be found in Tashjian (1995, 137–201).

14. Lamantia, a fifteen-year-old high school student, was discovered by *View* in 1943; he served briefly as an assistant editor (vol. 4, no. 2 [Summer 1944] through vol. 4, no. 4 [Winter 1944]) before becoming a contributing editor.

15. *View*'s attention to psyche and myth would certainly not have seemed wholly unorthodox to others familiar with the psychoanalytic myth criticism pioneered by Jung and Rank, adapted to cultural analysis by Frazer and Sir E. B. Tylor, and refined for literary study by Jane Harrison, Gilbert Murray, G. Wilson Knight, Maud Bodkin, Robert Penn Warren, Northrop Frye, and others. *View*'s emphasis on symbolic interpretation, though certainly drawn from surrealism, also extended an approach that many of the little magazines, encouraged by symbolism's tremendous impact on American authors (Melville, Whitman, Hart Crane), had actively pursued for many years.

16. Interestingly, the main difference between Tyler's critical interpretation of *Hide-and-Seek* and his 1944 poem inspired by the painting is that in the latter, the general interpretation is conveyed through repetition of key images and phrases, and that individual microinterpretations are less clearly identified with specific visual motifs in the work. (The poem, "Yesterday's Children," is reprinted in Tchelitchew [1967]).

17. Here James Frazer's monumental, groundbreaking work of cultural anthropology, *The Golden Bough*, had proven a major influence on Tyler, arguing that vestigial mythic belief also lives on within a wide variety of cultural artifacts, practices, and traditions.

18. I borrow the term from Bordwell (1989, 119–20).

19. Here Tyler has carefully qualified surrealism's own daydream metaphor. If the Hollywood cinema resembles a daydream, it is because it serves only to satisfy "a thousand small wishes," rather than the deep, chaotic desires addressed by night dreams. The analogy between the cinema and daydreaming, one central to much post-1970 film theory and criticism, is rooted in surrealist writing and in the larger romantic tradition. As early as 1762, Lord Henry Home Kames had likened spectatorial belief in the fictional realm to a "waking dream" ("because, like a dream, it vanisheth the moment we reflect upon our waking situation" [1824, 49]). For the surrealist Robert Desnos, the cinema would become a "twilight dream" (1978, 123) a term echoed by Tyler's own "daylight dream."

20. Here Bordwell (1989) might use the term "symptomatic" criticism: the critic interprets meanings as symptoms of the text's hidden, repressed psychoses.

21. In his consideration of Chaplin in relation to Kafka, Tyler (1950a) moves well beyond mythic iconography to compare thematic concerns and character traits in the work of these two figures, noting a similar innocence in the Tramp and *Amerika*'s Karl, as opposed to the guilt associated with Chaplin's Verdoux and Kafka's K.

CHAPTER FIVE
FROM TERMITES TO AUTEURS: CULTISM
GOES MAINSTREAM

1. The figures for 1940, 1948, and 1955 are from Bachmann (1955, 48–49) and Ellis (1955, 30–31). The figure for the 1960s is from Lynes (1985, 380).

2. Here I speak only of Sarris's vanguard cultism: he continued to pursue a far more detailed examination of auteur cinema in critical pieces, interviews, and his editorial contributions to the *Hollywood Voices* compendium (Sarris 1967).

CHAPTER SIX
HEAVY CULTURE AND UNDERGROUND CAMP

1. In "What Are the New Critics Saying?" (1966, 79).

2. Ross (1989) calls this trend as "Pop camp," but he regards it quite differently—as an elitist reappropriation of camp sensibilities by an intellectual class determined to maintain its cultural distinction in the face of pop's dangerous egalitarianism (148–56). I find Ross's argument here (and hence his term) rather problematic, insofar as he buys into a radically democratic notion of pop art (downplaying the dealers and critics who helped sell the movement) and fails to explain adequately how the tastemaking of an American elite specifically defined and controlled the new pop camp's "bad" taste, or even its "re-creation of surplus value from forgotten forms of labor" (151, italics omitted). I would argue instead that the new vanguard camp was at once elitist *and* democratic: like pop art, it still needed highbrow artist-leaders, but those leaders now refined their vanguard populism in a manner that made camp spectatorship of pop culture available to a wider audience, even as it jeopardized their continued leadership.

3. Tyler continued to be extremely active as a poet, playwright, art and literary critic, and biographer throughout the postwar period. His image was that of a cosmopolitan American intellectual and aesthete, a veteran of both the nascent New York scene and, before that, the heyday of the "little magazine" during the American poetry renaissance of the 1920s. His art studies include critical biographies of Florine Stettheimer and Pavel Tchelitchew, and monographs on Van Gogh, Renoir, Cézanne/Gaugin, and Degas/Lautrec. Much of his best postwar literary criticism is collected in Tyler (1964).

4. A revised version of Panofsky's "Style and Medium in the Motion Picture" had recently surfaced in *Critique* 1, no. 3 (January–February 1947). Deren had recently written a number of pieces for *New Directions* (1946a), *Popular Photography* (1946b), and *Dance Magazine* (1946c), and had published a small-circulation monograph entitled *An Anagram of Ideas on Art, Form and Film* (Yonkers, N.Y.: Alicat Book Shop Press), reprinted in Clark, Hodson, and Neiman (1988). For an in-depth analysis of Deren's antirealist stance, see Rabinovitz (1991), especially 72–75.

5. Because they confused apparent truth with real truth, such movies might substitute "archeological documentation" (Tyler 1949c, 528) of setting for a more psychologically revealing examination of the dramatic material (*The Snake Pit* [1948]), or narcissistically revel in the camera's assumed privileged access to psychological or sociological Truth (*Citizen Kane* [1941], *Boomerang!* [1947], *The Men* [1950], *The Big Lift* [1950]) (Tyler 1950c; 1960a).

6. Tyler was by no means the first or only critic to discuss the American avant-garde in detail during the immediate postwar years. See, for example, Arledge (1947), Knight (1950), and the 1946 Deren articles cited in n. 4, above.

For detailed discussion of the aesthetic and institutional development of the American avant-garde cinema, see Curtis (1971), Sitney (1979), James (1989; 1992), Rabinovitz (1991), and Suárez (1996).

7. In this case, Tyler's fears were apparently justified: according to Renan (1967), Markopoulos attempted to shoot *Serenity* in 1958 but then spent three

years fighting for access to this footage. Though he finally managed to piece together two versions of the film, he was again forced to relinquish it after editing
(166).

8. Nevertheless, Tyler continued to practice such criticism—albeit more spo-
radically—throughout his career. See, for example, "The Myth of the Great Lovers" (1960h, 83–89); "The Awful Fate of the Sex Goddess" (1969d, 18–26); "The
Horse: Totem Animal of Male Power" (1969d: 27–36), and especially *Screening
the Sexes: Homosexuality in the Movies* (1972a), which moves significantly beyond Hollywood, examining erotic mythos in films as varied as *The Great Escape*,
If . . . , *Strangers on a Train*, and *Ivan the Terrible*.

9. Here again Tyler's assumptions echo those of Lionel Trilling, who was himself fond of recalling Matthew Arnold's notion of art as a "criticism of life." Indeed, in his criticism of the 1950s and 1960s Tyler often expresses a Trilling-ish
regard for social insight and moral integrity—albeit in works whose elaborate
form Trilling might have found somewhat excessive.

10. I should note that my own discussion of Mekas's criticism here is meant
primarily to illustrate the ongoing development of vanguard approaches, and to
contextualize Tyler's violent reaction to the Underground. A thorough treatment
of Mekas's broader significance as a filmmaker, activist, and critic can be found
in James (1992).

11. The emphasis on vitality had itself been crucial to the New Wave's own
self-promotion. Godard, for instance, had in 1958 praised Jean Rouch's *Je suis
un noir* as a "text of wonderful verve and spontaneity" (1986, 104). For Mekas,
Rouch's film epitomized the New Wave's attempt to "develop a spontaneous dialogue and a spontaneous action" (1960, 5).

12. For an alternative take on Mekas's European sensibilities, see Pruitt
(1992).

13. *Myra Breckinridge* also helped to revive more serious interest in Tyler's
1940s books: *The Hollywood Hallucination* and *Magic and Myth of the Movies*
were reissued by Simon and Schuster in 1970.

14. In 1970, *Variety* reported that campus contacts employed by the major
studios had "accumulated enough downbeat reaction to the concept of 'youth-
oriented' films to not be surprised at the snail-paced b.o. for certain recent pix
combining such themes as drugs, sex, politics and young people. Beyond merely
avoiding such formalized 'now generation' films, many youths take affront at
what they consider to be patronizing, or pandering" (Spilker 1970, 3).

15. Hoberman and Rosenbaum (1983) still provide the best introduction to
the "midnight movie" phenomenon, with enlightening in-depth discussions of
Eraserhead, *El Topo*, *The Rocky Horror Picture Show*, and other cult films of the
1970s.

16. The film's second anniversary at the Westgate had been protested by disgruntled former patrons carrying signs reading, "Neighborhood theaters should
offer variety" and "Why must the show go on . . . and on . . . and on" (Jones
1974, B1).

17. Some readers will suspect that this sort of activism is beginning to sound
less like traditional avant-gardism, and suspiciously close to the kind of audience
involvement cultural studies critics have found in devoted fans of *Dallas*, *Star
Trek*, and *Cagney and Lacey* (reinstated after a ferocious letter campaign). In

truth, traditional avant-gardism had advocated spectatorial activism, too—yet in insisting that potential supporters embrace the difficult art necessary to sustain an ideal society, it assured its own political failure and subcultural success. Parker Tyler's erotic spectatorship of the 1940s and Manny Farber's increasingly esoteric film cultism had dutifully maintained this obscurity, limiting access to vanguard transformation to those able to understand and accept the aesthetic extremes of their methods. But as we have seen, the Underground changed all this, opening up the vanguard approach by rendering camp and cultist appropriation more accessible. If this in effect brought vanguard activity close to the sort of empowering endeavors fans of pop culture had been engaging in for years, it also gave the vanguard what it had always purported to desire: a means of mobilizing large numbers of spectators against the numbing effects of Commercial Art.

18. A number of highbrows within the New York Underground itself did manage to spearhead a reactionary drive for a return to a more exclusionary aesthetic discernment. This movement culminated in the December 1970 opening of Anthology Film Archives and the Invisible Cinema: the archive was intended to serve as a museum housing "the monuments of cinematic art" (Sitney 1975, v); the cinema was the accompanying ideal venue for the projection of the archive's holdings. The curious manifesto marking the opening reveals a tension between a lingering need to preserve Underground community and a fervent, almost desperate desire to retreat from cult/camp excess into contemplative aestheticism. This tension is most strongly felt in the justification of the cinema's rather unorthodox design:

> What do we want from a film theater? The creation of an audience spirit and the possibility of experiencing intensely the cinematic reality. Since the communal spirit is strongest and most effective in the absence of disturbance from one's neighbors, the special features of the new Cinema are tools to this end. One can hear the sound of the audience, but that sound is subdued. The film artist demands the eyes and ears of his audience. The seat hoods make concentration possible without destroying the sense by which a person senses the presence of others in a room, even in the dark. (vii)

Individual sightlines are preserved by elevating rows, patrons are actually physically separated by blinders, the entire interior is painted black—and, in a classic touch, foreign films are shown in "pure," untitled versions. ("There is a sacrifice involved in the substitution of the purity of the image for the sense of the words, but it is a necessary one" [viii].)

CHAPTER SEVEN
RETREAT INTO THEORY

1. Kael (1970, 123).
2. Michelson (1969, 63).
3. Kael's own awareness of (and sympathy for) experimentalism and foreign films had been shaped by her background in philosophy, poetry, and drama, her association with artists such as Robert Duncan and filmmaker/poet James Broughton (with whom she had a child in 1948), and her experience founding

and managing a groundbreaking art house in the 1950s. Further biographical information, and several revealing interviews, can be found in Brantley (1996).

4. For Barbara Rose, an "increasing uniformity of the environment and repetitiveness of a circumscribed experience" had induced artists to "find variety in repetition where only the nuance alters" (1968, 289).

5. See, for instance: Manny Farber, "Jack Levine," *Art News* 54, no. 1 (March 1955): 33+; "Eilshemius: Artist behind Mahatma," *Art News* 58, no. 2 (April 1959): 26–27+; and "New Images of (ugh) Man," *Art News* 58, no. 6 (October 1959): 38–39+.

6. Farber's painting of the late 1950s and early 1960s is discussed in "Manny Farber" (1956), Sawin (1956), and Sandler (1962). For a more general overview of Farber's oeuvre, see Amy Goldin, "Manny Farber," in La Jolla Museum of Contemporary Art (1978, 4–10).

7. By 1967, the term "funk" had become au courant in West Coast art circles to describe the loose, cluttered work of artists such as Robert Hudson, Bruce Nauman, and Wally Hedrick. See Monti (1967).

8. For those unfamiliar with this film, I offer Snow's own description:

> The film is a continuous zoom which takes 45 minutes to go from its widest field to its smallest and final field. It was shot with a fixed camera from one end of an 80 foot loft, shooting the other end, a row of windows and the street. This, the setting, and the action which takes place there are cosmically equivalent. The room (and the zoom) are interrupted by 4 human events including a death. The sound on these occasions is sync sound, music and speech, occurring simultaneously with an electronic sound, a sine wave, which goes from its lowest (50 cycles per second) note to its highest (12000 c.p.s.) in 40 minutes. (1967, 1)

9. The book, entitled *The Shadow of an Airplane Climbs the Empire State Building: A World Theory of Film* (1972), now defends Tyler's taste for the aesthetically sophisticated and ethically critical modernist cinema of Bergman, Antonioni, and Kurosawa by appealing to a theoretical notion of cinematic space/time. (Here he actually dips not simply into surrealist mythos but into his own "Elements of Film Narrative" [1948b].) Whereas art filmmakers offered a difficult but rewarding engagement with "cosmic" (imaginative, perceptual) space/time, they did so within a new "global village" of instantaneous communication, which provided the public a dangerously facile symbolic abatement of the atomic age's "time/space paranoia," an illusory sensation of social unity and safety. Space becomes a "measurable, secure box," time a "measurable, closed circle": "the conquest of that box, the world's space, is equivalent mythically to the conquest of fear" (1972b, 124). Together, McLuhanism, pop art, even the space program suggested a zeitgeist of neurotic escapism, willing submission to an amoral, an-aesthetic wash of vapid entertainment. Cinema, on the other hand, offers a medium of infinite space and "absolute" time: an intellectual, even cosmic notion of space and time much closer to mental (as opposed to physical or scientific) reality. A film literally records its maker's imagination: the medium's true destiny is thus "to photograph this mental process; indeed, millimeter by millimeter, to *be* this mental process, to produce the organism of this induplicable and supreme object" (287). The "true theory of film," Tyler suggests, "is simply the photograph of

what man's mind can bring of goodness and grace, aesthetically whole and victorious, to the spectacle of the world" (284).

10. Indeed, through the 1970s, Farber was able to enjoy an elevated status as a respected intellectual critic with wide and varied tastes, without needing theory to bolster his authority. If he seemed to inch closer to the middlebrow arena with pieces on Rainer Werner Fassbinder and Martin Scorsese for *Film Comment*, he also continued to face the radical edges of film appreciation with articles and university courses on the likes of Jean-Marie Straub, Michael Snow, Oshima, and Jacques Rivette, and in his ongoing friendship with French filmmaker (and sometime Godard collaborator) Jean-Pierre Gorin. (Most of Farber's critical pieces were now coauthored with his wife, Patricia Patterson, whose influence on his critical shift had been significant.) Farber's reputation as an elder statesman of Hollywood connoisseurship had not diminished, but his intersecting interest in cinematic modernism could make him a model of refined intellectual taste—a critic now equally attuned to high and low film art, Europe and America, form and ideology, art history and film history, and able to perceive with informed hindsight the errors of his former ways. (Two excellent interviews with Farber can be found in Thompson [1977] and Gorin et al. [1982].) Farber also continued to work as a practicing artist, finally gaining considerable recognition for his talents; in his "Auteur series" of the late 1970s, he even integrated his film criticism into his art in quirky, highly personal still lifes of critical notes and associated toys, household objects, and human figures on a desk pad (titles included *Preston Sturges, A Dandy's Gesture [Howard Hawks], Wim Wenders's "Kings of the Road", The Films of R. W. Fassbinder*). For discussions of Farber's artwork since the 1960s, see La Jolla Museum of Contemporary Art (1978) and Yard (1991).

11. What Noël Carroll (1988) has called the "specificity thesis" in classical film theory is certainly relevant here as well: *2001*, for Michelson, uniquely epitomizes the cinema's aesthetic uniqueness.

12. In her review of Bazin's *What Is Cinema?* Michelson attributes Bazin's rejection of modernist disjunction to an "intransigent religious sensibility" (1968, 70) yet still hopes to rescue the phenomenological approach itself by focusing on issues of cognition central to the Eisenstein/Vertov tradition of political and modernist radicalism, and compatible with much American minimalist criticism. By accepting the medium's inherent "bipolarity" and discarding the very category of "manipulation," radical modernists such as Godard and Resnais free cinema "to re-define the nature and possibilities of cinematic 'realism' itself" (71).

13. Again, Tyler's own theory is an exception here: its narrow modernist canon actually brings it much closer to classical theory than to those of his contemporaries (Tyler 1972b).

14. At the *Cahiers*, writings and films spanning Eisenstein's complex career were reprinted and/or discussed, often with less consideration given to immediate political relevance than to inherent aesthetic interest. Noël Burch's ambitious theory of film, serialized in the journal and later published as *Praxis du cinéma*, introduces Eisenstein's montage and formal dialectics alongside the work of Antonioni, Bresson, and the American experimentalists, in order to more fully elaborate the stylistic parameters of the medium. (The installments ran continuously from issue no. 188 [March 1967] through issue no. 197 [December 1967–January

1968]; *Praxis* was published in France in 1969 [Editions Gallimard], and in English in 1973, as *Theory of Film Practice*, trans. Helen R. Lane [New York: Praeger]). Barthélemy Amengual's August 1968 analysis of the lost *Bezhin Meadow* reveals a critic eager to defend Eisenstein's deployment of conventions of mysticism, legend, and sacred art throughout his career (Amengual 1968). In issue no. 217 (December 1969), part 2 of Comolli and Narboni's explicitly dialectical-materialist "Cinema/Ideology/Criticism" appears alongside Eisenstein's "Music of the Countryside: The New Type of Counterpoint" and Jean-Pierre Oudart's structuralist analysis of color. Even the special Eisenstein issue (January–February 1971) juxtaposes Jean-Louis Baudry's criticism of *Alexander Nevsky*'s "aestheticism" (41) with Leonid Kozlov's spirited ideological defense of *Ivan the Terrible*'s analytical historiography. (Kozlov concludes by noting that Eisenstein is "not content to show and analyze history: he expresses and forms *social and historical sentiment*" [38, my translation].)

15. For a thorough examination of the editorial stances of the *Cahiers* and *Cinéthique* in relation to both contemporary French politics and Soviet culture of the 1920s, see Harvey (1978).

16. By this I hardly wish to discount Barthes's substantial influence on French, British, and (eventually) American materialism, only to note that critical approaches and stances associated with him predate his ascent to prominence and derive from broader vanguard precepts. That said, it is hard to overstate Barthes's particular importance as a vanguard critic and theorist in his own right—as manifested variously in his cultist attachment to neglected "texts" such as wrestling and Balzac's *Sarrasine*, and his ferocious commitment to camp liberation of (frequently oppositional) textual meanings. His sizable debt to the "critic-as-artist" tradition, and his grounding in modernist aesthetics, are both highlighted by Sontag (1982): she notes, for instance, that his "notions of 'text' and 'textuality' . . . translate into criticism the modernist ideal of an open-ended, polysemous literature; and thereby make the critic, just like the creators of that literature, the inventor of meaning" (xi).

17. The specific articles referred to here are Editors of *Cahiers du cinéma* (1970) and Bellour (1974–75). The *Cahiers* piece is a landmark analysis in which Lincoln's authoritative countenance and demeanor are isolated as inept, uncontrolled symbolic elements that both boost the film's intended ideological project (to assist in electing a Republican president in 1940) and inadvertently derail that project by going overboard, suggesting a monstrous demeanor and withering "castrating stare." Bellour's structural analysis is less clearly political: he finds in twelve shots from a conversation scene in Hawks's film (Vivian and Marlowe in a car, on their way from Eddy Mars's garage to Geiger's house) complex patterns of repetition and variation that seem primary to the very process of storytelling which most of the movie's viewers will focus on. ("It is not surprising . . . that it should be the regulated opposition between the closing off of symmetries and the opening up of dissymmetries which gives rise to the narrative, to the very fact that there is a narrative" [16].)

The sheer body of critical work from this period is simply so immense and complex that I cannot hope to do it justice here. I wish only to suggest that the key structuralist and psychoanalytic critical methods employed in many of these pieces allow the highbrow critic, in effect, to heighten the symbolic and formal richness of a given movie, thus implicitly aligning it with—and indeed surpassing—the richness of European art films of the 1950s and 1960s. We must not forget that the French critics who pioneered this politicized vanguard criticism had been intimately familiar with the stylistic tropes of Bergman, Antonioni, Resnais, and of course Godard. It thus makes perfect sense that complex, semiautonomous patterning should crop up not simply in *Last Year at Marienbad, Muriel,* and *Vivre sa vie,* but in Bellour's analyses of *The Big Sleep* and *The Birds* (Bellour 1969)—and that prolonged emphasis on countenance, even staring, is played up not simply by Bergman and Antonioni, but by the *Cahiers* editors (in the *Lincoln* piece), and later by Mulvey (1975). In seeking to assert their own creative authority, these critics drew from models of cinematic art making with which many of them had grown up, even as they sought to offer critical spectatorship itself as a properly politicized aesthetic alternative.

18. Already in 1968, René Micha had seized on *Wavelength,* which had been awarded the Grand Prix at Knokke-le-Zoute's 1967 Experimental Film Festival (an event vociferously protested by Maoist students), setting Snow alongside Eisenstein, Kuleshov, Pudovkin, and Vertov while praising his film's "concrete expression of the relation between man and the world" (169).

19. For an extended discussion of Michelson's appeal to phenomenological "interpretive schemata" in her criticism of minimalist films (especially those of Michael Snow), see Peterson (1994, 77–80).

20. Michelson would go on to discuss both unrealized projects separately, in "Reading Eisenstein Reading *Capital*" (*October,* 1976) and "Reading Eisenstein Reading Joyce" (*Art and Text,* 1989).

21. The discussion of Japanese cinema is by Noël Burch—"To the Distant Observer: Towards a Theory of Japanese Film," printed in the first issue of *October* (Spring 1976), became the basis for his book *To the Distant Observer: Form and Meaning in the Japanese Cinema* (Berkeley and Los Angeles: University of California Press, 1979), which Michelson edited and revised.

22. Here Michelson is playing off the currency of recent forays—by Jean-Louis Baudry, Christian Metz, Laura Mulvey, and others—into Freudian and especially Lacanian flavored materialist film theory. Mulvey (1975), for instance, cites scopophilia and fetishism as two primary sources of (male) spectatorial pleasure.

23. Coincidentally, in American universities, film criticism and theory became the domain of humanities, not art departments; ironically, many art departments would not begin teaching cinema studies in earnest until modern art theory had itself absorbed the highbrow vanguard approach.

CONCLUSION
LOVE, DEATH, AND THE LIMITS OF ARTISTIC CRITICISM

1. See, for instance, Bassett (1997), Champagne (1997), Fonarow (1997), and Jenkins (1992).

2. Well over a decade ago, art critic Donald Kuspit seemed to be nailing the coffin shut on modern artistry when in heralding deconstructionism ("the art which imaginatively works upon art" [1984, xviii]), he proclaimed that while "it

used to be that one could think of 'the critic as artist,' if not as an actual artist," it was now inevitable that "one acknowledge, however reluctantly—for both critic and artist—that 'the critic is artist,' in the fullest sense that the eroding idea of 'artist' retains"(xi). He has since recanted somewhat (see Kuspit 1993).

3. A recent, passionate defense of such a "public" criticism within the Arnoldian tradition may be found in Dickstein (1992).

4. Film criticism may even have helped to influence a larger shift in criticism's role and importance in neighboring fields. Intriguing claims for a larger "crisis of criticism" are found in Berger (1998); one might also note Harold Bloom's complaint of a "flight from the aesthetic" (1994, 17) in literary studies and the accompanying abandonment of the Western Canon and core principles of discernment (summarized as the "ancient and quite grim triple question of the agonist: more than, less than, equal to?" [35]). The notion of a "crisis" in literary criticism, however, dates at least as far back as 1952, when Randall Jarrell disparagingly characterized the times as an "age of criticism." "People still read, still write— and well," he noted, "but for many of them it is the act of criticism which has become the representative or Archetypal act of the intellectual" (187). Jarrell's main concern is actually similar to my own: he worries that the writer and the work may get smothered in the process, with literature and poetry serving merely as " 'raw material' which the critic cooks up into understanding." Critics, he warns, are "often useful and wonderful and a joy to have around the house; *but* they're the bane of our age, because our age so fantastically overestimates their importance and so willingly forsakes the works they are writing about for them" (199).

REFERENCES

Agee, James. 1958. "What Hollywood Can Do." *Nation*, 7 December 1946. In *Agee on Film: Reviews and Comments*, 229–31. Boston: Beacon Press.

Alloway, Lawrence. 1968. "Systemic Painting." In *Minimal Art: A Critical Anthology*, edited by Gregory Battock, 37–60. New York: E. P. Dutton & Co.

Amengual, Barthélemy. 1968. "A Propos du *Pré de bézine*" (About *Bezhin Meadow*). *Cahiers du cinéma* 203 (August): 6–12.

Andrew, Dudley. 1978. *André Bazin*. New York: Oxford University Press.

Arledge, Sara Kathryn. 1947. "The Experimental Film: A New Art in Transition." *Arizona Quarterly* 3, no. 2 (Summer): 101–12.

Arnold, Matthew. 1949a. "Culture and Anarchy." In *The Portable Matthew Arnold*, edited by Lionel Trilling, 469–573. New York: The Viking Press.

———. 1949b. "The Function of Criticism at the Present Time." In *The Portable Matthew Arnold*, edited by Lionel Trilling, 234–67. New York: The Viking Press.

Ashton, Dore. 1979. *The New York School: A Cultural Reckoning*. New York: Penguin Books.

Bachmann, Gideon. 1955. "Film Societies in the U.S.A." *Film Culture* 1, no. 2 (March–April): 48–49.

Bart, Max. 1950. Letter to the editor. *Nation*, 2 December, 516.

Barthes, Roland. 1973. "The Third Meaning: Notes on Some of Eisenstein's Stills." Translated by Richard Howard. *Artforum* 11, no. 5 (January): 46–50.

Bassett, Caroline. 1997. "Virtually Gendered: Life in an On-Line World." In *The Subcultures Reader*, edited by Ken Gelder and Sarah Thornton, 537–50. London: Routledge.

Baudry, Jean-Louis. 1971. "Notes sur *Alexander Nevsky*" (Notes on *Alexander Nevsky*). *Cahiers du cinéma* 226–27 (January–February): 39–41.

Bazin, André. 1981. *French Cinema of the Occupation and Resistance: The Birth of a Critical Esthetic*. Translated by Stanley Hochman. New York: Frederick Ungar Publishing Co.

Baziotes, William. 1990. "I Cannot Evolve Any Concrete Theory." *Possibilities*, 1947–48. In *Issues in Abstract Expressionism: The Artist-Run Periodicals*, edited by Ann Eden Gibson, 241. Ann Arbor, Mich.: UMI Research Press.

Becker, Howard S. 1982. *Art Worlds*. Berkeley and Los Angeles: University of California Press.

Bell, Daniel. 1991. "Modernism Mummified." In *Modernist Culture in America*, edited by Daniel Joseph Singal, 158–173. Belmont, Calif.: Wadsworth Publishing Company.

Bellour, Raymond. 1969. " 'Les Oiseaux': Analyse d'une séquence" (*The Birds*: Analysis of a sequence). *Cahiers du cinéma* 216 (October): 24–38.

———. 1974–75. "The Obvious and the Code." Translator unknown. *Screen* 15, no. 4 (Winter): 7–17.

Berger, Maurice, ed. 1998. *The Crisis of Criticism*. New York: The New Press.

Bloom, Harold. 1994. *The Western Canon: The Books and School of the Ages.* New York: Harcourt Brace & Company.

Bordwell, David. 1985. *Narration in the Fiction Film*. Madison: University of Wisconsin Press.

———. 1989. *Making Meaning: Inference and Rhetoric in the Interpretation of Cinema*. Cambridge: Harvard University Press.

Bourdieu, Pierre. 1984. *Distinction: A Social Critique of the Judgement of Taste.* Translated by Richard Nice. Cambridge: Harvard University Press.

———. 1993. "The Market of Symbolic Goods." Translated by R. Swyer. In *The Field of Cultural Production*, 112–41. New York: Columbia University Press.

Brantley, Will, ed. 1996. *Conversations with Pauline Kael*. Jackson: University of Mississippi Press.

Breton, André. 1972. *Manifestoes of Surrealism*. Translated by Richard Seaver and Helen R. Lane. Ann Arbor: University of Michigan Press.

———. 1991. "Lighthouse of the Bride." *View*, 1945. In *View: Parade of the Avant-Garde, 1940–1947*, edited by Charles Henri Ford, 123–30. New York: Thunder's Mouth Press.

Brooks, Van Wyck. 1920. *The Ordeal of Mark Twain*. New York: E. P. Dutton & Co.

Bürger, Peter. 1984. *Theory of the Avant-Garde*. Translated by Michael Shaw. Minneapolis: University of Minnesota Press.

Calinescu, Matei. 1987. *Five Faces of Modernity*. Durham, N.C.: Duke University Press.

Camper, Fred. 1973. "*Western History* and *The Riddle of Lumen*." *Artforum* 11, no. 5 (January): 66–71.

Carroll, Noël. 1988. *Philosophical Problems of Classical Film Theory*. Princeton, N.J.: Princeton University Press.

"Catalogue of the Hans Hofmann Exhibition." 1975. Kootz Gallery, 1955. In *Readings in American Art, 1900–1975*, edited by Barbara Rose, 148. New York: Praeger.

Caughie, John, ed. 1981. *Theories of Authorship*. London: Routledge and Kegan Paul.

Chamberlain, Dorothy, and Robert Wilson, eds. 1982. *The Otis Ferguson Reader*. Highland Park, Ill.: December Press.

Champagne, John. 1997. " 'Stop Reading Films!': Film Studies, Close Analysis and Gay Pornography." *Cinema Journal* 36, no. 4 (Summer): 76–97.

Cheney, Sheldon. 1941. *The Story of Modern Art*. New York: The Viking Press.

Chipp, Herschel B. 1968. *Theories of Modern Art*. Berkeley and Los Angeles: University of California Press.

Clark, VeVe A., Millicent Hodson, and Catrina Neiman. 1988. *The Legend of Maya Deren: A Documentary Biography and Collected Works*. Vol. 1, pt. 2, *Chambers (1942–1947)*. New York: Anthology Film Archives / Film Culture.

Cockroft, Eva. 1974. "Abstract Expressionism, Weapon of the Cold War." *Artforum* 12, no. 10 (June): 39–41.

Cohen, Phoebe. 1973. "Scenes from under Childhood." *Artforum* 11, no. 5 (January): 51–55.

Collins, Jim. 1989. *Uncommon Cultures: Popular Culture and Post-Modernism.* New York: Routledge.

Crane, Diana. 1987. *The Transformation of the Avant-Garde: The New York Art World, 1940–1985.* Chicago: University of Chicago Press.

Curtis, David. 1971. *Experimental Cinema: A Fifty-Year Evolution.* New York: Dell Publishing Co.

Deren, Maya. 1946a. "Cinema as an Art Form." *New Directions*, no. 9 (Fall): 111–20.

———. 1946b. "Creative Movies with a New Dimension—Time." *Popular Photography* 19, no. 6 (December): 130–32.

———. 1946c. "Ritual in Transfigured Time," *Dance Magazine* 20, no. 12 (December): 9–13.

Desnos. Robert. 1978. "Eroticism." *Paris-Journal*, 1923. In *The Shadow and Its Shadow: Surrealist Writings on Cinema*, edited by Paul Hammond, 122–23. London: British Film Institute.

Dickstein, Morris. 1992, *Double Agent: The Critic and Society.* New York: Oxford University Press.

Editors of *Cahiers du cinéma*. 1970. "*Young Mr. Lincoln* de John Ford" (John Ford's *Young Mr. Lincoln*). *Cahiers du cinéma* 223 (August): 29–47.

Ellis, Jack. 1955. "Film Societies Federate." *Film Culture* 1, no. 3 (May–June): 30–31.

Eysteinsson, Astradur. 1990. *The Concept of Modernism.* Ithaca, N.Y.: Cornell University Press.

Farber, Manny. 1942a. "Gallery and Theatre." *New Republic*, 8 June, 798.

———. 1942b. "The Movie Art." *New Republic*, 26 October, 546–47.

———. 1942c. "Thomas Benton's War." *New Republic*, 20 April, 542.

———. 1942d. "Twice Over Heavily." *New Republic*, 10 August, 173.

———. 1942e. "Two European Painters." *New Republic*, 9 November, 610–11.

———. 1943a. "Between Two Worlds," *New Republic*, 12 July, 48.

———. 1943b. "The Cardboard Star." *New Republic*, 8 November, 653.

———. 1943c. "The Gang's All Here." *New Republic*, 27 December, 915–16.

———. 1943d. "One for the Ages." *New Republic*, 12 April, 476.

———. 1943e. "Tessa's Last Stand?" *New Republic*, 23 August, 255.

———. 1943f. "Two Shorts and a Wrongo." *New Republic*, 15 November, 686–87.

———. 1943g. "Young Mr. Pitt." *New Republic*, 22 March, 382.

———. 1943h. "Zanuck at the Front." *New Republic*, 5 April, 447.

———. 1944a. "The Art of Contrast." *New Republic*, 13 November, 626.

———. 1944b. "Movies in Wartime." *New Republic*, 3 January, 16–20.

———. 1944c. "Theatrical Movies." *New Republic*, 14 February, 211–12.

———. 1945. "Jackson Pollock." *New Republic*, 25 June, 871.

———. 1946a. "An American Show." *New Republic*, 14 October, 485.

———. 1946b. "Caper of the Week." *New Republic*, 30 September, 415–16.

———. 1946c. "Crime without Passion." *New Republic*, 3 June, 806.

———. 1946d. "Maya Deren's Films." *New Republic*, 28 October, 555–56.

———. 1946e. "Nervous from the Service." *New Republic*, 2 December, 723.

———. 1946f. "Open City." *New Republic*, 15 July, 46.

Farber, Manny. 1949. "Films." *Nation*, 7 May, 538.

———. 1950. "Films." *Nation*, 28 October, 397–98.

———. 1951a. "Art." *Nation*, 27 January, 92.

———. 1951b. "Art." *Nation*, 17 February, 162–63.

———. 1951c. "Art." *Nation*, 21 April, 384.

———. 1951d. "Art." *Nation*, 19 May), 476–77.

———. 1951e. "Art." *Nation*, 16 June,: 572–73.

———. 1951f. "Films." *Nation*, 13 January, 45–46.

———. 1951g. "Films." *Nation*, 10 March, 237–38.

———. 1951h. "Films." *Nation*, 31 March, 306.

———. 1952. "Films." *Nation*, 11 October, 337–38.

———. 1953a. "Films." *Nation*, 17 January, 57–59.

———. 1953b. "Films." *Nation*, 17 October, 318–19.

———. 1953c. "Films." *Nation*, 26 December, 574–75.

———. 1954. "Films." *Nation*, 9 January, 37–38.

———. 1958. "Star-Gazing for the Middlebrows." *New Leader* 41, no. 45 (8 December): 14–15.

———. 1959a. "Bathroom Mirror Sinceratease." *New Leader* 42, no. 5 (2 February): 27.

———. 1959b. "Home Screen Jabberwocky." *New Leader* 42, no. 12 (23 March): 27–28.

———. 1959c. "Three Art-y Films." *New Leader* 42, no. 10 (9 March): 27–28.

———. 1959d. "Underground Magic, Eccentric Vitality and Artful Direction Salvage Banal Stories." *New Leader* 42, no. 16 (20 April): 27–28.

———. 1962–63. "White Elephant Art vs. Termite Art." *Film Culture* 27 (Winter): 9–13.

———. 1968a. "Film." *Artforum* 6, no. 5 (January): 66–67.

———. 1968b. "Film." *Artforum* 6, no. 6 (February): 63.

———. 1968c. "Film." *Artforum* 6, no. 7 (March): 68–69.

———. 1968d. "Film." *Artforum* 6, no. 9 (May): 73–75.

———. 1968e. "Film." *Artforum* 6, no. 10 (Summer): 65–67.

———. 1968f. "Film." *Artforum* 7, no. 1 (September): 71–74.

———. 1968g. "The Films of Jean-Luc Godard." *Artforum* 7, no. 2 (October): 58–61.

———. 1969a. "Film." *Artforum* 7, no. 5 (January): 70–73.

———. 1969b. "Film." *Artforum* 7, no. 8 (April): 79–82.

———. 1969c. "Film." *Artforum* 8, no. 2 (October): 80–82.

———. 1969d. "Film." *Artforum* 8, no. 3 (November): 85–87.

———. 1970a. "Film." *Artforum* 9, no. 5 (January 1970): 81–82.

———. 1970b. "Film." *Artforum* 8, no. 7 (March): 89–92.

———. 1970c. "Film." *Artforum* 8, no. 9 (May): 87–88.

———. 1971a. "The Cold That Came into the Spy." *Cavalier*, 1966. In *Negative Space: Manny Farber on the Movies*, 170–74. New York: Praeger.

———. 1971b. "Day of the Lesteroid." *Cavalier*, 1966. In *Negative Space: Manny Farber on the Movies*, 160–64. New York: Praeger.

———. 1971c. "The Decline of the Actor." *Commentary*, 1963, as "The Fading Movie Star." In *Negative Space: Manny Farber on the Movies*, 145–54. New York: Praeger.

———. 1971d. "Hard Sell Cinema." *Perspectives*, 1957. In *Negative Space: Manny Farber on the Movies*, 113–24. New York: Praeger.

———. 1971e. "Pish-Tush." *Cavalier*, 1966. In *Negative Space: Manny Farber on the Movies*, 180–83. New York: Praeger.

———. 1971f. "Rain in the Face, Dry Gulch, and Squalling Mouth." *Cavalier*, 1965 and 1967. In *Negative Space: Manny Farber on the Movies*, 175–79. New York: Praeger.

———. 1971g. "Raoul Walsh: 'He Used to be a Big Shot.' " *Artforum* 10, no. 3 (November 1971): 78–80.

———. 1971h. "The Subverters." *Cavalier*, 1966. In *Negative Space: Manny Farber on the Movies*, 184–87. New York: Praeger.

———. 1971i. "Underground Films: A Bit of Male Truth." *Commentary*, 1957. In *Negative Space: Manny Farber on the Movies*, 12–24. New York: Praeger.

———. 1971j. "The Wizard of Gauze." *Cavalier*, 1966. In *Negative Space: Manny Farber on the Movies*, 165–69. New York: Praeger.

Ferguson, Otis. 1971. *The Film Criticism of Otis Ferguson*, edited by Robert Wilson. Philadelphia: Temple University Press.

Fiedler, Leslie. 1957. "The Middle against Both Ends." *Encounter*, 1955. In *Mass Culture: The Popular Arts in America*, edited by Bernard Rosenberg and David Manning White, 537–47. New York: The Free Press.

Fiske, John. 1989. *Understanding Popular Culture*. Boston: Unwin Hyman.

———. 1991. "Popular Discrimination." In *Modernity and Mass Culture*, edited by James Naremore and Patrick Brantlinger, 103–16. Bloomington: Indiana University Press.

Fonarow, Wendy. 1997. "The Spatial Organization of the Indie Music Gig." In *The Subcultures Reader*, edited by Ken Gelder and Sarah Thornton, 360–69. London: Routledge.

Freeman, Judi. 1989. *The Dada and Surrealist Word-Image*. Cambridge: MIT Press.

Gans, Herbert. 1974. *Popular Culture and High Culture: An Analysis and Evaluation of Taste*. New York: Basic Books.

Gardner, Paul. 1949. Letter to the editor. *Nation*, 23 July, 97.

Gibson, Ann Eden. 1990. *Issues in Abstract Expressionism: The Artist-Run Periodicals*. Ann Arbor, Mich.: UMI Research Press.

Gilbert-Rolfe, Jeremy, with Rosalind Krauss and Annette Michelson. 1976. "About *October*." *October* 1:3–5.

Gitlin, Todd. 1997. "The Anti-Political Populism of Cultural Studies." In *Cultural Studies in Question*, edited by Marjorie Ferguson and Peter Golding, 25–38. London: Sage.

Godard, Jean-Luc. 1986. "Jean Rouch Wins the Delluc Prize." *Arts*, 1958. In *Godard on Godard*, edited and translated by Tom Milne, 104. New York: Da Capo.

Goodman, Nelson. 1978. *Ways of Worldmaking*. Indianapolis: Hackett Publishing Company.

Gorin, Jean-Pierre, O. Assayas, S. Le Péron, and S. Toubiana. 1982. "Manny Farber—Critique et peintre du cinéma" (Manny Farber—Critic and painter of cinema). *Cahiers du Cinéma* 334–35 (April): 54–56+.

Greenberg, Clement. 1986. *Clement Greenberg: The Collected Essays and Criticism*, vol. 2, *(1945–1949)*, edited by John O'Brien. Chicago: University of Chicago Press.

———. 1990. "The Avant-Garde and Kitsch." *Partisan Review*, 1939. In *Twentieth Century Art Theory: Urbanism, Politics and Mass Culture*, edited by Richard Hertz and Norman M. Klein, 336–50. Englewood Cliffs, N.J.: Prentice Hall.

Grossberg, Larry. 1997. "Another Boring Day in Paradise: Rock and Roll and the Empowerment of Everyday Life." In *The Subcultures Reader*, edited by Ken Gelder and Sarah Thornton, 477–93. London: Routledge.

Guggenheim, Peggy, ed. 1942. *Art of this Century: Objects, Drawings, Photographs, Paintings, Sculpture, Collages, 1910 to 1942*. New York: Arno Press.

Gunning, Tom. 1992. " 'Loved Him, Hated It': An Interview with Andrew Sarris." In *To Free the Cinema: Jonas Mekas and the New York Underground*, edited by David E. James, 62–82. Princeton, N.J.: Princeton University Press.

Hadjinicolaou, Nicos. 1982. "On the Ideology of Avant-Gardism." *Praxis* 6:39–70.

Hammond, Paul. 1978. "Off at a Tangent." In *The Shadow and Its Shadow: Surrealist Writings on Cinema*, edited by Paul Hammond, 1–22. London: British Film Institute.

"Harold and Maude." 1971. Uncredited review. *Variety*, 15 December, 35.

Harvey, Sylvia. 1978. *May '68 and Film Culture*. London: British Film Institute.

Hoberman, J. 1992. "The Forest and *The Trees*." In *To Free the Cinema: Jonas Mekas and the New York Underground*, edited by David E. James, 100–120. Princeton, N.J.: Princeton University Press.

———. 1998. "The Film Critic of Tomorrow, Today." In *The Crisis of Criticism*, edited by Maurice Berger, 71–89. New York: The New Press.

Hoberman, J., and Jonathan Rosenbaum. 1983. *Midnight Movies*. New York: Harper & Row.

Hoffman, Frederick J., Charles Allen, and Carolyn F. Ulrich. 1947. *The Little Magazine: A History and a Bibliography*. Princeton, N.J.: Princeton University Press.

Horak, Jan-Christopher, ed. 1998. *Lovers of Cinema: The First American Film Avant-Garde, 1919–1945*. Madison: University of Wisconsin Press.

Hutcheon, Linda. 1988. *A Poetics of Postmodernism: History, Theory, Fiction*. New York: Routledge.

Huyssen, Andreas. 1986. *After the Great Divide: Modernism, Mass Culture, Postmodernism*. Bloomington: Indiana University Press.

Hyman, Stanley Edgar. 1948. *The Armed Vision: A Study in the Methods of Modern Literary Criticism*. New York: Alfred A. Knopf.

"The Idea of Art: Fourteen Sculptors Write." 1990. *Tiger's Eye*, 1948. In *Issues in Abstract Expressionism: The Artist-Run Periodicals*, edited by Ann Eden Gibson. Ann Arbor, Mich.: UMI Research Press.

James, David E. 1989. *Allegories of Cinema: American Film in the Sixties*. Princeton, N.J.: Princeton University Press.

———, ed. 1992. *To Free the Cinema: Jonas Mekas and the New York Underground*. Princeton, N.J.: Princeton University Press.

Jarrell, Randall. 1952. "The Age of Criticism." *Partisan Review* 19, no. 2 (March–April): 185–201.

Jenkins, Henry. 1992. *Textual Poachers: Television Fans and Participatory Culture*. New York: Routledge.

Jones, W. 1974. "After Last Night." *Minneapolis Tribune*, 21 March, B1.

Kael, Pauline. 1959. "Movies, the Desperate Art." In *Film: an Anthology*, edited by Daniel Talbot, 189–209. New York: Simon and Schuster.

———. 1965. "Circles and Squares: Joys and Sarris." *Film Quarterly*, 1963. In *I Lost It at the Movies*, 292–319. Boston: Little, Brown & Co.

———. 1966. "Movie Brutalists." *New Republic*, 24 September, 23–24+.

———. 1970. "Trash, Art and the Movies." *Harper's*, 1969. In *Going Steady*, 85–129. Boston: Little, Brown & Co.

Kames, Lord Henry Home. 1824. *Elements of Criticism*. London: G. Cowie & Co.

Kammen, Michael. 1996. *The Lively Arts: Gilbert Seldes and the Transformation of Cultural Criticism in the United States*. New York: Oxford University Press.

Karl, Frederick R. 1988. *Modern and Modernism: The Sovereignty of the Artist 1885–1925*. New York: Atheneum.

Kazin, Alfred. 1965. *Starting Out in the Thirties*. Boston: Little, Brown & Co.

Kelly, Richard. 1943. Letter to the editor. *New Republic*, 25 January, 121.

Knight, Arthur. 1950. "Ideas on Film." *Saturday Review*, 27 May, 38–40.

Kootz, Samuel. 1930. *Modern American Painters*. New York: Brewer and Warren.

———. 1943. *New Frontiers in American Painting*. New York: Hastings House.

Kozlov, Leonid. 1971. "L'Unité" (Unity). *Cahiers du cinéma* 226–27 (January–February): 28–38.

Kuspit, Donald. 1984. *The Critic Is Artist: The Intentionality of Art*. Ann Arbor, Mich.: UMI Research Press.

———. 1993. *The Cult of the Avant-Garde Artist*. Cambridge: Cambridge University Press.

La Jolla Museum of Contemporary Art. 1978. *Manny Farber* (exhibition catalog). La Jolla, Calif.

Leblanc, Gérard. 1978. "Economic/Ideological/Formal." *Cinéthique* 3, 1969. In *May '68 and Film Culture*, edited by Sylvia Harvey, translated by Elias Noujaim, 149–64. London: British Film Institute.

LeGrice, Malcolm. 1977. *Abstract Film and Beyond*. Cambridge: MIT Press.

Levin, Meyer. 1960. "Tuesday Brown." *Clipper*, 1940. In *Introduction to the Art of the Movies*, edited by Lewis Jacobs, 239–46. New York: The Noonday Press.

Long, Scott. 1993. "The Loneliness of Camp." In *Camp Grounds: Style and Homosexuality*, edited by David Bergman, 78–91. Amherst: University of Massachusetts Press.

Lynes, Russell. [1949] 1980. *The Tastemakers: The Shaping of American Popular Taste*. New York: Dover.

Lynes, Russell. 1985. *The Lively Audience: A Social History of the Visual and Performing Arts in America, 1890–1950*. New York: Harper & Row.

MacCabe, Colin. 1974. "Realism and the Cinema: Notes on Some Brechtian Theses." *Screen* 15, no. 2 (Summer): 7–27.

Macdonald, Dwight. 1960. "Masscult and Midcult: II." *Partisan Review* 27, no. 4 (Fall): 589–631.

———. 1967. "Objections to the New American Cinema." In *The New American Cinema*, edited by Gregory Battock, 197–204. New York: E. P. Dutton & Co.

MacDonald, Scott. 1987. "Amos Vogel and Cinema 16." *Wide Angle* 9, no. 3: 38–51.

Maland, Charles J. 1989. *Chaplin and American Culture: The Evolution of a Star Image*. Princeton, N.J.: Princeton University Press.

"Manny Farber: Writing as Painting." 1956. *Art News* 55, no. 7 (November): 37+.

Margo, Boris, et al. 1990. "The Ideas of Art: The Attitudes of Ten Artists on Their Art and Contemporaneousness." *Tiger's Eye*, 1947. In *Issues in Abstract Expressionism: The Artist-Run Periodicals*, edited by Ann Eden Gibson, 134–39. Ann Arbor, Mich.: UMI Research Press.

Margulies, Edward, and Stephen Rebello. 1993. *Bad Movies We Love*. New York: Plume Books.

Marquis, Alice Goldfarb. 1989. *Alfred H. Barr, Jr.: Missionary for the Modern*. New York: Contemporary Books.

McGowan, John. 1991. *Postmodernism and Its Critics*. Ithaca, N.Y.: Cornell University Press.

McGuigan, John. 1992. *Cultural Populism*. London: Routledge.

McLuhan, Marshall. 1964. *Understanding Media: The Extensions of Man*. New York: McGraw-Hill.

McLuhan, Marshall, and Quentin Fiori, 1967. *The Medium Is the Massage*. New York: Bantam.

Mekas, Jonas. 1955a. "The Experimental Film in America." *Film Culture* 3 (May–June): 15–18.

———. 1955b. Untitled editorial. *Film Culture* 1, no. 1 (January): 1.

———. 1957. Untitled editorial. *Film Culture* 3, no. 4 (14) (November): 2.

———. 1959. "Editorial Note." *Film Culture* 20:1.

———. 1960. "Cinema of the New Generation." *Film Culture* 21 (Summer): 1–20.

———. 1972. *Movie Journal: The Rise of a New American Cinema, 1959–1971*. New York: Collier Books.

Meyer, Moe. 1994. "Introduction: Reclaiming the Discourse of Camp." In *The Politics and Poetics of Camp*, edited by Moe Meyer, 1–22. New York: Routledge.

Micha, René. 1968. "The Cinema Rises in Rebellion. The Cinema Is Liberty." In *Art and Confrontation: The Arts in an Age of Change*, translated by Nigel Foxell, 151–74. Greenwich, Conn.: New York Graphic Society.

Michelson, Annette. 1966. "Film and the Radical Aspiration." *Film Culture* 42 (Fall): 34–42+.

———. 1968. "What Is Cinema?" *Artforum* 6, no. 10 (Summer): 67–71.

————. 1969. "Bodies in Space: Film as 'Carnal Knowledge.' " *Artforum* 7, no. 6 (February): 54–63.

————. 1973. "Camera Lucida / Camera Obscura." *Artforum* 11, no. 5 (January): 30–37.

————. 1979. "About Snow." *October* 8 (Spring): 111–25.

Monti, James. 1967. " 'Making It' with Funk." *Artforum* 5, no. 10 (Summer): 56–58.

Mulvey, Laura. 1975. "Visual Pleasure and Narrative Cinema." *Screen* 16, no. 3 (Autumn): 6–18.

Museum of Modern Art. 1984. *The Museum of Modern Art, New York: The History and the Collection*. New York: Harry N. Abrams.

Neiman, Catrina. 1991. "Introduction." In *View: Parade of the Avant-Garde, 1940–1947*, edited by Charles Henri Ford, xi–xvi. New York: Thunder's Mouth Press.

Newman, Barnett. 1990. "The Ideographic Picture." Betty Parsons Gallery, 1947. In *Barnett Newman: Selected Writings and Interviews*, edited by John P. O'Neill, 107–8. Berkeley and Los Angeles: University of California Press.

Nichols, Dudley. 1943. Letter to the editor. *Nation*, 10 May, 640.

Perloff, Marjorie. 1986. *The Futurist Moment: Avant-Garde, Avant Guerre, and the Language of Rupture*. Chicago: University of Chicago Press.

Peterson, James. 1994. *Dreams of Chaos, Visions of Order: Understanding the American Avant-Garde Cinema*. Detroit: Wayne State University Press.

Philipson, Morris. 1963. *Outline of Jungian Esthetics*. Evanston, Ill.: Northwestern University Press.

Pleynet, Marcelin. 1977. "The 'Left' Front of the Arts: Eisenstein and the Old 'Young Hegelians.' " Translated by Susan Bennett. *Cinéthique*, 1969. In *Screen Reader 1*, 225–43. London: The Society for Education in Film and Television.

Poggioli, Renato. 1968. *The Theory of the Avant-Garde*. Translated by Gerald Fitzgerald. Cambridge: Harvard University Press, Belknap Press.

Polcari, Stephen. 1991. *Abstract Expressionism and the Modern Experience*. New York: Cambridge University Press.

Prince, Stephen. 1997. *Movies and Meaning: An Introduction to Film*. Boston: Allyn and Bacon.

Pruitt, John. 1992. "Jonas Mekas: A European Critic in America." In *To Free the Cinema: Jonas Mekas and the New York Underground*, edited by David E. James, 51–61. Princeton, N.J.: Princeton University Press.

Rabinovitz, Lauren. 1991. *Points of Resistance: Women, Power and Politics in the New York Avant-Garde Cinema, 1943–1971*. Urbana: University of Illinois Press.

Radway, Janice. 1988. "Book-of-the-Month-Club." *Critical Inquiry* 14, no. 3 (Spring): 516–38.

Renan, Sheldon. 1967. *An Introduction to the American Underground Film*. New York: E. P. Dutton & Co.

Richards, Janet. 1979. *Common Soldiers: A Self-Portrait and Other Portraits*. San Francisco: The Archer Press.

Robertson, Pamela. 1996. *Guilty Pleasures: Feminist Camp from Mae West to Madonna*. Durham, N.C.: Duke University Press.

Rose, Barbara. 1967. *American Art since 1900: A Critical History*. New York: Praeger.

———. 1968. "A B C Art." *Art in America*, 1965. In *Minimal Art: A Critical Anthology*, edited by Gregory Battock, 274–97. New York: E. P. Dutton & Co.

Rosenbaum, Jonathan. 1995. *Placing Movies: The Practice of Film Criticism*. Berkeley and Los Angeles: University of California Press.

Rosenberg, Bernard, and Norris Fliegel. [1965] 1990. *The Vanguard Artist*. New York: New Amsterdam Books.

Ross, Andrew. 1989. *No Respect: Intellectuals and Popular Culture*. New York: Routledge.

Rubin, Joan Shelley. 1992. *The Making of Middlebrow Culture*. Chapel Hill: University of North Carolina Press.

Russell, Charles. 1985. *Poets, Prophets, and Revolutionaries: The Literary Avant-Garde from Rimbaud through Postmodernism*. New York: Oxford University Press.

Sandler, Irving H. 1962. "Manny Farber." *Art News* 61, no. 6 (October): 13.

Sarris, Andrew. 1956. "Giant." *Film Culture* 2, no. 4 (10): 23–24.

———. 1959. "The Seventh Seal." *Film Culture* 19:51–61.

———. 1961. "The Director's Game." *Film Culture* 22–23 (Summer): 68–81.

———. 1962a. "Cactus Rosebud or The Man Who Shot Liberty Valance." *Film Culture* 25 (Summer): 13–15.

———. 1962b. "The High Forties Revisited." *Film Culture* 24 (Spring): 62–70.

———. 1962–63. "Notes on the Auteur Theory in 1962." *Film Culture* 27 (Winter): 1–8

———. 1963a. "The American Cinema." *Film Culture* 28 (Spring): 1–51.

———. 1963b. "Directorial Chronology 1915–1962." *Film Culture* 28 (Spring): 52–68.

———. 1964–65. "Random Reflections." *Film Culture* 35 (Winter): 10–14.

———. 1965. "Acting Aweigh!" *Film Culture* 38 (Fall): 47–61.

———. 1966. "Random Reflections—II." *Film Culture* 40 (Spring): 21–23.

———, ed. 1967. *Hollywood Voices: Interviews with Film Directors*. Indianapolis: The Bobbs-Merrill Company.

———. 1968. *The American Cinema: Directors and Directions 1929–1968*. New York: E. P. Dutton & Co.

———. 1969a. "L'Avventura." *Village Voice*, 1961. In *Confessions of a Cultist: On the Cinema, 1955–1969*, 34–35. New York: Simon and Schuster.

———. 1969b. "The Rose Tattoo." *Film Culture*, 1955. In *Confessions of a Cultist: On the Cinema, 1955–1969*, 19–20. New York: Simon and Schuster.

Sawin, Martica. 1956. Untitled review. *Arts* 31, no. 3 (December): 61.

Seeley, Carol. 1943. Untitled poem. *New Republic*, 8 February, 184.

Seldes, Gilbert. [1924] 1957. *The Seven Lively Arts*. New York: A. S. Barnes & Co.

Shapiro, David, and Cecile Shapiro. 1985. "Abstract Expressionism: The Politics of Apolitical Painting." *Prospects* 3, 1977. In *Pollock and After: The Critical Debate*, edited by Francis Frascina, 135–51. New York: Harper & Row.

Shattuck, Roger. 1968. *The Banquet Years*. Rev. ed. New York: Random House.

Sherwood, Robert E. 1972. "The Four Horsemen of the Apocalypse." *Life*, 1921. In *American Film Criticism: From the Beginnings to Citizen Kane*, edited by Stanley Kauffmann with Bruce Henstell, 113–15. New York: Liveright.

Simon, John. 1967. "A Critical Credo." In *Private Screenings*, 7–23. New York: Berkeley Publishing Corporation.

Sitney, P. Adams, ed. 1975. *The Essential Cinema*. New York: Anthology Film Archives and New York University Press.

———. 1979. *Visionary Film: The American Avant-Garde, 1943–1978*. Rev. ed. New York: Oxford University Press.

Snow. Michael. 1967. "A Statement on 'Wavelength' for the Experimental Film Festival of Knokke-le-Zoute." *Film Culture* 46 (Autumn): 1.

Sontag, Susan. 1966a. "Notes on 'Camp.' " *Partisan Review*, 1964. In *Against Interpretation and Other Essays*, 277–93. New York: Dell.

———. 1966b. "One Culture and the New Sensibility." *Mademoiselle*, 1965. In *Against Interpretation and Other Essays*, 294–304. New York: Dell.

———. 1982. "Writing Itself: On Roland Barthes." In *A Barthes Reader*, edited by Susan Sontag, vii–xxxvi. New York: Hill and Wang.

Spilker, Eric. 1970. "Majors Staff Up for Youth." *Variety*, June 24, 3+.

Staiger, Janet. 1992. *Interpreting Films: Studies in the Historical Reception of American Cinema*. Princeton, N.J.: Princeton University Press.

Suárez, Juan. 1996. *Bike Boys, Drag Queens, and Superstars: Avant-Garde, Mass Culture, and Gay Identities in the 1960s Underground Cinema*. Bloomington: Indiana University Press.

Sweeney, James John. 1991. "Iconographer of Melancholy." *View*, 1942. In *View: Parade of the Avant-Garde, 1940–1947*, edited by Charles Henri Ford, 47–48. New York: Thunder's Mouth Press.

Tashjian, Dickran. 1995. *A Boatload of Madmen: Surrealism and the American Avant-Garde 1920–1950*. New York: Thames and Hudson.

Tchelitchew, Pavel. 1967. *Thirty Studies for Hide and Seek*. New York: Catherine Viviano Gallery.

Tellotte, J. P. 1991. "Beyond All Reason: The Nature of the Cult." In *The Cult Film Experience: Beyond All Reason*, edited by J. P. Telotte, 5–17. Austin: University of Texas Press.

Thompson, Richard. 1977. "Manny Farber and Patricia Patterson interviewed by Richard Thompson." *Film Comment* 13, no. 3 (May–June): 36–45+.

Trilling, Lionel. 1950. "Manners, Morals and the Novel." *Kenyon Review*, 1948. In *The Liberal Imagination*, 193–209. New York: Harcourt Brace Jovanovich.

Tyler, Parker. 1935. "Beyond Surrealism." *Caravel* 4:2–6.

———. 1940. "Hollywood in Disguise: Gods and Goddesses Paid to be Alive." *View* 1, no. 2 (October): 1+.

———. 1942a. "The Endless Island." *View* 2, no. 3 (October): 9–13.

———. 1942b. "A Gift from Max Ernst." *View* 2, no. 1 (April): 16.

———. 1944a. "The Erotic Spectator: An Essay on the Eye of the Libido." *View* 14, no. 3 (Fall): 74–77+.

———. 1944b. *The Hollywood Hallucination*. New York: Simon and Schuster.

———. 1945a. *The Granite Butterfly: A Poem in Nine Cantos*. New York: Bern Porter.

Tyler, Parker. 1945b. "The Limit of the Probable in Modern Painting." *View* 5, no. 1 (March): 39–41.

———. 1945c. "Nature and Madness among the Young Painters." *View* 5, no. 2 (May): 30–31.

———. 1946. "Fourteen Minus One." *View* 7, no. 1 (Fall): 35–37.

———. 1947a. *A Little Boy Lost: Marcel Proust and Charlie Chaplin*. Prospero Pamphlets. New York: QVS Press.

———. 1947b. *Magic and Myth of the Movies*. New York: Henry Holt and Company.

———. 1947c. "Movie Letter." *Kenyon Review* 9, no. 2 (Spring): 317–24.

———. 1948a. *Chaplin: Last of the Clowns*. New York: The Vanguard Press.

———. 1948b. "The Elements of Film Narrative." *Magazine of Art* 41, no. 4 (April): 137–41.

———. 1949a. "The Experimental Film: A Layman's Guide to Its Understanding and Enjoyment." *Theatre Arts* 33, no. 6 (July): 46–48+.

———. 1949b. "Experimental Film: A New Growth." *Kenyon Review* 11, no. 1 (Winter): 141–44.

———. 1949c. "Movie Letter: *Hamlet* and Documentary." *Kenyon Review* 11, no. 3 (Summer): 527–32.

———. 1950a. "Kafka's and Chaplin's 'Amerika.' " *Sewanee Review* 58:299–311.

———. 1950b. "Movie Letter: Lament for the Audience—and a Mild Bravo." *Kenyon Review* 12, no. 4 (Autumn): 689–96.

———. 1950c. "Violating Reality via the Fact-Fiction Film." *Films in Review* 1, no. 4 (May–June): 9–11+.

———. 1958. "Stan Brakhage." *Film Culture* 4, no. 3 (18) (April): 23–25.

———. 1959. "Willard Maas." *Film Culture* 20:53–58.

———. 1960a. "The Eyewitness Era in Film Fiction." *American Quarterly*, 1949. In *The Three Faces of the Film*, 23–35. New York: Thomas Yoseloff.

———. 1960b. "Film Form and Ritual as Reality." *Kenyon Review*, 1948. In *The Three Faces of the Film*, 74–82. New York: Thomas Yoseloff.

———. 1960c. "Harrington, Markopoulos and Boultenhouse: Two Down and One to Go?" *Film Culture* 21 (Summer): 33–39.

———. 1960d. "Movies and the Human Image." *Forum*, 1958. In *The Three Faces of the Film*, 139–44. New York: Thomas Yoseloff.

———. 1960e. "The Movies as Fine Art." *Partisan Review*, 1958. In *The Three Faces of the Film*, 17–22. New York: Thomas Yoseloff.

———. 1960f. "A Preface to the Problems of the Experimental Film." *Film Culture*, 1958. In *The Three Faces of the Film*, 56–63. New York: Thomas Yoseloff.

———. 1960g. "*Rashomon* as Modern Art." *Cinema* 16, 1952. In *The Three Faces of the Film*, 36–43. New York: Thomas Yoseloff.

———. 1960h. *The Three Faces of the Film*. New York: Thomas Yoseloff.

———. 1961. "Declamation on Film." *Film Culture* 22–23 (Summer): 26–32.

———. 1962a. *Classics of the Foreign Film: A Pictorial Treasury*. New York: The Citadel Press.

———. 1962b. "For *Shadows*, against *Pull My Daisy*." *Film Culture* 24 (Spring): 28–33.

————. 1964. *Every Artist His Own Scandal: A Study of Real and Fictive Heroes.* New York: Horizon Press.

————. 1966. "Is Film Criticism Only Propaganda?" *Film Culture* 42 (Fall): 29–34.

————. 1967a. *The Divine Comedy of Pavel Tchelitchew.* New York: Fleet Publishing Corporation.

————. 1967b. *The Three Faces of the Film.* Rev. ed. New York: A. S. Barnes & Co.

————. 1969a. "*La Dolce Vita* and the Monster Fish." In *Sex Psyche Etcetera in the Film*, 106–13. New York: Horizon Press.

————. 1969b. "Masterpieces by Antonioni and Bergman." In *Sex Psyche Etcetera in the Film*, 114–31. New York: Horizon Press.

————. 1969c. "Maze of the Modern Sensibility: An Antonioni Trilogy." In *Sex Psyche Etcetera in the Film*, 83–96. New York: Horizon Press.

————. 1969d. *Sex Psyche Etcetera in the Film.* New York: Horizon Press.

————. 1969e. *Underground Film: A Critical History.* New York: Grove Press.

————. 1972a. *Screening the Sexes: Homosexuality in the Movies.* New York: Holt, Rinehart and Winston.

————. 1972b. *The Shadow of an Airplane Climbs the Empire State Building: A World Theory of Film.* New York: Doubleday & Company.

Tyler, Parker, and Charles Henri Ford. 1930. "Round." *Blues* 9 (Fall): 25.

Vertov, Dziga. 1984. *Kino-Eye: The Writings of Dziga Vertov*, edited by Annette Michelson. Berkeley and Los Angeles: University of California Press.

Vidal, Gore. 1968. *Myra Breckinridge.* New York: Bantam Books.

Ware, Caroline F. 1935. *Greenwich Village, 1920–1930.* New York: Houghton Mifflin.

Warshow, Robert. 1970a. "The Anatomy of Falsehood." *Partisan Review*, May–June 1947. In *The Immediate Experience*, 155–61. New York: Atheneum.

————. 1970b. "The Legacy of the 30's." *Commentary*, December 1947. In *The Immediate Experience*, 33–48. New York: Atheneum.

————. 1970c. "Statement of Project." Guggenheim Fellowship application, October 1954. Reprinted as "Author's Preface" in *The Immediate Experience*, pp. 23–29. New York: Atheneum.

Waters, John. 1986. *Crackpot, the Obsessions of John Waters.* New York: Vintage Books.

Watson, Steven. 1991. *Strange Bedfellows: The First American Avant-Garde.* New York: Abbeville Press Publishers.

Wellington, Fred. 1966. "Film '65—Thirteen Panel Discussions." *Film Culture* 40 (Spring): 25–30.

"What Are the New Critics Saying?" 1966. *Film Culture* 42 (Fall): 76–88.

Wilde, Oscar. 1981. "The Critic as Artist." In *The Portable Oscar Wilde*, rev. Ed., edited by Richard Aldington and Stanley Weintraub, 51–137. New York: Viking Penguin.

Willemen, Paul. 1973. "Eisenstein/Brakhage." *Studio International* 185, no. 956 (June): 252–53.

Wollen, Peter. 1982. "The Two Avant-Gardes." *Studio International*, December 1975. In *Readings and Writings: Semiotic Counter-Strategies*, 92–104. London: Verso.

Yard, Sally. 1991. *Manny Farber: Paintings of the Eighties*. La Jolla, Calif.: Quint-Krichman Projects.

Zolberg, Vera L. 1990. *Constructing a Sociology of the Arts*. New York: Cambridge University Press.

INDEX